# Spirit Matters

# Spirit Matters

*Occult Beliefs, Alternative Religions,
and the Crisis of Faith
in Victorian Britain*

J. Jeffrey Franklin

Cornell University Press
Ithaca and London

Copyright © 2018 by Cornell University

All rights reserved. Except for brief quotations in a review, this book, or parts thereof, must not be reproduced in any form without permission in writing from the publisher. For information, address Cornell University Press, Sage House, 512 East State Street, Ithaca, New York 14850.

First published 2018 by Cornell University Press

Printed in the United States of America

Library of Congress Cataloging-in-Publication Data
Names: Franklin, J. Jeffrey, author.
Title: Spirit matters : occult beliefs, alternative religions, and the crisis of faith in Victorian Britain / J. Jeffrey Franklin.
Description: Ithaca : Cornell University Press, 2018. | Includes bibliographical references and index.
Identifiers: LCCN 2017028029 (print) | LCCN 2017051440 (ebook) | ISBN 9781501715457 (pdf) | ISBN 9781501715464 (ret) | ISBN 9781501715440 | ISBN 9781501715440 (cloth : alk. paper)
Subjects: LCSH: English prose literature—19th century—History and criticism. | Occultism in literature. | Spiritualism in literature. | Occultism—Great Britain—History—19th century. | Spiritualism—Great Britain—History—19th century. | Religion and culture—Great Britain—History—19th century. | Great Britain—Religion—19th century.
Classification: LCC PR788.O33 (ebook) | LCC PR788.O33 F73 2018 (print) | DDC 823/.91209034—dc23
LC record available at https://lccn.loc.gov/2017028029

Cornell University Press strives to use environmentally responsible suppliers and materials to the fullest extent possible in the publishing of its books. Such materials include vegetable-based, low-VOC inks and acid-free papers that are recycled, totally chlorine-free, or partly composed of nonwood fibers. For further information, visit our website at cornellpress.cornell.edu.

Dedicated to William Henry Trotter
and Selmon Theodore Franklin,
my grandfathers, patriarchs of faith

# Contents

Preface ix

Acknowledgments xix

1. Orthodox Christianity, Scientific Materialism, and Alternative Religions — 1

**Part I: Challenges to Christianity and the Orthodox/Heterodox Boundary**

2. The Evolution of Occult Spirituality in Victorian England and the Representative Case of Edward Bulwer-Lytton — 27

3. Anthony Trollope's Religion: The Orthodox/Heterodox Boundary — 45

4. The Influences of Buddhism and Comparative Religion on Matthew Arnold's Theology — 67

## Part II: The Interpenetration of Christianity and Buddhism

5. Interpenetration of Religion and National Politics in Great Britain and Sri Lanka: William Knighton's *Forest Life in Ceylon* — 85

6. Identity, Genre, and Religion in Anna Leonowens's *The English Governess at the Siamese Court* — 115

## Part III: The Turn to Occultism

7. Ancient Egyptian Religion in Late Victorian England — 141

8. The Economics of Immortality: The Demi-immortal Oriental, Enlightenment Vitalism, and Political Economy in Bram Stoker's *Dracula* — 164

## Part IV: The Origins of Alternative Religion in Victorian Britain

Conclusion: From Victorian Occultism to New Age Spiritualities — 185

Notes — 213

Bibliography — 229

Index — 251

# Preface

There was a widespread urgency in the Victorian period (1837–1901) to defend the continued existence of and belief in "Spirit" against the growing forces of what was called "materialism." As Hudson Tuttle summarized in his "Manual of Spiritual Science and Philosophy" in 1867: "There is no alternative, and material science is fast driving Christianity to the wall. It has taken all the thinkers of the world. The church holds only those who do not think. Spiritualism is the last stronghold against the tide of materialism, and if it fails to establish its claims, the former will be supremely triumphant" (56). From the remove of twenty-first-century postindustrial society and postmodern culture, it may be difficult to appreciate how dire that urgency was, concerning as it did nothing less than the negation of the continued existence of the human soul and of God's loving dispensation for human beings as his privileged creation. "Spirit" had multiple connotations, but it might be summarized as faith in or claimed proof of the existence at the most fundamental level of any type of anthropocentric spiritual entities or realms. Those ranged from the immortal soul to the

"Spirit World" to ranks of supernatural beings (angels, demons) to a divine vital force resonant throughout the natural universe. Materialism, summarized as the disavowal of any transcendent being or realm that supersedes empirical reality or natural law, also came in multiple forms. Those included the reduction of individual spirituality to institutionalized dogma or ritual, the economic materialism of consumer capitalism, or the worst extreme of metaphysical materialism, but its most frequently decried form was as "natural philosophy": science. Science might presume to explain the order of the universe, or human evolution, without reference to the divine, reducing its subjects to nothing more than matter. The contest between orthodox Christianity and science that had developed in the eighteenth century resulted in the formation of "physicotheologies," such as Enlightenment Deism, in part to allow Christian faith and natural science to coexist (Brooke and Cantor 149). In the nineteenth century, this contest pitted the predominant physicotheology, Natural Theology, which eventually would be stretched to accommodate divine creation to evolutionary science, against what was rapidly becoming the dominant truth-telling authority in modern society, scientific naturalism. This contest was a primary expression of the spiritual-versus-material dialectic that runs throughout the chapters of this book.

*Spirit Matters* may appear on the basis of the table of contents to be wide-ranging, and it is. It spans the long Victorian period, from the 1830s to the first decades of the twentieth century; traverses multiple locations in that century's great empire, from England to Egypt to Southeast Asia; analyzes authors and texts that might at first glance appear to share little with one another; and treats religious and spiritual topics ranging from Spiritualism to the Church of England to Buddhism to Western occultism. Yet the highly diverse chapters that make up *Spirit Matters* are knitted together by recurring historical, theological, and literary patterns, one of which is participation by all of the texts in the aforementioned cultural contest between spiritualism and materialism. The chapters are sequenced purposefully to tell a cumulative story about the evolution of nonorthodox spiritual and religious discourses from the beginning to the end of the century.

To give a single representative example, consider the following dialogue that appears in one of many spiritual romance novels by Marie Corelli (1855–1924), among the most famous and best-selling novelists across the English-speaking world at the fin de siècle. The novel is *The Life Everlasting: A Romance of Reality* (1911). The speakers are Santoris, a spiritual adept, and Catherine, an initially skeptical neophyte who it seems will come under his mentorship—two character types typical in Corelli (as is their gendering). Santoris offhandedly refers to "wiser forms of study" than those he encountered at Oxford, and Catherine asks if he means "occult mysteries and things of that sort." He answers: " 'Occult' is a word of such new coinage that it is not found in many dictionaries. . . . I do not care for it myself; I prefer to say 'Spiritual science.' " She says, "You believe in that?," and he responds, "Assuredly! How can I do otherwise, seeing that it is the Key to the Soul of Nature?" (133). Corelli wrote this novel at the end of the period considered in *Spirit Matters*, and this dialogue reflects the cumulative influence of Romantic *naturphilosophie*, the midcentury Spiritualism movement, the establishment of Theosophy in the 1870s–1880s, and the emergence of a "new occultism" unique to the end of the nineteenth century (Owen, *Place* 4). "Spiritual science" had been a motif in Spiritualism and a defining feature of Theosophy, as subsequent chapters will explore, yet Corelli repeatedly disclaimed those sources and all occultism, always asserting that "my creed has its foundation in Christ alone" (*Romance* xvii). Her corpus is dedicated to demonstrating that "Materialism does not, and can never still the hunger of Immortal Spirit," but for that purpose her writing eschews orthodox Christian diction and doctrine, champions an afterlife more akin to reincarnation than heaven, and portrays astral travel through a planetary system of "higher worlds" (xvi). This one piece of dialogue digests a century of religious and spiritual discourse with such multivalent ambivalence that reading *Spirit Matters* (or the scholarship behind it) is necessary in order to be equipped to trace all of the allusions and unpack all of the contradictions.

*Spirit Matters* is about nonmainstream or heterodox religious and spiritual beliefs—what in the twentieth century would come to be called "alternative religions"—in nineteenth-century Great Britain. These beliefs were alternatives to orthodox Protestant Christianity, of which the large majority of British citizens would have claimed to be adherents, and which came in many denominations and subdenominations while sharing an identified set of beliefs and doctrines. The ideas and events analyzed in the chapters that follow were outside of the domain of orthodox religion yet still religious or spiritual, neither atheistic nor materialistic. The territory explored in this book lay between orthodox Christianity on one side and atheism or materialism on the other side. In that territory, there arose throughout the nineteenth century a very wide variety of alternative religious positions, ways of believing that gained sufficient currency to be consistently reproduced and broadly circulated through social discourse and cultural media. That variety ranged from heterodox Christian beliefs to European esotericisms to new "scientific" spiritual movements to Buddhist doctrines adapted to Western beliefs, among many others. This book investigates representative case studies across that spectrum. It presents them semichronologically and thematically in order to provide something approaching a historical survey of how alternative religious thought developed in the course of the Victorian period. It ends by demonstrating how all of those varied pieces—the diverse works and subjects covered in the chapters of this book—tell a story about the origins of modern alternative religion and how they provided the necessary elements for the emergence in the twentieth century of New Age spiritualities.

The method of *Spirit Matters* is a kind of cultural historicism, analysis of diverse texts in relationship to the religious, political, economic, literary, and other contextualizing social and cultural events and discourses of the time and place in which they were written and read. Thus, in terms of disciplinary orientation and style, this book falls somewhere in between the history of ideas, literary studies, and comparative religious studies. In one sense, the types of written works that I have chosen to analyze are less important than that they all compellingly represent how many people acted and thought about their vitally important religious and spiritual concerns. Some of the works are novels of varying subgenres, some are travel writing or autobiography, some are religious studies or theological treatises, and some combine these and other genres of writing. I treat all of the texts analyzed in *Spirit Matters* equally as exceedingly rich cultural artifacts, whatever their genre. They all teach us about the history and development of religious and spiritual thought throughout a period and in a multilocational place, the British Empire of the nineteenth century, that were crucial in determining how twenty-first-century peoples still think, talk, and practice religion and spirituality to this day.

Among the primary texts analyzed in this book are the following, in the order treated: Edward Bulwer-Lytton's Gothic-romance novels *Zanoni* (1842) and *A Strange Story* (1862); Anthony Trollope's realist novel, *The*

*Vicar of Bullhampton* (1870), in the context of his nonfiction work *The Clergymen of the Church of England* (1866); Matthew Arnold's work of theological criticism, *Literature and Dogma: An Essay Towards a Better Apprehension of the Bible* (1873); William Knighton's novelistic travelogue, *Forest Life in Ceylon* (1854); Anna Leonowens's fictionalized autobiography, *The English Governess at the Siamese Court; Being Recollections of Six Years in the Royal Palace of Bangkok* (1870); H. Rider Haggard's Gothic romance, *Cleopatra, Being an Account of the Fall and Vengeance of Harmachis, the Royal Egyptian, as Set Forth by His Own Hand* (1889); Bram Stoker's *Dracula* (1897); H. P. Blavatsky's seminal works of Theosophy, primarily *Isis Unveiled: A Master-Key to the Mysteries of Ancient and Modern Science and Theology* (1877); and selected Theosophical works by Annie Besant, including *The Evolution of Life and Form: Four Lectures delivered at the Twenty-Third Anniversary Meeting of the Theosophical Society at Adyar, Madras, 1898*.

All of these works bear the influences of the major spiritual movements of the first half of the century, the key historical events that influenced religion in Great Britain after midcentury, and the formation of new syncretic or "hybrid religions" near the end of the century (Franklin, *Lotus* 59). The early century movements were Mesmerism and Spiritualism (following Swedenborgianism), which I treat especially in chapter 2 on Bulwer-Lytton. After midcentury, the frequently noted catalytic events included these:

1) the rise to global preeminence of the British Empire, which precipitated a "counterinvasion" of England by world religions other than Christianity, especially Buddhism, as I explore in chapters 5 and 6 on Knighton and Leonowens and further delineate in chapters 7 and 8 on Haggard and Stoker;
2) the resulting formation of the field of comparative religious studies, which took Buddhism as a primary object and disseminated foreign religious ideas and an evenhanded methodology of studying religions throughout British culture, as I discuss especially in chapter 4 on Arnold, chapter 7 on Haggard, and the concluding chapter on Theosophy and New Age spirituality;
3) the Darwinian revolution, especially after the 1859 publication of *On the Origin of Species*, and the maturation of modern scientific

naturalism, which I detail in chapter 1 and which is foundational for understanding the spirit/matter dualism throughout; and,
4) what amounted to the proclamation of modern latitudinarian Broad Church Anglicanism within the Church of England in 1860, the major religious upheaval in nineteenth-century Britain that opened the dominant denomination to integration with heterodox and foreign elements, as I analyze in chapters 3 and 4 on Trollope and Arnold, who mark the orthodox/heterodox boundary in this study.

The end of the century saw a proliferation of new hybrid religions, such as Theosophy, the stated purpose of which was to defend Spirit against materialism; to bolster or supplant the institutions of orthodox Christianity, which were felt to be losing the fight against materialism; and to defend against the threat in particular of scientific naturalism. The founders of hybrid religions did this by integrating doctrines of Hinduism and Buddhism, the Goddess from ancient Egyptian religion, the methods of comparative religion, the Christ figure from Christianity, and elements of scientific naturalism itself. The intent was to produce a scientific spirituality and a spiritual science, thereby dissolving the spiritualism/materialism dichotomy without collapsing either side into the other. All of the texts analyzed in *Spirit Matters* were influenced by these events and discourses and provided materials for the late century culmination of hybrid religions, as I show in the concluding chapter.

A word about genre: although I said above that in one sense the types of works that I have selected to analyze here do not matter, in another sense they do matter. A review of the above list of works reveals that three genres of writing recur: religious study or theology, for obvious reasons; the Gothic-romance novel; and travel writing. The reason for the focus on the second of these is that the widespread Victorian cultural contest between Natural Theology and scientific naturalism, which is crucial throughout *Spirit Matters*, found expression especially in the literature of the Gothic-romance novel. That genre was shaped by this contest and became a consistently replicated "cultural form" and vehicle for the circulation and debate of it (Franklin, *Serious Play* 6–7). Bulwer-Lytton's novels directly influenced and set the pattern for later generations of Gothic-romance novelists, such as Marie Corelli. Authors in this genre strove mightily to reconcile religion and science through the construction of fictional physicotheologies, and their "battle to maintain faith without rejecting science—or to pursue science without the traditional consolations of faith—continues in both popular science writing and science fiction," even in the twenty-first century (Fuller 104). Thus, genre formation is a significant recurring concern in this book. The chapters on Bulwer-Lytton, Haggard, and Stoker trace the historical trajectory of the Gothic-romance novel, and the chapter on Leonowens analyzes her switching between genres, one of which is Gothic romance, as a primary indicator of her conflicting meanings. As many have observed, the maturation of the literary Gothic paralleled the growing fascination with esoteric and then occult spirituality, as on the opposed side novelistic realism has been said to express the growing dominance of scientific empiricism and middle-class values, though these generalizations of course oversimplify.

The third genre that recurs in this collection is travel writing, which in the nineteenth century frequently was a hybridization of multiple genres. Two works treated here, Knighton's *Forest Life in Ceylon* and Leonowens's *English Governess*, merge the travelogue with the novel, the diary or autobiography, the anthropological notebook, the fable or tale, and the treatise on comparative religious studies, in this case of Christianity and Buddhism. These two works, ostensibly grounded in actual places and historical events, even so bear many similarities to "imperial Gothic" novels, and their authors fictionalized freely (Brantlinger, "Imperial Gothic" 184). Haggard and Stoker, alike with Knighton and Leonowens, portray Christianity under the threat of cultural "counterinvasion" by foreign religions whose own homelands the British were actively trying to colonize (Franklin, *Lotus* 7). The novels and the travel writing alike of the period represented the pervasive ambivalences about the "civilizing" violence of empire—"The horror! The horror!" as Kurtz summed it up in *The Heart of Darkness* (1899). International travel, whether actual or fictional, brought contact with indigenous practices within other world religions, as well as with Christian missionaries from home. These contacts flooded England with artifacts and ideas especially from Hinduism and Buddhism that many orthodox Christians perceived as fantastical if not horrifying, but they also brought awareness of the limitations of the servants of Christ in the mission fields and prompted the comparative analysis of Christianity relative to other belief systems. These contacts could not but stimulate consideration of the historical and doctrinal, as well as geographical, boundaries of Christianity. Buddhism was the non-Judeo-Christian religion that had the biggest influence on religion in Britain in the nineteenth century. These are among the reasons why *Spirit Matters* includes two chapters focused on works of travel writing and three that investigate the dialogue between Christianity and Buddhism.

Although I selected the works analyzed in this book with care and because I find them both fascinating and representative, I have no doubt that I could choose ten entirely different works that would be similarly representative. Thus, for instance, I could have chosen to analyze, from the early to mid-Victorian years, translations of writings by Emanuel Swedenborg or Lucretius, any of the Bridgewater Treatises on Natural Theology, novels by Charlotte Brontë or Charles Dickens, treatises on mesmeric medicine by C. H. Townshend or Harriet Martineau, early missionary reports about Buddhism, or theological criticism by George Eliot. From the mid-Victorian decades, I could select essays from the Broad Church manifesto *Essays and Reviews*, or rejoinders to them; novels by Charles Kingsley or poems by Robert or Elizabeth Barrett Browning; séance narratives, collections of spirit writing, or popular treatises on Spiritualism; the early works of comparative religion focused on Buddhism; documents debating T. H. Huxley's coining of the word "agnosticism"; or Charles Bradlaugh's defenses of freethought and atheism. In the late Victorian period and up to World War I, the choices would be further multiplied: loss-of-faith novels by Mrs Humphry Ward or Edmond Gosse, among others; defenses of Christian faith by North England physicists; defenses of Spiritualism by Alfred Russel Wallace or Arthur Conan Doyle; fairytales by George MacDonald or reports and photographs of fairy encounters; spiritual romances by Maria Corelli or spiritual autobiographies by Florence Marryat; religious poetry by Dante Gabriel Rossetti or Christina Rossetti; Society for Psychical Research reports; novels set in Asian countries by Somerset Maugham, Leonard Woolf, or James Hilton; popular science writings on the spiritual universe, such as *The Unseen Universe* or *Flatland*; secret documents from the Hermetic Order of the Golden Dawn; anything published in spiritualist or occult journals such as *Medium and Daybreak*, *Light*, or *Borderland*; or poetry by W. B. Yeats or T. S. Eliot. As any scholar of the period knows, I have only brushed the surface (and I have not even touched the vast subjects of the influences of Hinduism or Islam, which I leave to other scholars). It is no exaggeration to say that thousands of works were published in nineteenth-century Great Britain that were outside the domain proper of orthodox Christianity and represented spiritual positions defined between it and scientific naturalism or foreign faiths. That is the territory I have claimed for *Spirit Matters*, and I could have chosen to analyze many other texts to which my observations and conclusions in this book still would apply.

*Spirit Matters* is about how immense pressure came to bear upon traditional religious belief in nineteenth-century Great Britain for identifiable historical reasons, how the struggle to retain faith generated evolutionary adaptation of it into an array of alternative religious positions that in their number, variety, and inventiveness would have been unimaginable at any prior moment in nineteen centuries of Western history, and how that array of variations succeeded in keeping Spirit alive through a compromise with materialism and science such that it would be reborn in the subsequent century as widespread sociocultural phenomena called "New Age."

# Acknowledgments

My thanks to the editors and publishers who supported my work along the path toward *Spirit Matters*, in particular those associated with *The Ashgate Companion to Spiritualism and the Occult in the Nineteenth Century*, *The Routledge Research Companion to Anthony Trollope*, and the journals *Literature Compass* and *Cahiers victoriens et édouardiens*, which published previous versions of what are now chapters 2, 3, 4, and 8, respectively, as cited in the bibliography.

I am indebted and grateful to the community of fellow scholars at the University of Colorado Denver, the College of Liberal Arts and Sciences, and the Department of English for their example and moral support; Robert Damrauer of the CU Denver Office of Research Services and Michelle Comstock, chair of English, for financial support; the librarians at the Auraria Library, who procured many sources from afar; the colleagues and friends in the Victorian Interdisciplinary Studies Association of the Western United States; Bernard Lightman, who gave me useful criticism of chapter 1; two anonymous outside readers, who were both generous and incisively critical; my editor at Cornell University Press, Mahinder Kingra, who gave invaluable guidance and spurred me to take additional steps that I had not realized were necessary, which made *Spirit Matters* the book that it is; and, finally, she who ungrudgingly grants the necessary distance, unstintingly applies the balm of love, and beautifully embodies a life lived with Spirit, my lifetime friend and wife, Judy Lucas.

# Spirit Matters

# 1

# Orthodox Christianity, Scientific Materialism, and Alternative Religions

Nineteenth-century Great Britain witnessed and was transformed by a confluence of world-historical trends in science, economics and industry, and empire. These in turn converged with—and in part caused—a set of historically predicated obsessions about God's relationship to the natural world and the proper functions of religion in modern society. The resulting volatile amalgamation was especially characteristic of the Victorian period (1837–1901). This period experienced what could be considered the second wave of the Protestant Reformation, its individualization of faith, which had been building momentum in Europe since the Enlightenment. Thus Protestant individuals, driven by a widely perceived crisis of faith in orthodox Christianity, subject to modern science's rise to dominance in truth-telling authority, and fully exposed for the first time in history to the panoply of world religions, generated an unprecedented proliferation of new and often hybrid religions and spiritualities. This book treats that diverse array of alternative beliefs, which until now have been considered largely as disparate events and discourses, as parts of a century-long, collectively experienced cultural phenomenon. That phenomenon was a culture-wide striving to reclaim a spiritual certainty that for the first time in history a critical mass of Britons suspected could be lost.

In one sense, this is a book about what William James called *The Varieties of Religious Experience* (1902). Though James (1842–1910) was American and this book focuses on England, he encountered and studied many of the same religious experiences that I analyze in the contemporaneous context of Victorian Britain. He was born into a culture rooted in New England Puritanism, haunted by the Spiritualism movement, and infused with American Transcendentalism. His father was a theologian of the mystical Christianity of Swedenborgianism, and he himself experimented with drug-induced mystical states, cofounded the American Society for Psychical Research (modelled on the London SPR), and attended séances to commune with the spirits of the departed. This variety of religious and spiritual experiences only begins to suggest the full range that existed in nineteenth-century Britain, even more so than in North America. This book investigates a broad spectrum of those experiences through a series of representative case studies that, although highly varied, tell a chronological story about the development of unorthodox religious and spiritual discourses in Britain over the course of the nineteenth century.

## The Territory of Spirit

The Victorian period—often characterized as the "age of doubt," the "age of agnosticism," the "age of materialism," and the "age of scientific naturalism"—was an age of the most intense private angst and public debate about the states of faith and doubt, perhaps the age of the most intense religious controversy in history not typified by widespread physical violence or religious war.[1] As the familiar story goes, the primary contestants were the "old orthodoxy" of mainstream Christianity and the "new orthodoxy of materialistic science," especially after Charles Darwin's *On the Origins of Species* (1859) (Turner, *Between* 2). My opening premise is that there was a third contestant, which some Victorians called "Spirit," in the form of an array of esoteric and occult beliefs and practices, and that the Victorian period was the age of the proliferation of alternative religions, the beginning of New Age spiritualities, although that term was not widely adopted until the subsequent century. The story this book tells concerns the formation of that array of alternative beliefs within the context of their triangular positioning in relationship to orthodox Christianity on one side and scientific naturalism and its associated materialism on the other. Thus one thread that ties this story together is the recurrence throughout the century of the foundational, Western metaphysical opposition between the spiritual and the material. That dualism was continuously contested throughout the century and remained ever fluid and noncategorical. The boundaries between religion and science never were unequivocal, and, in fact, the faithful produced their own scientific foundations and empirical proofs and the scientists produced their own religious positions and secularized theologies. That is part of the story this books tells. Another part is the unexpected influence of the encounter with non-Western religions as a byproduct of imperialism, in particular the profound influence of Buddhism in the West. The encounter with Buddhism linked the frontiers of missionary contacts with indigenous religions to debates within the Church of England to the appropriation of elements of Hinduism and Buddhism by the syncretic or "hybrid religions" that proliferated in Great Britain at the end of the century (Franklin, *Lotus* 59). Yet another part of the story is the historical arc from the early century popular spiritual movements—Mesmerism and Spiritualism—to those hybrid religions late in the century.[2] The story ends with its culmination in Theosophy, which drew all of the influences covered in this book into a synthesis that deconstructed the dualisms of spiritualism versus materialism and Natural Theology versus scientific naturalism, thereby forging the template for twentieth-century New Age spiritualities.

Returning to the early nineteenth century for an opening example, consider the range of religious positions represented in *Jane Eyre* (1847). Charlotte Brontë (1816–55), who grew up in a rural parish as the daughter of an Evangelical Church of England clergyman, wrote at a time of significant religious upheaval. The end of the eighteenth and first half of the nineteenth century saw a major evangelical revival that spanned Protestant denominations and, at the same time, the rapid encroachment upon the dominance of the established church by Nonconformist denominations such a Congregationalism, Methodism, and multiple Baptist varieties. These events conditioned the emergence, beginning in the 1830s, of the Anglo-Catholic Tractarian movement, led by Oxford divines, and the resulting schism within Anglicanism between those Rome-leaning High Churchmen and Low Church evangelicals. In that same period, a comparable burgeoning of spiritual discourses occurred at or outside the boundaries of orthodox Christianity. Starting in the 1830s, the Mesmerism movement began to spread to London from the Continent, saturating popular culture in England by the 1850s. Close upon its heels came the Spiritualism movement, having originated in 1840s New England. By the 1860s, many thousands of Europeans, including royalty, famous authors, eminent scientists, and even clergymen, had held hands around a séance table to invite communications from the Spirit World. Add to this the persistence through several millennia of pagan beliefs and practices within indigenous British Isle cultures. These had merged or syncretized with Christianity such that "it involved no inconsistency for a villager to attend the parish church on Sunday morning . . . and with equal conviction to . . . ask the permission of the 'Old Gal' before chopping elder wood" (Obelkevich 305–6). It should be no wonder, then, that Brontë's writings, like those by her siblings and many others, portrayed a variety of religious and spiritual experiences, as well as syncretism among them.

*Jane Eyre* is a novel in which spirits abound, "spirit" having connotations more varied than the traditional Christian conceptions of the immortal soul or the Holy Spirit. The novel invokes spirit in Christian ways, pagan and other non-Christian supernatural ways, and, most tellingly, ways that blur those boundaries. It stages a contest between and, ultimately, a merging of multiple spiritualities.[3] In the following exemplary excerpt, Jane is in flight across the moors from the temptations that Rochester has proffered of living with him out of wedlock:

> She broke forth as never moon yet burst from cloud: a hand first penetrated the sable folds and waved them away; then, not a moon, but a white human form shone in the azure, inclining a glorious brow earthward. It gazed and gazed and gazed on me. It spoke to my spirit: immeasurably distant was the tone, yet so near, it whispered in my heart—"My daughter, flee temptation!" . . . We know that God is everywhere; but certainly we feel His presence most when His works are on the grandest scale spread before us. . . . I had risen to my knees to pray for Mr. Rochester. Looking up, I, with tear-dimmed eyes, saw the mighty Milky Way. Remembering what it was—what countless systems there swept space like a soft trace of light—I felt the might and strength of God. Sure was I of His efficiency to save what

He had made: convinced I grew that neither earth should perish nor one of the souls it treasured. I turned prayer to thanksgiving: the Source of Life was also the Saviour of spirits. (281, 285)

In certain ways this reads as a Christian reconversion experience. Brontë was a devout Christian, as nearly all early Victorian readers would have professed to be. Her readership exerted tremendous pressure upon heroines to exemplify Christian faith and morals. *Jane Eyre* represents Christian discourse especially through four characters, two Anglican clergymen, Mr. Brocklehurst and St. John Rivers, and two female characters, Helen Burns and Jane herself. Brocklehurst and Rivers are both evangelicals, though of two significantly different strains within Anglicanism, and the novel ultimately shows them and their brands of Christianity to be unworthy of Jane's powerful, female spirituality. This could not but trouble many of Brontë's readers, as it did a well-known reviewer who famously tarred the novel as "eminently an anti-Christian composition" (Rigby in Brontë 442). Helen Burns, frail and dying of tuberculosis, is the figure of Christlike sacrifice in the novel, but Jane's spirit is too vital to embrace such self-abnegation. Although Helen is a Christian paragon, her devotion itself incorporates beliefs outside of orthodox Christianity, as when she says: "Besides this earth, and besides the race of men, there is an invisible world and a kingdom of spirits: that world is round us, for it is everywhere; and those spirits watch us, for they are commissioned to guard us" (60). Jane is the remaining spokesperson for Christian faith in the novel, yet she more than anyone is figured throughout in terms of pagan spirituality, and she directly experiences the reality of a natural supernatural event. Thus the above passage, rather than casting off the pagan in order to herald the Christian, merges God the Father with Mother Nature. The "Source of Life" is both divine and the natural universe (explained to Jane by the science of astronomy), whether worshiped directly in paganism and pantheism or taken as proof of God's design as in Natural Theology. The "Saviour of Spirits" signals at once both the redeemer of souls, Jesus Christ, and the Spirit World, a state or location outside of traditional heaven and Christian orthodoxy.

William James and Charlotte Brontë, representative of a large number in the nineteenth century, explored beliefs beyond the boundaries of orthodox Christianity, but they did so necessarily in reference to and using terms drawn from that dominant cultural register. A comprehensive consideration of religious and spiritual positions during that period would have to focus largely on those within Christian orthodoxy. That in itself would entail consideration of a very broad variety, given that "the foremost characteristic of Victorian religion was its unabashed, unapologetic denominationalism" and "religious controversy [was] the 'spectator sport of Victorian England'" (Turner, *Contesting* 23; Schlossbert 286). A wide range of contested positions existed just within the Church of England, as well as within non-Anglican Protestantism, and then there was Catholicism. But, none of these many religious positions is of primary concern here. This book is not about Christianity, not directly, but cannot help being indirectly about it. The focus here is on heterodox, non-Christian or borderline-Christian religious and spiritual positions in nineteenth-century Britain. In order to locate those positions, however, one must be able to identify the boundary of orthodoxy against which heterodoxies defined themselves.

For the purposes of this study, "orthodox Christianity" designates an immensely complex, grossly generalized amalgamation of nineteenth-century British Christianities. Despite the hotly contested schism within the state church, both High Church and Low Church "espoused the quest for holiness of living . . . , both agreed on the divine inspiration of scripture, both agreed on the essentiality of the doctrines of divine judgment and eternal punishment, both held uncompromisingly supernatural views of Christianity, and both firmly believed in miracles, revelation and the literal fulfillment of prophecy" (Parsons 34). The more evangelical congregations, both Anglican and Nonconformist, emphasized biblical literalism, individualism of faith, human fallenness through sin, and God's judgment. All denominations, including the minority Catholics, experienced the common threat to truth-telling authority posed by scientific naturalism, signaled especially by Darwin's *On the Origin of Species*, as a crisis within the faith as a whole. It is this whole—the historical and doctrinal consensus of Christianity concerning the birth and crucifixion of Jesus of Nazareth and some version of sin, redemption, and heavenly reward—which I refer to as "orthodox Christianity" or "Victorian Christianity." The territory of this study is largely outside that domain. Even the chapters on Matthew Arnold and Anthony Trollope find unorthodox religious positions tied to paganism and Buddhism.

## Materialism and Scientific Naturalism

The territory of this study is bounded on the side opposite orthodox Christianity by atheism and what was called "materialism," one of the master terms underlying debate about religion in the nineteenth century. The following chapters are no more concerned directly with atheism and materialism than they are with orthodox Christianity, but it is similarly necessary for understanding the religious and spiritual discourses analyzed in this book to locate them in relationship to the beliefs that marked the outer boundary against which they were defined.

Both atheism and materialism were as much theoretical foes—boogeymen to frighten those with wavering faith or freethought leanings—as actual foes on the ground in England. The number of Britons who publicly professed atheism was very much smaller than the number of Christian apologists who cited the dangers of atheism. Though after midcentury there were infamous self-proclaimed atheists, such as Charles Bradlaugh, the founder of the Secular Society in 1866, most cited examples of atheists were not Englishmen at all but rather were the classical progenitors—Epicurus, Democritus, and Lucretius—or modern Continental philosophers such as Baruch Spinoza or Denis Diderot, on the basis of whom Britons thereafter linked atheism to revolutionary politics. Similarly, "during the nineteenth century . . . European materialism was limited almost exclusively to Germany in the form of the scientific materialism of men such as Vogt, Büchner, Moleschott and the dialectical materialism of Marx and Engels" (Lightman, *Origins* 25). Self-proclaimed materialists were few and far between in Britain. Despite that fact, "materialism was widely perceived as the archvillain of the age" and "an expression of support for materialism of any sort was still not tolerated in Britain in the 1870s" and subsequent decades (Oppenheim 61; Lightman, "On Tyndall's" n.p.).

Materialism is of particular relevance here because it was a linchpin concept that locked religion and science in dialogue within one of the most significant cultural contests of the nineteenth century and, indeed, throughout "Western Civilization." In the second half of the century, those most accused of materialism were the "scientific naturalists," especially Charles Darwin, Herbert Spencer, John Tyndall, and T. H. Huxley, but also W. K. Clifford, Francis Galton, Frederic Harrison, G. H. Lewes,

Edward Tylor, and Leslie Stephen, among others. Huxley, the great polemicist on behalf of science, "coined 'scientific naturalism' as an antithetical term to 'supernaturalism'" because it was "preferable to the considerably more contentious term *scientific materialism* coined by his close friend John Tyndall" (quoted in Dawson and Lightman 1).[4] Tyndall, the prominent Irish physicist, had inflamed the Christian opponents of Darwinism and science generally in his "Belfast Address" of 1874 and handed them an advantage by using the term "materialism" in defense of scientific method. The scientific naturalists placed themselves in the position of defending a precarious distinction between science as a *method* of "observation and experiment which explains phenomena only through natural laws and processes, without direct appeal to supernatural or divine agency" and science as a *metaphysics* that eschews or dismisses the divine in claiming to explain absolutely everything from the conscience to the cosmos in purely materialistic terms (Fuller 8).

Huxley strove to maintain this distinction in his "two-spheres position"—that the domains of religion and science are separate and so need not be in conflict—as well as in the word he coined for a religious position suitable to scientific naturalists: agnosticism (Lightman, "Victorian Sciences" 347). He strategically distanced agnosticism from atheism and materialism by defining it on the basis of the limited scope of human knowledge, which excused adherents from any and all knowledge claims about the divine. Thus, as Frank Miller Turner summarizes, "in their metaphysics despite their rather loose and continuously misunderstood polemical vocabulary Spencer, Tyndall, Huxley, and others of the camp of scientific naturalism presented themselves as opponents of any form of reductionistic materialism" (*Contesting* 82). They, like eminent predecessors such as Thomas Hobbes and "like most other English materialists, in contrast to their French counterparts, did not consider atheism to be a logical implication of materialism"; they strove to reconcile scientific methodological materialism with the divine, though not with religious dogma (van Huyssteen and Vrede, 540.). Nevertheless, the distinction they precariously maintained between science as method and science as metaphysics, and therefore between science and atheism, was "often quite understandably lost on [their] audience" (Turner, *Contesting* 264). Christian apologists "scoured their public pronouncements for evidence of infidel materialism" and found sufficient evidence to tar scientific materialism with the brush of atheism (Endersby 178). The stakes could not have been higher: the traditional truth-telling authority of orthodox Christianity versus the increasingly empowered truth-telling authority of science.

The scientific naturalists could not disencumber themselves of the history—or histories—of materialism. Perhaps the oldest historical foundation was that of the Epicurean fathers of Western materialism, especially Lucretius (ca. 99–ca. 55 BCE). His *De rerum natura*, a seminal work of philosophical materialism in verse, experienced a wave of renewed interest in the mid-nineteenth century. It followed Democritus in presaging modern atomic theory, appeared to predict Darwinian evolutionary theory, was "monistic" in positing the universe as "a single, unified, material substratum," and was baldly atheistic in denying the existence of anything external to or transcendent of that material continuum (Vitzthum 18). For Lucretius, "humans, along with the souls that inhabit them, are nothing more than complex physical systems" (B. Morgan vii). Especially after Tyndall's "Belfast Address," both he and Huxley were paired with Lucretius to brand them as abject materialists. Despite Tyndall's denials that his form of materialism was part of the tradition originated by Lucretius, "Lucretius became a pawn in the struggle for cultural domination between the men of science and the men of religion and idealism" (Turner, *Contesting* 272).

The Victorian interest in Epicurean physics—signaled by references to "monism" and the "uniformity of nature"—was contemporaneous with the culmination of modern thermodynamics in a series of groundbreaking statements by physicists in Germany and England between 1840 and 1850. Statements about the impossibility of creating or destroying matter, the fixed amount of available energy in the universe, and entropy appeared to preclude external—divine—intervention: "Rejecting the old dualism of matter and force, in which force was applied to matter by an extrinsic being (God), the two were now seen as immanent within one another. . . . These materialist principles challenged—and would ultimately succeed—the metaphysical basis of natural theology" (Crook 203). As Bernard Lightman has observed, "this interpretation of the law of the conservation of energy was probably more destructive of religious explanations involving miracles, spirits, or God than the theory of evolution by natural selection" ("Victorian Sciences" 354). Thus Dimsdale Stocker, a popular author on diverse spiritual and ethical topics, lamented in his *Spirit,*

*Matter, and Morals* (1908) that "this monistic conception of life and mind is destined, within a very short space of time, to completely revolutionize the unwarranted assumption that there can be any *fundamental* difference . . . between matter and spirit" (53). On the other hand, theistic scientists such as James Clerk Maxwell, William Thomson, Lord Kelvin, and other "North England" physicists (as distinguished from the London scientific naturalists) "accept[ec] the concept of nature as a self-contained system" but still "regarded the operations of divine providence as occurring within the natural order": God's will expressed as natural laws (Heimann 76).[5] For them, the "unity of nature was a theological concept as well as a scientific one," and so James Ward, a geologist who wrote a manual on Natural Theology, countered materialistic science with his theory of a "spiritualistic monism" (Stanley, "Where Naturalism" 248; Turner, *Between* 233).

The most significant of the historical backgrounds of materialism was that of Christianity itself, in particular the historical context of Protestant antimaterialism. If the biblical creation story is about a fall of humanity from unity with the divine it also is a story of the fall of humanity from unity with nature through expulsion from Eden. In ways much more complex than I am going to do justice to here, one of the master narratives of Christianity is the story of this tripartite relationship between the divine, the natural, and the human. This master narrative cycles unceasingly through the answers to this question: to what extent is each one of these unified with, divided from, transcendent of, or immanent within each of the others? In Genesis, God creates the natural universe for the use of humanity as his privileged creation that transcends the natural by possession of an immortal soul. This is the *externality of the human from the natural*, not subject to but lord of nature. Revelation, as in the Mosaic story or the Resurrection, is about transcendence, the *externality of the divine* from the natural and the human. The Jesus story, both human and divine, is about healing this very separation, if through paradox shading into contradiction. In contrast to transcendence, immanence is about the identity of the natural and the divine, as in pantheism, and thus it is outside of Christian orthodoxy. God, nature, and humankind always must be at once part of and separate from one another, or in constant oscillation between spirit and matter.

One product of this Christian master narrative is the traditional, Western body/soul dualism in which the body is matter, wed to nature, divorced from the divine. Catholic mortification of the flesh and Protestant defilement of the body as sin incarnate are the results. This is why the root meaning of "materialist," as in this eighteenth-century definition, is "one who denies spiritual substances," most crucially God and the immortal soul but also spirits and the supernatural of all sorts (Johnson n.p.). This is why, as Peter Pels summarizes, " 'materialism' emerges in the late seventeenth and early eighteenth centuries as an accusation, a Protestant critique of a way of thinking that, since the early Christian patriarchs, was identified with Epicurean philosophy and its perceived tendency to liberate human lust and gluttony" ("Modern Fear" 273).

## Physicotheologies and the Religion of Science

Yet it was during that same European historical period—the Enlightenment—that the emergence of modern philosophy and science revived or built complementary, legitimizing discourses of materialism in the form of "physicotheologies," such as Deism and Natural Theology (Brooke and Cantor 149). The seventeenth through the nineteenth centuries witnessed the formation of a series of modern European physicotheologies, theologies defined in relationship to rationality or an empirical understanding of the natural world, and this series is another of the contextualizing histories of materialism.

Enlightenment Deism, to summarize briefly, preserved God's creating and, in some accounts, judging authority but by rationalizing revelation and miracle out of the natural universe, which now would be the purview of reason. This places Deism on or outside the boundary of orthodoxy. As Henry Baildon bemoaned in his 1880 work, *The Spirit of Nature, Being a Series of Interpretive Essays on the History of Matter from the Atom to the Flower*, "Thus, in his anxiety to avow his deism, he banished the action of his Deity to a remote period of the past, leaving Him as it were at the very verge of His own universe, in such a position, too, that He must recede continually before the advance of science" (41). The "absentee landlord" God of Deism is the externalized creator of natural laws who is unwilling to intervene in or violate them with supernatural phenomena, surrendering that field as the domain of science.[6]

The most successful form of physicotheology, Natural Theology, has classical and medieval origins but bloomed in England especially in the seventeenth and eighteenth centuries as a carefully arranged marriage, or truce, between the Church and science. Both were not infrequently represented in the same person: an Anglican clergyman whose Oxbridge education also bred interest in natural science. As Turner summarizes: "Anglican culture as it touched upon the larger intellectual life of the nation and in particular the pursuit of sciences was very closely associated with exposition of natural theology"; "scientists, who were of course also often clergymen, in turn appropriated a new emphasis on natural theology to demonstrate that science and rational thought correctly understood would lead not to materialism, atheism, and revolution as in France but rather to reverence for God and support for the existing political and social order" (*Contesting* 47, 77). Built in part on a "two-spheres position," Natural Theology eschewed revelation theology, yet, unlike Deism, it argued for the discernibility of God's ongoing presence in his creation through unaided human reason in observation of nature. William Paley's *Natural Theology: or, Evidences of the Existence and Attributes of the Deity, Collected from the Appearances of God* (1802) made the watchmaker analogy and the "argument from design" as proof of God's existence commonplaces in the nineteenth century. The golden age of Natural Theology in England was marked by the Bridgewater Treatises, a series published in the 1830s–1840s of expositions on the efficacy of that belief, initiated by a bequest from the Earl of Bridgewater.

Then came Charles Darwin. He, among others, showed that species might evolve without divine plan, even randomly, and suggested that the human species may not be external to nature but rather very much a part of it. Thus a severe blow fell upon the anthropomorphism and optimism of Natural Theology, which had come to underwrite the superiority not only of the species but of the social, commercial, and imperial practices of British wealth as the manifest destiny of "progress" designed by God especially for the English.[7] Even with so much riding upon Natural Theology, the scientific naturalists were driven to defeat it in order to exercise the authority to make scientific claims free of reference to divine intention. In this they demonstrated their methodological materialism and opened themselves to the charge of metaphysical materialism.

Natural Theology was far from the only nineteenth-century physicotheology. Indeed, a historically unique proliferation of physicotheologies arose in nineteenth-century Europe, though all had roots in previous eras.

German and then English Romanticism (and then American Transcendentalism) were, among many other things, a wedding of the natural and the divine in which the sublimity of nature became God's immanent investiture. Thomas Carlyle rearticulated this as "natural supernaturalism," spiritualizing nature by materializing the spiritual, while at the same time he became the foremost critic of the materialism of the Industrial Revolution, damning "Mechanism" and the "Age of Machinery."[8] Charles Dickens further popularized this critique in such novels as *Hard Times* (1854). In the same decades, the Mesmerism movement modernized occult belief in the form of a universal "vital fluid," the divine essence of all life, and transformed that belief into a science of "animal magnetism," which generated research studies and mesmeric hospitals in Paris and London. It was championed by some on materialist grounds as soon-to-be-verified science and by others with very different motives on spiritualist grounds as empirical proof of the soul. In a different cultural domain, John Ruskin's widely influential criticism combined a "reverent respect for the material world," as manifested in natural beauty and the beauty of great art, with a "ferocious hostility to [any] materialism" that threatened to deny the origins of such beauty in divine creation and inspiration (Levine, *Realism* 80, 81). Ruskin's physicotheological aesthetics contributed later in the century to the Aestheticism movement, which he would have damned for stripping the worship of beauty of its ethical and spiritual dimensions by hedonistically materializing it.[9]

Victorian scientists, effectively driven by the context of these debates to declare a religious position, participated as much if not more than others in the fashioning of physicotheologies. Many scientists publicly took religious or spiritual stances, and those ranged across the spectrum from orthodox to heterodox to pantheistic to spiritualistic. Theistic physicists, such as the North England physicists, strove to find God's design even in the entropy described by the second law of thermodynamics and to credit a lawful uniformity of nature that evidenced rather than excluded God's participation in it. Balfour Stewart and Peter Guthrie Tait wrote, in addition to physics textbooks, *The Unseen Universe* (1875) "to show that the presumed incompatibility of Science and Religion does not exist," placing themselves among "those who have a profound belief that the true principles of science will be found in accordance with revelation, and . . . believe that the Author of revelation is likewise the Author of nature" (n.p.).

They saw "in London-based scientific naturalism a form of anti-Christian materialism" (Lightman, "Victorian Sciences" 352).

Theistic biologists, alike with a larger number of "Christian Darwinians" in other walks of life, strove similarly to find a divine order in evolution, one not yet explicated by science, to counter random natural selection (England 277). As one popular science writer described a not uncommon position, "My general aim is not so much to discredit Darwinism proper . . . as to attack and if possible demolish that materialistic and atheistic system . . . that involves the extension of what may be called a mechanical evolution not only to the whole organic world, but also to matter and force in their most simple and primitive forms . . . without any direction, control or assistance from creative power or intelligence" (Baildon vii). Perhaps the most notable evolutionary theist next to Herbert Spencer was Alfred Russel Wallace, co-originator of the theory of evolution through natural selection and, later in his career, one of the most outspoken proponents of Spiritualism. Wallace's "evolutionary theism explicitly maintains that the Divine Being continues to sustain relations to His creation"; more significant, "in contrast to pantheists—who view God as identical with the totality of nature or the laws of nature or a world soul immanent in nature and not in any way transcending it—Wallace's deity is a purposeful eternal being, transcending the world but also immanent in it" (Fichman 228).[10] In addition to maintaining this split view of God as at once both external and internal to the natural universe, Wallace, like many spiritualists, claimed evidence for Spiritualism in observable phenomena and adhered to a theory of spiritual evolution, a Lamarckian model of the soul's intentional progression, sometimes conceived as occurring over the course of multiple incarnations (thanks to European exposure to Hinduism and Buddhism).

As monism was to physics, the human mind was the boundary-marking issue from a biological perspective. Surely nature could not have created such complexity unaided by divine design. This argument from cerebral design found support across the full spectrum of theistic positions. Thus Wallace declared in 1870 that "natural selection could not account for the mental and moral nature of human beings," that "self-consciousness, reason, the moral sense, free will, and religiosity" could not but be the fingerprint of God—a tautology that because we believe in God he must exist (Turner, *Between* 73; Fichman 239). Even as a bridging concept in the professionalization of modern psychology as a science in the latter part of the century, "one of the most popular interpretations of the unconscious mind . . . was, in fact, the soul" (Reed 119). A number of prominent public intellectuals, such as the psychologist James Ward and the novelist Samuel Butler, generalized this understanding of mind to a panpsychist view of the interconnection between the natural and the divine. In that model, the universe itself and all beings within it share a vital, integrated, purposeful sentience; "whereas the psychical researcher or spiritualist saw mind as external to the physical world [transcendent of it, as with revealed divinity], the panpsychist saw mind as immanently present in physical nature" (Turner, *Between* 133).

What is more, the scientific naturalists themselves constructed physicotheologies, if somewhat more secularized versions. Contrary to their own claims about having progressed beyond the need for metaphysics, contrary to the charges by their opponents that they were thoroughgoing materialists and atheists, and contrary to a predominant master narrative among some twentieth-century historians that portrayed science and Christianity as monolithic and polarized and culminated in the "secularization thesis," according to which in the nineteenth century science had emerged victorious over religion, scientific naturalism itself was a metaphysical, ideological, and even religious position.[11]

Scientific naturalism rested on a nonempirical metaphysical foundation only less by degree than did the theologies that its adherents criticized on that very basis. If, as skeptics argued, appeals to an invisible Holy Spirit or a sacred text or an inner sense of right and wrong provided but flimsy proof of the eternal soul or Jesus's Resurrection or God's law, so appeals to atoms, which could not (yet) be seen, or to the existence supposedly millions of years prior of extinct species provided but flimsy proof of scientific claims about force and matter or evolutionary theory or the origins of life. The scientific naturalists "were fully aware that their anti-metaphysical stance, and the work of science, were dependent on metaphysically unprovable assumptions" (Levine, "Paradox" 85). Their foundational axioms, such as "the universality of the law of causation, the uniformity of nature, and the existence of an objective, external natural world . . . became articles of faith, for the agnostics could no more justify certainty in their existence than orthodox Christians could scientifically prove the actuality of the Son, the Father, and the Holy Ghost" (Lightman, *Origins* 146). Thus late Victorians, feeling their most cherished beliefs under attack especially by Huxley, the "self-consecrated 'bishop' of the 'Church scientific,' " who had adopted his polemical style from Protestant evangelicalism, countered in kind by pointing out that the "Priests of Science" should temper the claims for their "creed of science" accordingly (Moore 177; Lilly, *Ancient Religion* 254, 327).

Not only did scientific naturalism have metaphysical foundations, but those foundations were alloyed with *theological* metaphysics. Perhaps the point is that there is no physics entirely free of metaphysics, and that any metaphysics, even that of science, cannot but be physicotheological. Further, the admixing of naturalistic metaphysics with more traditionally theological metaphysics occurred in a range of complex ways that may have varied on a person-by-person basis. Scholars of Darwin and Huxley have analyzed their religious upbringings and identified the religious elements in their writings.[12] Another point, then, is that no one escapes the dominant cultural discourses of their time. Even Tyndall, "who called himself a 'materialist' . . . still contended that matter had been 'defined and maligned by philosophers and theologians, who are equally unaware that it is, at bottom, essentially mystical and transcendental' " (Turner, *Between* 147). Perhaps unavoidably, the thought of many scientific naturalists was laced with Natural Theology or pantheism or transcendental materialism—various strains of physicotheologies. In this I follow not those historians who subscribed to the "secularization thesis" but those, such as Robert Young and Bernard Lightman, who see not a clear-cut paradigm shift but rather the continuities between Natural Theology and scientific naturalism. The scientific naturalists revered nature, and nature for them was either God or next to God, the matter of spirit.

This is of course partly explained by the history of social relationship between scientific naturalists in England and the Church. Huxley and other radical intellectuals were contesting cultural authority, as Turner puts it; their stance was in juxtaposition to that of the ruling intellectual, political, and class-based establishment, the Church of England. They worked to build the professionalism of science, disambiguating themselves from the amateur gentlemen scientists, and to carve a place for scientific education in the traditionally locked academy of the public (private) schools and Oxbridge. The scientific naturalists were not trying to destroy Christianity or Anglicanism but rather to replace them with a more modern form, in effect to become them. And so their ambition was patterned upon the very religion in opposition to which they positioned themselves. Huxley in 1889 wrote of the "New Reformation" brought on by modern science, a break from Protestant Christianity that also was a continuation of it ("Agnosticism" n.p.). It was this "ambivalence about the Established Church especially—a coveting of its power and authority coupled with a loathing for its creed, an inclination to reform the institution tempered by an impulse to abolish it—that made the Protestant Reformation a potent metaphor for the dissident intellectuals" of scientific naturalism (Lightman, *Origins* 175). Thus Huxley's "original agnostics were not atheists, nor were they materialists or Positivists" but rather shaped "a species of agnosticism which is Christian, theistic, and religious, a thought that jars the modern sensibility," which tends to assume a clean opposition (16, 28). Although defenders of Christianity had reason for viewing agnosticism as only one step removed from atheism, it was in fact, or also, itself a heterodox religious position.

Even like Martin Luther in this regard, some agnostics were motivated by the sense that the Church of England had lost the pathway of pure religious truth—in which they were in consensus with many Nonconformists—and that science might lead the way to a surer truth for the future. On one side, the institution of the Church, the foundation of English religious and civil stability for centuries, seemed threatened by defection back to Catholicism, reversing the Reformation, and on the other side it seemed harried by fire-and-brimstone dogmatism and biblical literalism, which some critics viewed as tantamount to a materialism of another sort. Schism and dissension were rampant. Within this context, one can conceive how some agnostics believed that "the best aspirations of an earlier religious tradition . . . would be better fulfilled by a new 'priesthood'—the term was Francis Galton's as well as Comte's—who would place progress on a 'better intellectual and social basis' with the creed of scientific naturalism" (Moore 179). One liability of this belief, as some liberal intellectuals recognized even then, is that science might become the basis for a new religion of progress, a simplified teleology of manifest destiny blind to its own metaphysical assumptions, ideological motives, and unforeseen social and ecological consequences.[13]

## Summary Observations

A number of conclusions issue from the foregoing discussion. First, as may be obvious by now, religion and science did not fall neatly into discrete domains. In the nineteenth century in particular but perhaps in all periods, the two are imbricated to the extent that they cannot be cleanly separated. As Turner predicted in 1993, "When that world of concrete specificity is recovered for Victorian religious life as it has been for Victorian science, the categories of the religious and the secular as generally understood at present will largely dissolve" (*Contesting* 35). Both the scientific naturalists and the Christian defenders had their own science and their own religion, and both claimed to be able to reconcile, if not harmonize, the two.

Second, there are reasonable grounds for viewing agnosticism and even scientific naturalism itself as religious positions, as physicotheologies of the nineteenth century. Nonbelief was less a threat to Christian faith than was another, rapidly growing belief system, scientific naturalism. "The question, therefore, was not whether Victorian Britain would have a religion, but merely how it would be expressed"; "everyone agreed with Francis Newman that 'the age is ripe for . . . a religion,' a religion that would combine the best of Christian ethics with the intellectual rigour of 'the schools of modern science'" (Moore 173).

Third, the pervasive, diffuse, and richly various discourses of spiritualism versus materialism performed absolutely crucial cultural work. They were the processing of a tremendous cultural and social upheaval in the transition between mainstream Christianity and a proliferating array of physicotheologies, by which orthodox faith was being partially replaced.

Fourth, therefore, materialism was neither merely a threat to nor a negation of spiritualism; it functioned as the preserver of the spiritual. Peter Pels asks, "What does the Protestant fear of matter . . . do for Victorians, caught as they are between the icons of Protestant worship and the contemporary idols of 'materialism'?" ("Modern Fear" 266). The answer is that it weds the bride of religion to the groom of science, positing "materialism" as a shared problematic that inextricably links the two.[14] As Pels concludes, "the modern fear, or contempt, of matter, is a this-worldly materialization of a desire for an other-than-this-worldly existence" (278). In the nineteenth century, science saved Christianity, materialism saved spiritualism, and vice versa.

## An Opening Example: Ancient Religion and Modern Thought

The preceding section attempts to chart the territory within which the case studies in the chapters of this book should be located. That territory is bounded on one side by orthodox Christianity and on the other side by philosophical materialism and atheism (as well as by beliefs from non-Christian religions that were considered utterly heretical or inconceivable and thus were inassimilable). For the purposes of this book, those boundaries mark the cultural and historical context of Victorian heterodox religious and spiritual discourses. Understanding this context is necessary for comprehending the analyses that follow as parts of a loosely cohesive historical narrative.

To illustrate the ways in which that context shaped thinking about religion and spirituality and to prepare the way for the rest of this book, let us briefly consider one exemplary text that it would be difficult to comprehend without understanding that context, *Ancient Religion and Modern Thought*, published in 1884 by William Samuel Lilly (1840–1919). Lilly trained in the law, served in the Indian Civil Service as secretary to the government of Madras before returning to England, converted to Catholicism, and served for twenty years as the secretary to the Catholic Union of Great Britain, but he was most known as the author of a number of widely read essays and books on religious, ethical, and political issues of the day. The *Times* obituary of 1919 described *Ancient Religion and Modern Thought* as a "once famous" book ("Death of Mr. W. S. Lilly" 13), and in 1886 Lilly famously debated Huxley in the pages of *The Fortnightly Review* on the issues he first had developed in that book ("Message of Buddhism" n.p.). Lilly's overarching aim was to anatomize and refute "Modern Thought" and its "Gospel of Materialism," which in his view and that of many for whom he wrote threatened to undermine Christian faith (*Ancient Religion* iii, viii). Here was the problem as he saw it: "It seems to me that the issue before the world is between Christianity and a more or less sublimated form of Materialism, which is most aptly termed Naturalism; a system which rejects as antiquated the ideas of final causes, of Providence, of the soul and its immortality; which allows of no other realities than those of the physical order, and makes of Nature man's highest ideal: and this issue is not in the least affected by decking out Naturalism in some borrowed garments of Spiritualism, and calling it 'Natural Christianity'" (237). The unifying theme of Lilly's book, which otherwise ranges across topics from Tractarianism to Natural Theology to Buddhism, is the same as that I have chosen to foreground in this introduction: the spiritual versus the material.

My reading here of *Ancient Religion* will focus only on its two closing sections, written as a one-hundred-page-long dialogue between the classical figures of friendship, Damon and Pythias, now modern gentlemen who meet for dinner at the Apollo Club, having last opened their minds to one another twenty years prior while at college. In the interim, Damon has converted to Catholicism, and Pythias has become an adherent of skeptical "modern thought." Lilly's intention is to portray a genuine dialogue around faith and doubt that is not only civil but mutually empathetic and that captures the range of questions that crossed the minds if not the tongues of virtually every critically thinking Victorian Briton. Damon, Lilly's spokesperson, demonstrates the breadth of his liberal-mindedness in quoting not only Plato, St. Augustine, Thomas Aquinas, Cardinal John Henry Newman, and the pope (Leo XIII) but also skeptical philosophers and scientists, including René Descartes, Arthur Schopenhauer, John Stuart Mill, Darwin, Spencer, Clifford, and Stephen. Lilly further demonstrates the courage of his faith by having Pythias challenge Damon to answer a skeptic's hardest questions and to do so rationally and dispassionately if he wishes to demonstrate the grounds for faith through means more defensible than personal testimony or assertion of religious dogma.

Pythias directs their conversation by proffering a series of perhaps thirty questions overall, many as challenges to faith, under two chapter titles: "Naturalism and Christianity" and "Matter and Spirit." To analyze them point by point would be to catalog many of the most common skeptical questions of the Victorian period (and take more time than appropriate here). Those questions include consideration of the following: the relationship of doubt to faith; the Natural Theology argument from design, in particular the argument from cerebral design; traditional questions about faith in a world in which evil abounds and unmerited suffering is common; the general Victorian movement away from Calvinistic hell-and-damnation theology; the topical problems of historicism, the New Criticism, and biblical literalism; and the key issue that might be called "the problem of miracles," which goes straight to the question of the existence of the supernatural and the divine (and in relationship to which I discuss the Broad Church Anglican responses in subsequent chapters on Trollope and Arnold).

It is significant that Damon's responses often are discernible as directed toward the scientific naturalists and upon the very topics that I summarize in the previous section. He challenges in return the unproved metaphysical bases of science's most ambitious and controversial theories, the "dogmatic Materialism" with which some scientists defended those, and the shortsightedness of believing that all truths derive from empirical methods (Lilly, *Ancient Religion* 248). When Pythias invokes the "spectre of Evolution," "the bearing of the doctrine of Evolution upon the Theistic controversy," Damon neither decries Darwinism nor takes refuge in biblical literalism (249). Rather, he accepts the basic premise of the "development of species in time from less complicated organisms" as "almost proved" (250). But, he argues, evolutionary theories remain "nude hypotheses" without any explanation of why the evolutionary process takes place, thereby opening the way for God's design of natural selection itself. Darwin is a brilliant scientist—"we owe much, both to Mr. Darwin and to Mr. Spencer"—but science is limited in its purview to material phenomena, as Huxley's own "two-spheres" position argued (252). Thus the theories of St. George Mivart, a biologist who strove to reconcile Darwinism with Catholicism by denying the former's applicability to the human mind, are "more truly scientific, than that which has been followed by the authors of the brilliant but loosely-knit speculations so popular for the moment," namely evolutionary theory (252).

One other point that deserves note is Damon's allusions to and uses of Buddhism throughout. European missionaries and scholars had "discovered" Buddhism in the 1820s–1830s, and the field of comparative religions studies, which formed after midcentury, took Buddhism as a primary object of investigation.[15] As a result, Buddhism "hit" Europe in the 1860s, becoming a widespread topic that peaked in London's "Buddhism-steeped Nineties" (Caracciolo 30). Buddhism's Christlike founder and rigorous ethics cast it as the "Protestantism of Asia" and attracted sufficient interest that alarmed theologians launched the "Christianity-versus-Buddhism debate" in the periodical press, in which Lilly participated (Clausen 7; Franklin, *Lotus* 23). He was reading widely not only in science writing but in comparative religious studies on Buddhism, such as the works by Max

Müller and the Rhys Davidses. He, like many others, linked Buddhism with scientific naturalism and materialism and especially with Darwinian evolutionary theory, given a Western assumption that reincarnation was a kind of spiritual evolution in which one might progress from lifetime to lifetime. Thus in defending the doctrine of sin, for example, Damon draws an analogy both to scientific law—"What do the researches of the physicists bring out more than inexorableness of the 'laws of Nature,' as they speak? . . . Law reigns everywhere"—as well as to the Buddhist doctrines of karma, according to which one inescapably will experience the consequences of one's actions, and of dharma, which those writing about Buddhism frequently translated as "the Law" and likened to the Darwinian law of evolution (Lilly, *Ancient Religion* 264).[16] Damon subsequently defends a nonliteral, "literary" reading of the Bible (not unlike Matthew Arnold's *Literature and Dogma*, as I will show) by expounding what amounts to an evolutionary theory of religious history, saying: "And why not? To live is to change," such is part of God's "divinely ordained law" (267, 268). One can imagine that many of Lilly's readers would not have felt comfortable with his appeals either to evolutionary theory or to non-Christian religions, as when he defends against the assault by New Criticism upon the Bible by saying, "I should deeply resent such irreverent treatment of the *Dhammapada* or the *Qur'ân*," holy books within Buddhism and Islam respectively (277). Were I to provide a full reading of Lilly's responses to Buddhism, at once fascinated and repulsed, it would complement the readings I provide in the subsequent chapters on Mathew Arnold, William Knighton, and Anna Leonowens and further illustrate the impacts of the assimilation of Buddhism in shaping syncretic religious beliefs in the West, starting in the nineteenth century.

By allowing Pythias his skepticism, by allowing him to ask the hardest questions without ridicule, and by working to moderate the authoritative or monological voice of orthodox dogma, Lilly allows the voice of his nemesis, materialism, to speak within an almost genuinely dialogical exchange.[17] This intentional demonstration of open-minded critical thinking is no mean accomplishment in the melee of religious debates in nineteenth-century Britain. To accomplish this, however, through the rationalization of Christian orthodoxy to the truth claims of science (and Buddhism), Lilly drives himself to a position so near the border that he is defending that many of his mainstream readers would not have followed him there, even while applauding his intention to defend the faith. His "modern" Christian, not dissimilar from the Broad Church Anglican liberal intellectual, embraces Darwinism, Buddhism, the nonliteralism of the Bible, the historicity of religions, and the historical fallibility of the Catholic Church, as for instance in the Inquisition. Pythias finally pushes him to the extent of asking, "You maintain that the Catholic Church does not proscribe, denounce, or reject any truth of any kind which the modern mind has brought to light?," and Damon answers, "To do so would be to stultify herself as the representative of the God of Truth" (Lilly, *Ancient Religion* 287). Science has been fully integrated into God's law, but in the process that law has become very close to that of scientific metaphysics, Natural Theology.

This compromise, and the concomitant movement away from Christian orthodoxy toward what amounts to a form of Christian spiritualism, becomes only more apparent in the second dialogue between Damon and Pythias, titled "Matter and Spirit." Lilly is now ready to level distinctions between world religions in order to defend the existence of any "non-Material Power above ourselves, be it God, One in the Essence of Three in Persons, of Christianity; the Allah of Islâm; the Ahuramazda of Zoroastrianism; the Brahmâ of Hindu Pantheism; the Supremely Just Law ruling in the three worlds, according to the Buddhist conception" (*Ancient Religion* 308). Damon strives to close the gap between the metaphysics of science and the "vast body of quite irrefragable facts—facts which testify to the incorporeal nature . . . and the distinct personality of the soul" (319). He perhaps approaches, from the opposite direction, a position not unlike that of the North England physicists. He cites Tyndall's musings about "the miracle of vitality," the spiritual life force, stating: "No conclusion, I submit, is so reasonable in view of the facts of Physical sciences as this: that the life of the body depends upon an immaterial something that vivifies the material frame—a something which we call the soul" (322). Damon attempts to enlist physics and evolutionary biology in proofs of the "existence of a non-atomic enswathement of the soul," tracing the origins of that divine spark of spiritual life from its primordial origin in Creation to what amounts to a Darwinian spiritual evolution, the "law of spiral ascension" (332, 341). He approaches Wallace's evolutionary theism, combining with it hints of Buddhist reincarnation. The goal of evolution is "increased self-consciousness or development of the *Ego*, as a personage, individual, self-balanced, master of its resources" through a series of stages that will culminate, perhaps after eons, in full spiritual realization or enlightenment, "a society of immortal beings, physically, morally, and intellectually perfect, united in the immanent Cause of their existence" (342, 344). Thus Lilly undertakes to collapse the defining Western dualism of spiritualism versus materialism from which he started without reducing the former to the latter, with the resulting conclusions that "Nature is the allegory of spirit" and "Matter as distinct from spirit is an abstraction" (342, 343).

Lilly would have argued, strenuously, I suspect, that he was defending orthodox Christianity, Catholicism in particular. He was. In the process, however, the difference between his modern Christianity and the "modern thought" that he characterizes as atheistic materialism increasingly approached a vanishing point called "Spirit," the defense of the existence of the human soul and, based upon that, the spiritual truth of the traditional Christian narrative. In this, Lilly provides an example, consonant with the other texts that I analyze throughout this book, of the shifting boundary between the orthodox and the heterodox. *Ancient Religion and Modern Thought* is one guide to locating that boundary within nineteenth-century British discourse about religion. The underlying, multivalent master narrative of materialism versus spiritualism is an especially useful marker for locating that boundary. It is one of the connective threads that stitches together the chapters in *Spirit Matters*.

Part I

# Challenges to Christianity and the Orthodox/Heterodox Boundary

2

# The Evolution of Occult Spirituality in Victorian England and the Representative Case of Edward Bulwer-Lytton

"It was a dark and stormy night"—as I choose to imagine it—the setting Knebworth, the Tudor-Gothic mansion and maternal ancestral seat of Edward Bulwer-Lytton, who, as he passed the "yellow room," glanced in, thinking he might glimpse the ghost of the "fair-haired boy" whom he insisted haunted that room.[1] On the previous day, while in London, Bulwer-Lytton had taken his seat in Parliament, where he had exchanged observations both political and literary with his friend Benjamin Disraeli, beside whom he would serve in Lord Derby's government as secretary of state for the colonies.[2] Both he and Disraeli would be raised to the peerage and move to the House of Lords. He then had met briefly with one of his publishers, William Blackwood, about royalties. As the immensely popular author of *The Last Days of Pompeii* (1834) and *The Caxtons* (1849), among other bestsellers, and as a man on his way to becoming "one of the most successful writers of the nineteenth century" (at least financially), Bulwer-Lytton knew he could demand top dollar and get it (Mitchell 109). On the way to join his friend Charles Dickens for a midday repast, he had stopped into a rare-book shop specializing in esoteric and occult literature; he was searching for a first edition of Johannes Andreae's *Chymical Wedding of Christian Rosenkreutz* (1616).[3] He was conducting research for another occult romance novel, *A Strange Story* (1862). His earlier occult romance, *Zanoni* (1842), had become known as a "Rosicrucian novel," and Bulwer-Lytton would later become, by induction, "a member of the Society of Rosicrucians and Grand Patron of the Order" (Wolff 233). Dickens, whom Bulwer-Lytton was meeting near the offices of Dickens's popular periodical, *All the Year Round*, had invited Bulwer-Lytton to publish his next novel serially. Dickens also would consult him about the draft ending of his own novel-in-progress, *Great Expectations* (1860–61), and dedicate that novel to Bulwer-Lytton. *A Strange Story* would appear in *All the Year Round*. He and Dickens had been joined for lunch by Chauncy Hare Townshend, whom he had known since their school days at Ramsgate. Townshend had drawn both Bulwer-Lytton and Dickens toward Mesmerism and Spiritualism, and works of his like *Facts in Mesmerism* (1840) were significant in legitimating Mesmerism in the eyes of many Britons, as were the fictional and personal investigations of it by such notables as Dickens and Bulwer-Lytton. In the afternoon, Townshend and Bulwer-Lytton had called upon Dr. John Elliotson at the London Mesmeric Infirmary, which Elliotson had founded in 1849. There they observed ongoing experiments to test the efficacy of mesmeric medicine. Bulwer-Lytton already had defended Elliotson against the censure of the medical establishment.[4] He previously had urged Harriett Martineau to try mesmeric treatment, and Martineau then helped popularize the movement with her *Letters on Mesmerism* (1845).[5] In the evening, Bulwer-Lytton had met with Daniel Home, one of the most famous spiritualist mediums of the century, as well as Madame Home, with whom Bulwer-Lytton later would correspond, at their lodgings for drinks. Bulwer-Lytton "offer[ed] Knebworth as a venue for his séances" (Mitchell 148). Now back at Knebworth, he was walking with a flickering Egyptian oil lamp in hand toward a darkened room in which his guests that evening had been prepared for his arrival. As part of the evening's entertainment, he would tell their fortunes, performing a role for which he had become known by assuming the persona in which he called himself "Le Vieux Sorcier," the old wizard (Mitchell 147).

## The Variety of the Esoteric and Occult

A historical study of Victorian esoteric and occult beliefs and practices, or of that period's obsession with the spirit-matter dualism that runs throughout this book, might well begin with Edward Bulwer-Lytton (1803–73). While he of course was preceded in the century by many students of the esoteric and occult, and while many of his famous contemporaries also attended séances or consulted mesmeric physicians, few were as informed or as influential as Bulwer-Lytton. He was a dedicated, life-long student of occult spiritualities. He "had put himself through a wide-ranging course of experimentation in the practical investigation of the occult, leaving unexamined not even the most outré practices of the magicians, and simultaneously he had systematically educated himself in the latest works of physiologists, philosophers, and students of the supernatural as they appeared"; "astrology, alchemy, mesmerism, clairvoyance, hypnotism, spiritualism, and magic: he investigated them all at first hand, and wrote about them all" (Wolff 148–49). Thus his "metaphysical novels," as he called *Zanoni* and *A Strange Story*, drew upon and combined virtually all of the occultisms and mysticisms from the history of ancient, medieval, and contemporary practices. Though these novels were torturously written, crammed with diverse occultisms, and too didactic to be as popular as some of his other novels, they nevertheless were influential conduits through which the esoteric traditions underlying the Mesmerism and Spiritualism movements of his day were disseminated into popular discourse. Whatever their literary merits, these novels were a principle point of origin for the occult romance novel as subsequently written by authors such as Marie Corelli and H. Rider Haggard. More significant in relationship to the history of spiritualism and occultism, Bulwer-Lytton, in his life and his writings, demonstrated a pattern of scholarly sampling from many ancient esoteric traditions that would be replicated later in the century by founders of new syncretic religions, most of all by Helena Petrovna Blavatsky (1831–91) in building the Theosophical Society.[6]

The current chapter situates Bulwer-Lytton within the history of nineteenth-century occultisms. I think of that history very broadly as occurring in major overlapping waves: the Mesmerism movement followed by the Spiritualism movement followed by the founding of what I have analyzed elsewhere as "hybrid religions" (Franklin, *Lotus* 59). The first half of this chapter theorizes a broad evolutionary model for the stages of occult spiritual discourse in England over the course of the century. It summarizes the ways in which Mesmerism contributed to the form of Spiritualism and how each of those contributed to the formation of hybrid religions, such as Theosophy (1875), the Hermetic Order of the Golden Dawn (1887), and Anthroposophy (1912), which were the culmination of the centuries-old imbrication of science and the occult, as I outline in chapter 1. Recognizing the continuities across the century, I also argue that a seismic shift occurred in these discourses, beginning approximately in the 1860s, between the paradigms of Mesmerism and Spiritualism and that of the subsequent hybrid religions. I then locate Bulwer-Lytton at that 1860s pivot point and argue for his importance, first in translating previous waves of occult spirituality and science, such as medieval alchemy and Enlightenment vitalism, into Victorian occultism and Spiritualism and, second, in preparing the way for and even predicting the shape of the later hybrid religions. Perhaps more than any other single person in the first half of the century, Bulwer-Lytton was representative of that period's enthusiasms, reservations, and deep-seated fears concerning occult spiritualities.

## The Mesmerism and Spiritualism Movements

The first half of the nineteenth century witnessed first the arrival to England from the Continent of the "mesmeric mania" and then the invasion from the United States of Spiritualism, all during a period when the Church of England was losing congregation to Nonconformist denominations and experiencing internal revolutions both high and low, Tractarian and Evangelical.[7] The sensation that Franz Anton Mesmer (1734–1815) had created with his new science of "animal magnetism" in Vienna and Paris was contemporaneous with the French Revolution, which is why many Britons disparagingly associated Mesmerism with that event. Not until the late 1830s did the movement hit London, when it rapidly became a subject of intense public and medical interest in the mid-1840s, saturating popular culture by the 1850s. Hundreds of articles and books championed or criticized the claims made on behalf of mesmeric medicine and mesmeric spirituality.[8] Among the key events were the launching of *The Zoist* in 1843, after *The Lancet* refused further Mesmerism articles, and the founding of the London Mesmeric Infirmary in 1849, both initiated by John Elliotson, "the single Englishman most responsible for the spread of mesmerism in England" (Kaplan 696). A number of excellent recent histories fully treat Mesmerism; I will note here only that both the proponents and the opponents divided roughly into two camps: the "materialists" and the "spiritualists."[9] Like Mesmer himself, Elliotson and most medical practitioners were materialists; they viewed phenomena as grounded in nature and ultimately explainable by science, whether in terms of the physics of a "vital principle" transmitted as magnetism or electricity or in biological terms as a "vital fluid" or "life force" animating the entire organic universe (Fulford 62). On the other side, spiritualist interpretations of mesmeric phenomena were backed by centuries of popular discourse. The histories of esoteric Christianity, occult spirituality, and Enlightenment Deism or Natural Theology all had set the stage for Victorians to view mesmeric phenomena as evidence of the invisible presence of Spirit in the universe. As Maria Tartar summarizes, "the magnetic fluid that had once streamed so abundantly through Mesmer's clinic was transformed by mystics into a divine afflatus, by spiritualists into ethereal specters, and by metaphysicians into an impalpable force designated as the will" (xiii). Thus there were four nonexclusive camps: those who championed Mesmerism on materialist grounds as soon-to-be-proved science, those who questioned Mesmerism on materialist grounds as unsupportable weird science, those who embraced Mesmerism for spiritual purposes and therefore viewed materialist Mesmerism as shortsighted if not sacrilegious, and those who criticized Mesmerism on spiritual grounds, either as heretical to Christian orthodoxy or, conversely, as too materialist to be sufficiently spiritualist.

Following on the heels of Mesmerism, the Spiritualism movement had begun in New England in the 1840s before it swept "like a contagious infection" through England and the Continent (Brandon 43).[10] By the 1860s, "spiritualism had become a conspicuous and, to many, lamentable part of Victorian cultural life, with its mediums, specialist newspapers, pamphlets, treatises, societies and private and public séances" (Noakes 26). By the time it had been partially subsumed into late century hybrid religions, Spiritualism had drawn many Britons—including royalty, famous authors, eminent scientists, and even clergymen—to hold hands around a parlor table, sit in a darkened séance chamber, or, later, attend auditorium-style performances. It also was a primary impetus for the founding of the Society for Psychical Research in 1882, which was the scientific investigation not merely of paranormal phenomena but, ultimately, of the existence of the human soul. Given the plethora of recent histories of Spiritualism, I will only summarize several characteristics of the movement that stand out and that will prove relevant to my reading of Bulwer-Lytton.[11] First, Spiritualism shared with other religious and spiritual discourses of the time a primary mission to defeat materialism. In popular usage, "materialism" variously signified atheism, science, and "mammonism," one of Thomas Carlyle's several terms for it in *Past and Present* (1843) and elsewhere. Understood at the broadest level as abnegation of the human soul, "materialism was widely perceived as the archvillain of the age" (Oppenheim 61). Proponents of Spiritualism argued that it was a stronger defense against materialism than institutional religions could provide because it relied not on faith but, according to believers, on the empirical evidence of direct experience. As James Robertson wrote in his 1893 history of the movement, "one single echo, a tiny rap from the [deceased] loved ones, was more value than book revelations, more comforting than what without evidence were simply speculations" (66). Thus, spiritualists enlisted the method and imprimatur of the scientific materialism, whose truth-telling authority they otherwise denounced, and this points to the profoundly conflicted relationship of Victorian occult spiritualities in general to science.

Spiritualism also might be understood as a logical historical outcome of the Protestant Reformation's emphasis on individual faith. It asserted the right of the individual entirely to control her own spiritual practice; every spiritualist became, in effect, his own clergy, congregation, and divine Spirit. Having partially subsumed from God the responsibility of guaranteeing immortality, and motivated by the need to explain what spirits were doing loitering outside of the gates of heaven or hell, spiritualists responded by formulating models of progressive spiritual evolution. As Hudson Tuttle wrote in 1876 in his "manual" to Spiritualism, "Progressive evolution of intellectual and moral force is the endless destiny of individual spirits" (14). He and many others arrived at conceptions of spiritual evolution by combining elements of evolutionary science, progressivism, and Eastern religions, especially Buddhist reincarnation. Another feature of Spiritualism was that it emerged still bearing the influences of the long history of European occultisms and mysticisms of which it was a part. Frank Podmore's *Modern Spiritualism: A History and Criticism* (1902) traces its roots back to witchcraft, alchemy, magicianship, Rosicrucianism, and, most recently, Mesmerism. Finally, Spiritualism contributed to a shift of the locus of spiritual discourse away from the patriarchally controlled public sphere dominated by traditional religious institutions to more private and domestic spheres. As scholars following the groundbreaking work of Janet Oppenheim and Alex Owen have shown, full understanding of the movement requires reading it in relationship to the histories of conditions for women, women's sexuality, and women's spiritual practices.[12] While Mesmerism had been spearheaded almost exclusively by men and had most famously involved the treatment by male physicians of (often working-class) female subjects, Spiritualism was more woman-centered, in both origin and practice.

While one can trace a progression from the beginning to the end of the nineteenth century that links Mesmerism to Spiritualism to hybrid religions at the fin de siècle, there also was a significant paradigm shift in occult discourse that began around 1860. It is well established that Mesmerism provided a platform for Spiritualism and influenced its development.[13] Many elements of Mesmerism transferred almost directly into Spiritualism: the mesmeric trance translated into the séance medium's trance, mesmeric "table turning" morphed into table rapping by spirits, and the mesmeric "imponderable fluid" became the medium through which spirits communicated with the living. Spiritualism in turn was the starting point for a number of late century hybrid religions, most significantly Theosophy. Blavatsky and its other founders had begun by investigating and practicing Spiritualism, and they ever after defended the authenticity of contact with the Spirit World. But they soon disclaimed Spiritualism as crudely practical and populist, lacking the historical lineage, institutional organization, and doctrinal depth that they built into and claimed for their new world religion. Thus, on the one hand, all of the features of Spiritualism summarized in the preceding paragraph were incorporated and reemphasized in the seminal texts of Theosophy. On the other hand, hybrid religions constituted an evolutionary leap in occult spirituality, a fully " 'new' occultism" that took shape in that way toward the end of the century (Owen, *Place* 5).

## Bulwer-Lytton's Metaphysical Novels

Bulwer-Lytton's metaphysical novels are romance novels of ideas, which is to say that they are noncomedic satires in the sense of portraying types and ideals: the characters often stand, in a nearly allegorical sense, for philosophical, sociopolitical, and spiritual positions, the positions that Bulwer-Lytton felt were most lamentably representative of his era. He considered this type of novel "the '*noblest* sphere' of fiction," the form appropriate to a moral mission to save modern society from itself (in Christensen 18).[14] He furnished as vehicles for this mission stories that are romantic, mysterious, and action-packed—page-tuners of their time—but their most fascinating feature is the critical diagnosis they provide of the materialism of British culture and society of the 1840s to 1860s. In delivering this diagnosis, Bulwer-Lytton does not disguise his own beliefs and prejudices, which makes them easy to identify among the array of discourses about politics, recent history, science, and occult spirituality that he was actively exploring and even citing in footnotes in his novels.

*Zanoni* opens in January 1842 (the author's present) in a rare-book shop in Covent Garden that specializes in the "works of Alchemist, Cabalist, and Astrologer" (Bulwer-Lytton, *Zanoni* ix). In looking for books on Rosicrucianism, the frame narrator encounters an initiated elderly gentleman who entrusts him with a manuscript of his own, which the younger man agrees to shepherd into print. As the reader comes to suspect, the old man is one of the three main characters in the body of that story, an English painter named Clarence Glyndon. While on tour in Italy in the 1780s, Glyndon fell in love with a beautiful concert vocalist, Viola Pisani. Because of his inability to love spiritually, or against class difference, he lost her to a powerful occultist named Zanoni. But in order to experience human love, Zanoni had to compromise the spiritual discipline that permitted him to live as a young man for five thousand years—an example of the "demi-immortal oriental" character type.[15] Glyndon apprenticed himself to Zanoni's master, Mejnour, but failed in sorcerer's-apprentice fashion, with dire aftereffects. Near the end of the novel, Glyndon reencounters Viola and Zanoni in Paris, where the story climaxes at the height of the French Revolution. He finally escapes the Terror to a long life of relative conventionality in London, though as one who has witnessed alchemy, magic, clairvoyance, Mesmerism, demi-immortality, and demonic specters of the Spirit World. The plot thus weaves together four primary thematic strands: aesthetic, romantic, political, and spiritual/supernatural. Questions about what constitutes ideal art, ideal love, political harmony, and spiritual as opposed to materialistic existence are intertwined, and the answers converge. The novel hopes to demonstrate that debased art, instrumental love, and revolutionary politics are signs of "a *spiritual* rather than a merely social or political crisis" (J. Coates 226). All are symptoms of the spiritual malaise of modernity.

"Materialism" serves in the novel as the catch-all term for that modern spiritual malaise. *Zanoni* might be read as a taxonomy of the types of materialism that Bulwer-Lytton, like many of his contemporaries, felt were plaguing modern spirituality. In aesthetics, materialism is called "the Real." The old gentleman in the bookshop insists on the "distinction between the Real and the True, in other words, between the imitation of actual life and the exaltation of Nature into the Ideal" (Bulwer-Lytton, *Zanoni* xiii). The narrative associates the former with the "Dutch School" and the latter with Greek heritage (a debate that will be joined by George Eliot, Matthew Arnold, and Walter Pater, among many others). Bulwer-Lytton "made of the art of fiction a vehicle to carry on the idealist tradition of Romantic poetry and so helped not only to save the soul of man but also to save fiction to serve visions other than that of mimetic realism" (Christensen 221). Realism is for philistines, whereas the romance of the old gentleman's manuscript and, by implication, of the novel that contains it "is truth for those who can comprehend it, and an extravagance for those who cannot" (Bulwer-Lytton, *Zanoni* xviii). Thus, the novel's aesthetic theme reflects upon its own form—Gothic or occult romance—as it attempts to be a material medium through which its spiritual theme might be heard to speak, rap, or manifest. Within this framework, Viola and her singing function as emblems of this ideal beauty, in a familiar gender-stereotypical way. Glyndon's friend Mervale, the voice of "sober England" with a bulging bankbook, tries to persuade him against Viola on the grounds that "what men respect is the practical, not the ideal" of marrying for love beneath one's station (98). When Jean Nicot, a debased painter, atheist, and representative of the French Revolution, betrays Glyndon, Zanoni, and Viola to the Committee of Public Safety, sending the latter two to the dungeon to await the guillotine, the narrator chides him for "the False Ideal that knows no God, and the False Love that burns from the corruption of the senses, and takes no luster from the soul!" (338). Revolutionary politics, atheism, and sexually motivated love—all trade the ideal for the real, signifying the spiritual failure of modern materialism.

The novel's term for materialism in the realms of politics and religion is "philosophy," because since spiritual concerns "are out of fashion, nothing now goes down but scepticism and philosophy" (Bulwer-Lytton, *Zanoni* 24). While Glyndon, Nicot, and, against his better judgment, Zanoni are vying for Viola's hand in Naples, in Paris historical characters such as Nicolas de Condorcet (1743–94) and Guillaume-Chrétien de Malesherbes (1721–94) are shown talking philosophy. They concur on "the superiority of the Moderns to the Ancients," mock "religion as a fable," and await the fruits of the "Age of Reason!—Equality in instruction, equality in institutions, equality in wealth!" (29, 30, 40). They embody the views actively opposed by Bulwer-Lytton in his politics, in his theory of art, and in his defense of spiritualism against materialism. He, "in his scorn for the doctrine of equality and his hatred for revolutionary bloodshed, . . . was too ready to overlook the viciousness of the *ancien régime*" (Wolff 208). These characters, therefore, must suffer the historical irony of being shown to celebrate the advent of the Revolution that will imprison and guillotine them.

To drive his point home with unmistakable force, Bulwer-Lytton mirrors Maximilien Robespierre's character with its double in the Spirit World, called the "Dweller of the Threshold." Earlier in the novel, Glyndon, in his ambition to acquire the occult powers that he has witnessed in Zanoni, transgresses Mejnour's interdiction against tampering with the alchemical elixirs in the laboratory. Without knowing what he is doing, he opens himself to perceive and communicate with the nonhuman beings of a parallel dimension, chief among them the Dweller of the Threshold. This loathsome apparition with burning eyes is all the more frightful for the fact that it "was not all a spirit, but partook of matter enough, at least, to make it more deadly and fearful an enemy to material forms"

(Bulwer-Lytton, *Zanoni* 242–43). Zanoni and Mejnour, through long and arduous initiation, are fortified to live in constant awareness of this parallel realm but as masters of its inhabitants. The young Glyndon, like Robespierre in his pride and thirst for power beyond his abilities to control it, has now made himself susceptible to be haunted, literally, by the unforeseen consequences, until Zanoni finally exorcises the ghostly entities. Through the latter section of the novel, the Dweller of the Threshold stalks the blood-drenched streets of Paris, trailing Glyndon and Zanoni just as they are being trailed by Nicot and Robespierre's other spies. This materialistic spirit is the spirit of the Revolution, that monstrous offspring of skeptical philosophy, as opposed to the antimaterialistic spiritualism that the novel champions.

Thus "philosophy" is shorthand both for Enlightenment skepticism, which for many equated with atheism, and for "natural philosophy," namely science. In *Zanoni*, and even more directly in *A Strange Story*, Bulwer-Lytton struggles mightily to rationalize spiritualism to science, science to spiritualism. In this, he was representative of a complex, pervasive, but frequently unarticulated Victorian response to occult spirituality: a desperate longing to believe in the phenomena implicit in Mesmerism and explicit in Spiritualism combined with the skepticism that accompanied a growing conviction that science was now the ultimate truth-telling authority. At stake was nothing less than the existence of the immortal human soul, of which all spirit manifestations came to serve as evidence. As Dr. Julius Faber, the stand-in character for Bulwer-Lytton, says in *A Strange Story*, "Certainly I would rather believe all the ghost stories upon record than believe that I am not even a ghost" (429). For Bulwer-Lytton, as for the many he represented, spiritualism was too vital not to have a scientific basis, while science, too important to ignore, had to be made to underwrite spiritual phenomena. It would seem that he lived his entire adult life struggling to resolve the paradox of materialist spiritualism and spiritual materialism (akin to Thomas Carlyle's "Natural Supernaturalism"), refusing to surrender either his spiritual beliefs or his scientific skepticism about them.[16]

This is made allegorically explicit in *A Strange Story*. The protagonist is a medical scientist, Allen Fenwick, who must be led, in part by witnessing supernatural phenomena, to realize that his purely intellectual science is "the hallucination by which Nature is left Godless—because Man is left soulless" (242). His antagonist, Margrave, has used occult science, alchemy, to attain the demi-immortality of perpetual youth, though now as a soulless body, vitalized but amoral, the final killing of which is a mercy to the extent that death is thought to reconnect the soul to the body and then free it. Neither Fenwick's overly "philosophical" science nor Margrave's unholy science is tenable, yet disregarding science is not conceivable either. This is the dilemma. The attempt to resolve it is staged in the novel as a series of convoluted dialogues between Fenwick and his scientific-turned-spiritual mentor, Faber, an eminent pathologist and devout believer in the soul. In an early conversation, Faber convinces Fenwick that the paranormal phenomena he has witnessed were produced by retinal afterimages, "diseased imagination," and "strong mental impression" (298). He appeals to the physiological and psychological explanations that in actuality would demystify Mesmerism by turning it to a "scientific" application in James Braid's 1843 theorization of hypnotism as a clinical method.[17] Faber, like Braid, predicts the scientification of spiritualist concepts that would commence with the founding of psychology as a quasi-scientific discipline starting in the 1870s and of the Society for Psychical Research in 1882. Here Faber might appear as the representative of scientific skepticism debunking supernatural phenomena. But, no; the text uses the very same occasion to undercut that scientific authority, since the reader knows that Fenwick has in fact witnessed genuine supernatural events. Margrave does possess the power to place others in a mesmeric trance, to exercise clairvoyant thought-control, and to project from a great distance a seeing and speaking image of himself, a "luminous phantom," "Scin-Laeca, or shining corpse" (257). The text thus enacts the debate between spiritualism and science in which thousands of Victorians were engaged, internally and publicly, giving neither Spirit nor science the upper hand.

Having supposedly disillusioned Fenwick of mesmeric or alchemical supernaturalism, Faber later switches to advocating for *Christian* supernaturalism, "that link between life here and life hereafter which is found in what we call Soul" (Bulwer-Lytton, *Strange Story* 311). This is the alternative to the soulless demi-immortality of Margrave, who says: "I count on no life beyond the grave. I would defy the grave, and live on" (349). Yet Fenwick continues to witness further proofs of the supernatural, some coming even from his wife, Lillian, who is hysterically possessed by

Margrave but whose purity of love and peculiarly feminine sensitivity, in this highly gendered worldview, imbues her with a power to sense when Fenwick is in jeopardy and call out to him with her spirit (much as Jane Eyre does to Rochester). When Fenwick and Lillian next meet up with Faber, now in Australia where the action concludes, he surprises Fenwick and the reader yet again by explaining Margrave's magic wand in terms of "animal magnetism and electro-biology" (411–12). Here he seems to oscillate between John Elliotson's materialist defense of Mesmerism and Chauncy Hare Townshend's spiritualist defense of the same. As the final baffling move in an argument that is dispersed across two hundred pages, Faber then mounts a full *scientific* justification of the soul and the afterlife, employing a version of the Deist "argument from design" (447).[18] He argues, in short, that it would be unnatural and against the precepts of science if nature (God) produced capacities, such as that for spiritual devotion, that were deceptively useless because unmatched by an object to which they apply.

In the process of arriving at this final position, Faber's character has acted out, one after the other, the full range of contradictions that Bulwer-Lytton, and the many for whom he spoke, was struggling to resolve. *A Strange Story*, in the series of dialogues between Fenwick and Faber, gives voice to all four of the camps that I have identified in mid-Victorian discourse about Mesmerism and Spiritualism: *materialist champions* of a scientific basis for natural supernaturalism, even if one must wait for science to advance sufficiently to be able to explain the spiritual evidence; *materialist opponents* who as scientific skeptics deny the existence of anything supernatural, perhaps including the human soul; *spiritual champions* or true-believing spiritualists for whom anything supernatural may be proof of the existence of a Spirit World and, therefore, an afterlife; and *spiritual opponents* to occult supernaturalism on more orthodox religious grounds who may view belief in occult phenomena as a sacrilegious infringement upon that singularly privileged supernatural entity, the traditional Judeo-Christian soul.

A similar though less fully articulated pattern occurs in the earlier novel, *Zanoni*. Mejnour, though not evil in the way that Margrave is in *A Strange Story*, also represents occultism without the soul, without the physical death and spiritual rebirth promised by Christianity, and also without the warmth of human love. Zanoni breaks from Mejnour and surrenders his demi-immortality to model ideal love with Viola (though they appear to be living together out of wedlock) and to become a Christlike sacrificial figure. He sacrifices his mortal life in order to save Viola and their son, to defeat the Dweller of the Threshold and the Terror of the Revolution in one swoop, and, most importantly, to demonstrate that the earthly demi-immortality acquirable through alchemical means is less desirable than a heavenly afterlife. This is the predominant moral of both *Zanoni* and *A Strange Story*. But, while it is given precedence toward the ends of the novels, this ostensibly Christian moral fails to recuperate the plethora of occult phenomena that dominate the main bodies of the novels and that they strive to convince readers are genuinely real.

In this contradiction Bulwer-Lytton again was giving fictional expression to a pattern that existed more broadly in his culture. The perceived crisis in Christianity, which received empirical support from the 1851 Census of Religious Worship, was a primary impetus for the development of occult spirituality in the nineteenth century.[19] As the spiritualist Hudson Tuttle wrote in 1876: "There is no alternative, material science is fast driving Christianity to the wall. It has taken all the thinkers of the world. The church holds only those who do not think. Spiritualism is the last stronghold against the tide of materialism, and if it fails to establish its claims, the former will be supremely triumphant" (56). Bulwer-Lytton's metaphysical novels model the rescue of modern spirituality by occultism in order then to reempower a Christian spiritualism. More precisely, there is a three-stage movement. First, occultism is enlisted to demonstrate the reality of spiritual phenomena, which orthodox, institutional Christianity was failing to do. But occultism then is shown to be incomplete or materialistically flawed in its spirituality. Finally, it then is possible to return to a Christian belief, which through this process has been reinvigorated to stand up to materialism. The hard bargain for Christianity is that it has been largely stripped of most of its traditional doctrines. *Zanoni* and *A Strange Story* use occult spiritualisms to arrive at an esoteric Christianity from which God, heaven, sin and redemption, and even the word "Christianity" have been if not removed then muted. This pattern will be repeated throughout the nineteenth century, for example in W. S. Lilly's *Ancient Religion and Modern Thought* and in novels by Rider Haggard. In place of the expected elements of orthodox Christianity, one finds euphemisms such as "the Divine One" and "the Great Religion," and the predominant focus is on the individual soul and a free-floating conception of the afterlife that is divorced from the traditional, dualistic geography of heaven and hell (Bulwer-Lytton, *Zanoni* 301, 377). The Protestant Reformation appears to find its endpoint in this move to a deinstitutionalized focus on the utterly freed but potentially isolated individual Spirit.[20]

## The Rescue of Christianity by Spirit

In order to effect this rescue of spirituality for Christianity by the occult, Bulwer-Lytton draws upon extensive study and direct experience of Mesmerism and Spiritualism to superload these novels with nearly every historical and contemporary variety of esotericism and occultism. One driving mystery in *Zanoni* is which among these is foremost, which is the true origin of the protagonist's powers. Some scholars have argued that it is Rosicrucianism, since the frame narrator and Glyndon are Rosicrucian and it is invoked periodically throughout the novel.[21] But Zanoni and Mejnour appeal to a broader range of occultisms and give precedence not to Rosicrucianism but to a more ancient esoteric source, a move that will be replicated by Madame Blavatsky in building Theosophy. In the first place, Mesmerism is more pervasive in both novels than is Rosicrucianism. Zanoni influences others with his "haunting eyes," heals with the "deep sleep" of mesmeric medicine, and compels others "by a power not [their] own" (Bulwer-Lytton, *Zanoni* 18, 86, 92). Mejnour repeatedly alludes to mesmeric vitalism—"Life is the one pervading principle"—and he and Zanoni live indefinitely without aging by accessing an "all-pervading and invisible fluid resembling electricity" (224, 228). In addition, both novels mix in a substantial dose of alchemy and magic, regularly invoking Albertus Magnus, Paracelsus, magic potions, and the philosopher's stone. Sometimes Zanoni and Mejnour are presented simply as "the first Herbalists—the master-chemists of the world" (64). This is all part of the argument that supernaturalism is natural, that "magic (or science that violates Nature) exists not,—it is but the science by which Nature can be controlled" (225). One could continue this list of occultisms. It would have to include also allusions to "other worlds," the Dweller of the Threshold, Zanoni's spirit-familiar or angel, Adon-Ai, and even intimations of a spiritual evolutionary model—"grades and heavens of spiritualized being"—which would become a common feature first within Spiritualism and then in late century hybrid religions (193, 250).

Another way in which Bulwer-Lytton modeled in advance subsequent new occultisms is in the claim to an ancient occult origin that gains its authority in part by historical precedence over any institutionalized world religion. (The alternative to this strategy for religion builders is to claim a new direct transmission from a deity, as in the case of the Church of Jesus Christ of Latter-day Saints.) Though *Zanoni* invokes a broad range of occultisms, it also thereby effectively teases readers with the prospect of revealing which one of them is the purest source. Mejnour points toward it when he says to Glyndon: "I allow, however, that the Rosicrucians formed a sect descended from the greater and earlier school. They were wiser than the Alchemists,—their masters are wiser than they" (Bulwer-Lytton, *Zanoni* 214). What earlier school, and who are the masters of the masters? The Dweller of the Threshold gives a hint when it addresses Zanoni mockingly as "young Chaldean!"—merely five thousand years old! (296). The novel implies that Mejnour and Zanoni had in fact lived among the ancient Babylonian or Mesopotamian Chaldeans (and both Blavatsky in building Theosophy and Corelli in building her fictional spiritualism will later enlist the Chaldeans). But then the unnamed narrator draws back from a conclusive identification, saying "not to us of an aged and hoary world is vouchsafed the NAME which, so say the earliest oracles of the earth, 'rushes into the infinite world'" (130). The closest the novel gets to naming it is as the "holy and spiritual Theurgia,—of a magic that could summon the Angel, or the Good Genius, not the Fiend" (371).[22] Thus Bulwer-Lytton leaves his readers midway between this primal but obscure origin and a spiritually recharged but doctrinally stripped Christianity. Perhaps the real point is to keep the ultimate source mysterious by ever pointing backward and insisting that it only can be known to the fully initiated adept. This, after all, is the strategy used to effect by the adepts of Theosophy, the Golden Dawn, and, for that matter, the Church of Scientology, a more recent occult-scientific religion that rivals the hybridity of its late nineteenth-century antecedents.

## Bulwer-Lytton as Gatekeeper

I have attempted to highlight the ways in which Edward Bulwer-Lytton was a pivotal figure both in literary history and in the history of spiritualism and the occult in the nineteenth century. In literary history, he was a father—perhaps *the* father—of the occult or Gothic-romance novel. His metaphysical novels contributed to at least three trends in the representation of spiritualism that have been repeated in occult romances ever since. The first is in portraying an antithesis between romantic love and spiritual practice. This elaboration of the traditional Western body/soul dichotomy, with its history of "mortifying the flesh," serves to generate a huge amount of plot-productive sexual tension, not only between human lovers but especially between human and demi-immortal characters (many vampire examples come to mind). According to the same logic, truly ideal love, which most often means romance exquisitely heightened by sexual abstinence, correlates with spiritual advancement—though seldom does it remain unconsummated. Second, Bulwer-Lytton championed the signature Romantic creed that Art is a spiritual vocation, that aestheticism is akin to spiritualism, a claim that will be taken to one extreme by the Decadents of the Aestheticism movement later in the century, championed in a distinct but related way in the novels of Marie Corelli, and then problematized by the artists and theorists of modernism in the early twentieth century. His novels align true or ideal art with genuine spirituality, artistic channeling of "genius" or "imagination" with spirit channeling.[23] Whatever one may think of the quality of his art or his spirituality, he worked with dedication toward adepthood in both arenas. His own religious practice, aside from periodic church attendance and lip service to Anglicanism, "was therefore part aesthetic and part spiritual" (Mitchell 138). Finally, *Zanoni* and *A Strange Story* develop the character type that I call the demi-immortal oriental, a character whose bodily, material longevity originates in an "Eastern" source and often comes to figure as a blasphemous alternative to the traditional Christian spiritual immortality of the soul. This figure will reappear after Bulwer-Lytton in novels not only by Corelli and Haggard but also in those by Oscar Wilde, Bram Stoker, Richard Marsh, and James Hilton.[24] Bulwer-Lytton himself was engaged in the "cult of youth," as fictionalized in Margrave, Dorian Gray, and others (Mitchell 88). He was fascinated by the idea that some vitalistic power, at once spiritual and scientific, might permit life extension, as does the natural substance "vril" in his later novel *The Coming Race* (1871). But, then, was not and is not one of the primary motivations for interest in occult spirituality—and religion in general—the mystery of death and the profound wish for eternal life?

In the history of Victorian spiritualism and occultism, Bulwer-Lytton performed a dual gatekeeping function. Translating the past into the present, his work served as a siphon filtering ancient, medieval, and modern esoteric and occult precedents into the discourses underlying the Mesmerism and Spiritualism movements of his day. Projecting the present into the future, his work predicted and influenced the construction of the hybrid religions of the latter part of the century. Bulwer-Lytton was a pivotal figure in the historical evolution that I have argued occurred from the paradigms of Mesmerism and Spiritualism to those informing late century hybrid religions. He served this function less because of any brilliant prescience on his part than because he felt and mirrored back to his society one of the most widely shared and deeply troubling dilemmas of his age: profound longing for spiritualism coupled with ultimate belief in scientific materialism. To his credit, Bulwer-Lytton remained faithful to each while fiercely worrying the apparently irreconcilable differences. It is this very contradiction in him that is most representative of a predominant Victorian response to spiritualism and occultism throughout the century. His intensely focused ambivalence and the resulting, tortured solutions to the contradictions between spiritualism and science that his writings formulate modeled responses that would be enacted not only in subsequent fiction but throughout British culture and society.

# 3

# ANTHONY TROLLOPE'S RELIGION

## *The Orthodox/Heterodox Boundary*

> I have regarded my art from so different a point of view that I have ever thought of myself as a preacher of sermons, and my pulpit as one which I could make both salutary and agreeable to my audience.
>
> ANTHONY TROLLOPE, *AN AUTOBIOGRAPHY*

> It is very hard to come at the actual belief of any man. Indeed how should we hope to do so when we find it so very hard to come at our own? How many are there among us who, in this matter of our religion, which of all things is the most important to us, could take pen in hand and write down even for their own information exactly what they themselves believe?
>
> ANTHONY TROLLOPE, *CLERGYMEN OF THE CHURCH OF ENGLAND*

It will surprise readers of Anthony Trollope (1815–82) to find him in a book concerned with the heterodox religious and spiritual beliefs of his period. He has been thought of by many, both fans and critics, as a bastion of mainstream virtues and a pillar of traditional Church of England values, though scholars of Trollope will know that this is a reductionistic summary of an immensely complex man. In order to delineate the cultural territory of the heterodox and the occult it is necessary to understand its unavoidable debt to and interface with the orthodox. For the purposes of *Spirit Matters*, Trollope, as well as Matthew Arnold, is the marker of that interface at the boundary that cleaved the heterodox from and to the orthodox.

## Trollope's Religious Position and Schism within the Church of England

It is ironic, in a characteristically Trollopian way, that we can claim such limited certainty about the religious beliefs of a man who became famous as *the* novelist of the Church of England clergyman.[1] While thousands of contemporary readers felt that his novels accurately captured Anglican clergymen and their wives, Trollope stated that "no one at their commencement could have had less reason than myself to presume himself to be able to write about clergymen," that he "never lived in any cathedral city,—except London, never knew anything of any Close, and at that time had enjoyed no peculiar intimacy with any clergyman" (*Autobiography* 92). He was being falsely modest here, since "besides seven clerical ancestors by birth and seven clerical ancestors by marriage, [he] had at least nine clerical relatives sharing his surname and 14 other clerical relatives by marriage in his collateral family" (Durey 1). From boyhood he was more knowledgeable about and more interested in the ecclesiastical and political controversies that surrounded the Anglican Church than were the majority of Britons. He was deeply committed to maintaining the historical centrality of the Church of England to British society and culture. Even so, as far as we know, he did not "take pen in hand" and write down even for his own information exactly what he himself believed; he intentionally refrained from ever making his religious position fully explicit in public record. Moreover, no single fictional clergyman from the dozens portrayed in his novels could be said to fully represent either the author's personal beliefs or an exclusive stance on his part concerning Church politics. Perhaps the strongest public statement in relation to faith that he ever made was in reference to the founding editorial principles of *The Fortnightly Review*, that "nothing should appear denying or questioning the divinity of Christ" (*Autobiography* 189–90). However, he preceded this with a statement more broadly representative of his views: "The matter on which we were all agreed was freedom of speech, combined with personal responsibility. We would be neither conservative nor liberal, neither religious nor free-thinking, neither popular nor exclusive" (189). This sort of dialectical balancing act—call it the Trollopian dialectic—is quintessential throughout his writings. His oppositions seldom resolve into a comfortable synthesis but rather maintain an oscillation of positions while creating an occupiable space between them. Thus, all attempts to pigeonhole him as High Church or Broad Church (Low Church never having been a serious contender) have ended undecided,[2] and, even where one can discern his leanings in regard to these positions, his personal beliefs on questions of faith remain undisclosed. Trollope chose to keep his private thoughts on religion largely private, and this privateness is itself part of his position on religion.[3] Thus the Trollopian dialectic, combined with his choice to maintain a separation between the public and the private in these matters, has made the question of what he actually believed an enduring one.

Trollope wrote during a period of upheaval in the Church of England and in British Christianity in general. In short, "during the period from about 1800 to 1870 the Church of England underwent a transformation more rapid, dramatic and enduring than any which it had experienced since the Reformation" (Knight, *The Nineteenth-Century Church* 1). What is more, "by 1870 it would hardly be an exaggeration to say that it was the agnostics rather than the orthodox who had the sense of being official, an intellectual establishment more powerful than the church establishment," and "by 1900, the question 'What do Anglicans believe?' had become, in any straightforward sense, impossible" (Cockshut 11; Parsons 62). It appeared to Trollope and to those of his contemporaries in the Broad Church in particular that the Church of England was threatened simultaneously by dissolution from without and by violent schism from within, given the ongoing political action by Nonconformists for separation of the "establishment" Church from the state, the highly publicized scrutiny of ecclesiastical "abuses" within the Church in the distribution of clerical positions and benefits,[4] and the bitter doctrinal and legal disputes between the High Church or Anglo-Catholic Tractarians of the Oxford movement and the Low Church Evangelicals.[5] As any reader of his novels knows, Trollope was painfully aware of these disruptive currents, which appear throughout his writing but especially in those most concerned with religious characters and issues: *The Warden* (1855), *Barchester Towers* (1857), *The Bertrams* (1858), *The Clergymen of the Church of England* (1866), *The Last Chronicle of Barset* (1867), and *The Vicar of Bullhampton* (1870). He wrote these contemporaneously with three of the most paradigm-shifting books of the nineteenth century: *On the Origin of Species* (1859) by Charles Darwin, *Essays and Reviews* (1860) by a list of latitudinarian Oxbridge clergymen, and *The Pentateuch and Book of Joshua Critically Examined* (1862) by John William Colenso, Anglican bishop of Natal, South Africa. *Essays and Reviews*, which "initiated what was arguably the great theological and religious controversy of the Victorian era . . . called for a thoroughly historical and critical approach to the Bible, for recognition of the moral and spiritual worth of religious traditions outside the Bible, and for acceptance of the findings of science concerning both the age of the earth and its geological history, and the possibility (or impossibility) of miracles" (Parsons 40, 42). This was widely greeted by British Christendom, as here in the Methodist *London Review*, as a harbinger of "the steady onward and downward course of latitudinarianism, scepticism, infidelity, and the darkness without" (in Shea and Whitla 29).

Having been raised in a High Church–leaning household that also was "sharply intolerant of evangelicalism" and in which "evangelicalism and Dissent were considered vulgar and ungentlemanly," Trollope became known for his sympathetic portrayals of High Church–leaning characters, such as Mr. Harding, Dr. Grantly, or Mr. Arabin, and unsympathetic portraits of Low Church and Nonconformist characters, such as Mr. Slope and Mrs. Proudie (N. J. Hall 15; Neville-Sington 68).[6] While there are reasons for claiming that Trollope was a High Church proponent, he was no "ritualist" and strongly disapproved of the defections to Catholicism of eminent Tractarians, most notably John Henry Newman.[7] To the partial extent he was aligned with the High Church, he was more of what Newman described in his *Apologia* (1865) as a "Tory," what other Victorians called the "high and dry" Church: "Its members are neither Tractarians nor evangelical nor liberals; . . . for in the eyes of the world their principle trait is to be the advocates of *an Establishment*" and are "more ardent for the conservation of a national Church than concerned about the beliefs that this national Church professes" (in Bankert 154–55). Always defending the establishment as the historically justified vehicle for social unity based on shared culture and ethics, Trollope opposed the schismatic ramifications of extreme dogma, whether from ritualists or Evangelicals.[8] After all, "both Evangelicals and Tractarians," though opposites in crucial ways, "espoused the quest for holiness of living . . . , both agreed on the divine inspiration of scripture, both agreed on the essentiality of the doctrines of divine judgement and eternal punishment, both held uncompromisingly supernatural views of Christianity, and both firmly believed in miracles, revelation and the literal fulfillment of prophecy" (Parsons 34). In contrast, Trollope balanced holiness with worldliness (tipping the scale well toward the latter), was able to question the divine inspiration of scripture, preferred a loving to a judging God who would not condemn a fallen women or any repentant sinner to eternal punishment, and, though he may not have said so directly, thought miracles and prophesy unnecessary for Christian faith. Thus his religious position frequently is consistent with a tradition that includes Samuel Taylor Coleridge, Thomas Arnold, and Trollope's near contemporary F. D. Maurice, whom Margaret Markwick observes "is commonly seen as the central figure in leading a vanguard for the defence of a middle ground which, in eschewing the holding of either of the extremes, proposed an interpretation of Anglican belief which offered a spiritual home to the many for whom the asceticism of one side and the brimstone and hellfire of the other disinclined them to see any relevance of such beliefs to their day-to-day lives" (30).[9] This likewise aligns Trollope in varying degrees with his contemporaries Charles Kingsley, Thomas Hughes, and Matthew Arnold, which is to say not in the high nor even fully in the high-and-dry Church but somewhere in the minority position within the majority denomination, the Broad Church.[10]

Trollope shared the Broad Church concern for maintaining the establishment as "a more moderate form of Christianity, focusing on rational assent and moral behavior and eschewing strong religious emotions" (Melnyk 5). Strong religious emotions led to dogmatism and schism. Trollope's sympathetic clerical characters eschew strong emotions and doctrinal debates in favor of an emphasis on healing the community by doing what is ethically right, even when what is right may not adhere either to norms or to scripture. This has led some readers, contemporary and since, to accuse (or praise) Trollope of both "situation ethics," or casuistry, and discounting spirituality in favor of morality—but this only returns us to competing Victorian definitions of "religion" (apRoberts, "Introduction" 11). It is true that he "is fascinated by their marriages, their politics, and their moral decision-making—but generally not by their spiritual lives," that his clergymen "are professional men, not much different from [his] doctors and politicians, except in the details of their responsibilities" (Melnyk 111). This need not mean, however, that Trollope held no religious convictions, as some have reasoned.[11] Rather, given his deeply held and linked commitments to preservation of the Church establishment and to being a gentleman, he chose not to dwell upon doctrine or faith publically.[12] To do so is at once schismatic and impolite. Trollope "not only takes it for granted but frequently emphasizes that being a gentleman is connected with being a Christian" (Letwin 216).[13] A "gentleman is never immune" from "doubting how much he should allow to the convictions of others and how far he is justified in condemning those who reject his own" (219).[14] He is by definition moderate and tolerant if not latitudinarian—disposed toward the Broad Church for several related reasons.

Trollope owned, read, and commented favorably upon both *Essays and Reviews* and Colenso's *Pentateuch*. Colenso had followed the authors of *Essays and Reviews* in demonstrating that the initial books of the Bible cannot possibly be read literally because the facts simply do not add up. Trollope himself had subscribed for Colenso, donating money to fund Colenso's appeal to the national Privy Council for reversal of the judgment by the ecclesiastical Court of Arches that he was guilty of heresy and thereby deposed of his bishopric. Colenso and all such "free-thinking clergymen of the present time" were pointing out "the incompatibility of the teaching of Old Testament records with the new teachings of the rocks and stones," an allusion to evolutionary science (Trollope, *Clergymen* 120, 125). As A. O. J. Cockshut observes about cases such as that of Colenso: "it was a conflict between the authority of the Bible and private judgment. But the Church of England believes in both these principles. It was a battle between the authority of the bishops and the power of the State over the bishops. The Church of England accepts both. Throughout the Victorian controversies one is driven to wonder, not that the disputes were so violent, but that they were so long delayed" (Cockshut 98). Trollope believed in both the Bible and private judgment, both the authority of the bishops and the power of the state, but he gravitated toward private judgment and the power of the state, or rather private judgment moderated within the communal enclosure of the state Church.

## Faith and Ethics in *The Vicar of Bullhampton*

My choice of *The Vicar of Bullhampton* as a test case for the observations above is predicated upon the fact that it is an underanalyzed novel with significant religious concerns about which there are conflicting interpretations. Jill Felicity Durey reads this novel as one among the later novels, including *The Eustace Diamonds* (1873) and *The Way We Live Now* (1875), that chart Trollope's "growing disillusionment with the Church as an institution, despite his remaining a devout member of it," and his "vision of a downward moral spiral in society, if not in the Church" (12, 37). In her reading, Vicar Frank Fenwick is representative of a type that "indicates through their weaknesses that the gentleman clergyman of the late 1860s does not command the same respect as his predecessor, and that he probably does not deserve it" (101). In this reading, Fenwick is an example of a weak if not failed religious leader.

In contrast, William Cadbury argues that "because of Frank Fenwick's central part in the novel, because of his character, because of his concerns, and because of the emphasis on values [in their substance] rather than choices [by characters between competing sets of values] . . . , *The Vicar* is Trollope's most religious novel" (154–55).[15] He continues: "Unlike his handling of clerical life in *Barchester Towers,* presented only in terms of the social problems of being in holy orders, Trollope here treats of the central problems of religion in the world, and most successfully creates a character who is both clergyman and man. Frank's primary aim is to apply Christian doctrine to life in the world, and his constant attempt is to prevent social judgment from overcoming the requirements of Christian charity" (155). By "man" Cadbury means something like "regular male member of the community" who therefore relishes defending himself with physical force against assault by would-be robbers and who is willing to join with local community in worldly pleasures, even to "let his pastoral dignity go" by playing at rat catching with a favored young parishioner, Sam Brattle, and on a Sunday (Trollope, *Vicar* 116). It is this sort of behavior that Durey interprets as a failure of the codes of the gentleman and the clergyman, supported in the text by Fenwick's closest friend, Squire Harry Gilmore, who asks Fenwick if rat catching is not beneath his proper role. Durey overlooks the fact that Gilmore proves to be unmanly and that Fenwick is the epitome of the "manly Christianity," championed by the "muscular Christianity" movement and represented in Charles Kingsley's *Westward Ho!* (1855) and Thomas Hughes's *Tom Brown's Schooldays* (1857), that held "particular resonance for Trollope" (Vance 7; Markwick 35).

But the primary difference between Durey and Cadbury concerns definitions of "religion" and "values." For Durey the former is about spiritual devotion, faith, which should not be reduced to morality, and in this she is replicating Victorian criticisms of the Broad Church by those more evangelically fervent or more ritually devout. Cadbury conflates the two, as in "the religious basis on which life in the world should be carried on, the manifestation of theology in ethics" (158), and in this he is replicating a certain Broad Church strain represented in the novel by Fenwick. Trollope, being Trollope, wants his reader to struggle between these two perspectives, as the Trollopian dialectic situates readers "in the position, not simply of accepting as 'true' what the narrator has told us, but rather of acting as ultimate judge, weighing contrary judgments" of characters with competing views (Swingle 110).

### What Makes a Religious Hero?

Trollope being Trollope, *The Vicar* is provoking on the topic of heroes, and this is a small but significant key to the novel. The titular character is of course not named as the hero, though he is the unifying figure who connects the three primary subplots (combining seven distinct subplots). Fenwick also is proven right, if with equivocation, on three counts: in advocating for the forgiveness of Carry Brattle's sin as a fallen woman; in advocating for the innocence of Sam Brattle, her brother, who is implicated in a murder; and in representing his and the Church's position relative to Mr. Puddleham and his Methodist congregation, which has "a very strong holding" in Fenwick's parish (Trollope, *Vicar* 2). The first two of these threads constitute the "fallen woman/fallen man subplot," which also encompasses Fenwick's relation to the Brattle family, in particular the father, Jacob Brattle. Jacob is the village miller who is portrayed as a stern patriarchal judge of sin, especially in the cases of his children, but who is described throughout as an "Old Pagan, going to no place of worship, saying no prayer, believing in no creed" (35). It is for this subplot that the novel has been considered a "fallen-woman novel," and Trollope stated that he wrote it "chiefly with the object of exciting not only pity but sympathy for a fallen woman," especially among middle-class women readers (*Autobiography* 329), but in fact Carry is a minor character and hers is not the primary subplot in the novel. Perhaps Trollope did not have the same intention or courage on this subject as did George Eliot, Elizabeth Gaskell, or Thomas Hardy, whose novels more fully dwell upon the plight of fallen women.[16]

The second primary subplot is the "religion subplot," the Fenwick–Puddleham or Church–Nonconformist contest with which the novel opens. Puddleham brings the contest for congregation members into Fenwick's backyard, or rather literally into his front yard by beginning to erect a Methodist chapel across the lane from Fenwick's gate. Puddleham is aided in this insult to and assault upon the established Church by the Marquis of Trowbridge, the largest landowner in the parish. His daughters have Low Church Evangelical sympathies, which align them with the Methodists, and he is insulted by Fenwick's lax treatment of such sinners as Carry and Sam Brattle, as well as by Fenwick's presumption of equal footing as a gentleman with himself, who expects deference and fealty. The Fenwick–Trowbridge contest is an offshoot of the religion subplot, as is Fenwick's relationship with Jacob Brattle in that Brattle's "paganism" is a significant religious position competing with Fenwick's as well as with the others in the novel.

The primary subplot is the "romance subplot," involving a triangle of Mary Lowther, Harry Gilmore, and Walter Marrable. Frank and Janet Fenwick, friends with both Gilmore and Mary, attempt to compel Mary to wed Gilmore for reasons of community (with them) and practicality— she has modest resources, he is a wealthy landowner—even or especially after Mary falls in love with Walter, a dashing but not financially independent captain. The novel ultimately shows the Fenwicks and Gilmore to be wrong and Mary to be right in not marrying for practicality but rather for heartfelt love. Trollope created Mary as one of the most self-reflective and self-determining of his characters, with clearer vision than any of her elders, and in certain ways she is the real hero of this novel. However, she is a young woman, and so the text, whether perversely or pointedly, adopts romance convention by naming Gilmore as "our hero,—or at least one of two," when Trollope has him squander the reader's sympathy for his heartache by becoming a maudlin stalker who tries to pressure a woman who does not love him into marriage (*Vicar* 4). Walter is "another hero," likeable and honest enough to qualify, but he does not save Mary—she saves herself, and perhaps him as well—and really does nothing very heroic (84). That throws the reader back upon Fenwick as perhaps our hero and upon consideration of what other characters might be heroic, in a modest modern novelistic sense. I believe that Trollope intended this challenge for his readers, and regardless of authorial intention, the text invites us to compare and contrast the relative heroism of characters representing different religious positions, which is a persuasive reason to consider this Trollope's novel most concerned with religion.

The clergymen in the novel are of course the obvious representatives of religion. Puddleham is disqualified as religious hero on multiple counts: he is a Nonconformist, not a gentleman, a toady to the Marquis, and an unforgiving judge of Carry's sin. But he is true to his beliefs and his congregation. When finally defeated in his plan to locate the new chapel across from Fenwick's gate, he preaches that "it did not matter where the people of the Lord met . . . so long as they did meet to worship the Lord in a proper spirit of independent resistance to any authority [i.e., the Church] that had not come to them from revelation" (Trollope, *Vicar* 518). Puddleham functions primarily as a foil against which Fenwick demonstrates his tolerance, moderation, and Christian ethics in Broad Church fashion. Fenwick feels that "Mr. Puddleham's religious teaching was better than none at all; and he was by no means convinced—so he said,—that, for some of his parishioners, Mr. Puddleham was not a better teacher than himself" (116–17). The "so he said" is the sign that Trollope's narrator may not fully trust Fenwick's latitudinarianism. The reader knows that Fenwick does not much care for Puddleham or his religion. While he works upon commendable principles to avoid denominational squabbles in his parish, asking "was it not his special duty to foster love and goodwill among his people?," there is a touch of "hypocritical good humour" in Fenwick's public face about the ugly brick chapel going up opposite his house (245, 244). The narrative leaves the reader uncertain whether to applaud Fenwick's turning the other cheek or to shake him from his assumed "willingness to regard Mr. Puddleham's flock as being equal to his own in the general gifts of civilization" (240). Puddleham serves both to recommend by contrast and to cast doubt upon Fenwick's suitability for the role of religious hero.

Far from being a religious hero, Parson John Marrable is the uncle to cousins Walter Marrable and Mary Lowther and is the rector of Loring Lowtown. He is "a kindly-hearted, good, sincere old man,—not very bright, indeed, nor peculiarly fitted for preaching the gospel, but he was much liked, and he kept a curate, though his income out of the living was small" (Trollope, *Vicar* 82). He is the example of what Trollope portrays with some sympathy but very unflatteringly as "The Town Incumbent": "located among the growing outskirts of a manufacturing town," he is overworked without financial reward commensurate to the number of his parishioners and without the pastoral lifestyle benefits of the country vicar, "probably a very good man" who "probably fails" (*Clergymen* 71, 74). With neither High nor Low Church fervor, Parson John is worldly and overly tolerant of Walter's reprobate father, Colonel Marrable, and "yet the man was a clergyman, preaching honesty and moral conduct, and living fairly well up to his preaching, too, as far as he himself was concerned!" (Trollope, *Vicar* 106). The latter phrase and exclamation mark again signal the narrator's judgment. Parson John also is an inveterate bachelor, in part out of financial necessity, and sour on marriage; contrary to his intentions, he therefore serves as an example of why Mary's hesitation about marrying Walter under less than optimal financial conditions is problematic and why her final choice to marry him in faithfulness to her own deepest feelings is right (though Trollope eases her decision by having the finances come right too).

The next potential candidate for religious hero is Rev. Henry Fitzackerley Chamberlaine, a more complex but hardly more heroic cleric. He visits Bullhampton to dispense advice to Gilmore, his nephew, about the foolishness of romantic fixation on Mary and to Fenwick about the foolishness of his tolerance for a fallen women, the foolishness of not tolerating the pretensions of a marquis, and then, when it is proved that the marquis does not own the land on which the Methodist chapel is being erected, the foolishness of tolerating its presence. He arrives in his own carriage and pair of horses and has highly refined tastes in wine, coffee, and ideas.

He is "a prebendary of the good old times" who owns a stall at Salisbury Cathedral "worth £800 a year and a house" (Trollope, *Vicar* 163). In addition, he is "incumbent of a living in the fens of Cambridgeshire, which he never visited," upon which Trollope's narrator pointedly adds, "his health forbidding him to do so," when it is clear that he is in good health (163). Even though he donates money from the incumbency back to that parish, he is an exemplar of the abuses into which the Ecclesiastical Commission was probing at the time. Chamberlaine approaches the type of Dr. Grantly, but then he lacks Grantly's engaging pugnacity; he approaches the type of Mr. Arabin, but then he lacks both the spiritual devotion and the openness to female tutelage of Arabin. While Grantly and Arabin are thoroughly married, Chamberlaine, like Parson John, is an inveterate bachelor, a sign of unmanly self-centeredness for Trollope.

Though the novel is not explicit about Chamberlaine's refined ideas, we are told that "it suited his tastes and tone of mind to adhere to the well-bred ceremonies of life," which points to ritualism (Trollope, *Vicar* 163). As Fenwick describes him: "He is the most perfect philosopher I ever met . . . and has gone to the very centre depth of contemplation. In another ten years he will be the great Akinetos," a genuine pagan (166). This marks him as an example of the high-and-dry Church and of a kind with the "Normal Dean of the Present Day," whose duties are "difficult to define," who "shall have shown a taste for literature in some one of its branches," and who "is a gentleman who would probably not have taken orders unless the circumstances of his life had placed orders very clearly in his path" (Trollope, *Clergymen* 36). He has "great gifts of preaching, which he would exercise once a week during thirteen weeks of the year," and "many applications were made to him to preach here and there, but he always refused" (Trollope, *Vicar* 164). His definition of "work" is not Trollope's. Thus, the narrator comments that while he is considered a great man of the Church that he "was only a prebendary, was the son of a country clergyman who had happened to marry a wife with money, and had absolutely never done anything useful in the whole course of his life" (165). The novel's final judgment of him is sealed when he heartlessly responds to Fenwick's attempts to rehabilitate Carry and bring her back to her father's house and to the community by saying, "There are penitentiaries and reformatories, and it is well, no doubt, to subscribe to them" (186).

This leaves among the clergymen only Fenwick as candidate for religious hero. He would seem to qualify on the basis of Christian compassion and charity, in particular in working to save Carry. The problem from the perspective of Mr. Puddleham and his congregation, the marquis and his daughters, and even Fenwick's own more traditional parishioners is that he seems less concerned with saving her soul than with saving her in the worldly ways of body, family, and community. To Puddleham, who believes she must be cast out and allowed to suffer the full consequences of such a heinous sin, Fenwick responds in a Mauricean vein: "Have we not all so sinned as to deserve eternal punishment. . . . Then there can't be much difference between her and us. . . . If she believe and repents, all her sins will be white as snow. . . . Then speak of her as you would of any other sister or brother,—not as a thing that must be always vile because she has fallen once" (Trollope, *Vicar* 124).

On the one hand, Fenwick is only enacting his author's participation in a historical trend that was especially compatible with Broad Church principles. There was a movement throughout the century, even among evangelicals, away from the Calvinist emphasis on fallenness, a "shift of emphasis from the death of Christ to the life of Christ—from a theology centred on the Atonement to one centred on the Incarnation—and a shift from the wrath and judgement of God to the love and Fatherhood of God" (Parsons 109). Jacob Brattle, the marquis, and Mr. Puddleham, though very different, each practices the wrath of God. In contrast, and on the other hand, Fenwick practices liberality in the extreme, even within the historical trend. Janet Fenwick, in writing to Mary about the Jobian suffering of Jacob Brattle, asks: "Can it really be that the man is punished here on earth because he will not believe? When I hinted this to Frank, he turned upon me, and scolded me, and told me I was measuring the Almighty God with a foot-rule" (Trollope, *Vicar* 90). For Fenwick, Brattle is not excluded from God's love even in his apostasy. Thus, the marquis refers to Fenwick throughout, up until their final reconciliation, as an infidel, "and if an infidel, then also a hypocrite, and a liar [in claiming allegiance to the *Thirty-Nine Articles*, as required], and a traitor, and a thief" of the parish's tithes (178).

It only further weakens Fenwick's case in the eyes of those around him when he variously acknowledges sexuality as a natural human act, even for women; points out the greater culpability of men than women, as well as the double standard by which women even so are more harshly judged; and minimizes the severity of it as a sin, as when he says: "Think how easy it is for a poor girl to fall,—how great is the temptation and how quick, and how it comes without knowledge of the evil that is to follow! How small is the sin, and how terrible the punishment! Your friends, Mr. Brattle, have forgiven you worse sins than ever she has committed" (Trollope, *Vicar* 191).[17] Reminding people of their equal culpability and, worse, of their hypocrisy about it does not strengthen one's case, though it is clear that Trollope's narrative favors Fenwick's greater tolerance on religious issues and on women's issues.

Meanwhile, Fenwick has hypocrisy and credibility issues of his own. The novel foregrounds this first in relation to Fenwick's fishing and rat catching with Sam Brattle, which is known throughout the parish and casts doubt upon his objectivity concerning Sam's innocence of murder and upon his fitness for his office. The marquis and his family are under the impression that the vicar and Sam spend "the best part of their Sundays" in these sports, and though Trollope does not substantiate this claim he intimates it in order to bring in one of his pet peeves about evangelicals, which is their strict Sabbatarianism (*Vicar* 116). Fenwick says to Gilmore on the subject: "I understand it all, old fellow . . . and know very well I have got to choose between two things. I must be called a hypocrite, or else I must be one. I have no doubt that as years go on with me I shall see the advantages of choosing the latter" (116). Being a hypocrite means here both engaging in an activity one loves even if beneath the dignity of a vicar and, by implication at least, breaking the Sabbath, according to stringent Sabbatarians (such as Mrs. Proudie), even when training and norms compel one to preach observance of it. Trollope raises the latter issue in "The Clergyman who Subscribes for Colenso," whom he describes thus: "Now the special offence of the liberal preacher on this occasion was a thing conveyed in a sermon that the fourth commandment ["Remember the Sabbath Day to keep it holy"] in its entirely is hardly compatible with the life of an Englishman in the nineteenth century" (*Clergymen* 123).[18] Indeed, hypocrisy is the special cross to be borne by the liberal clergyman: "He is one who, without believing, cannot bring himself to think that he believes, or to say that he believes that which he disbelieves without grievous suffering to himself. He has to say it, and does suffer" (*Clergyman* 129). It may be that Fenwick is a clergyman who, like Trollope, subscribed for Colenso.

Fenwick, however, does not seem to suffer from his choice of hypocrisy. Perhaps he falls between that liberal clerical type and the type of "The Parson of the Parish," the old-school version of which Trollope describes as the most caring, genial, and gentlemanly of clerics. With an understanding of "the peccadilloes dear to the rustic mind he knows how to make compromises, and can put up with a little drunkenness, with occasional sabbath-breaking, with ordinary oaths, and with church somnolence," and he "hates . . . the over-pious young curate" (Trollope, *Clergymen* 62, 63). This type of clergyman has his own challenge of hypocrisy, because "it is his misfortunate that he must preach higher than his own practice":

> As the mealman in the description of his flours can never go below "middlings," knowing that they who wish to get the cheapest article would never buy it if it were actually ticketed as being of the worst quality, so is the parson driven to ticket all his articles [of faith] above their real value. He cannot tell his people what amount of religion will really suffice for them, knowing that he will never get from them all that he asks; and thus he is compelled to have an inner life and an outer,—an inner life, in which he squares his religious views with his real ideas as to that which God requires from his creatures; and an outer life, in which he is always demanding much in order that he may get little. (63–64)

If in the pulpit Fenwick preaches higher than his practice, which perhaps involves even Sabbath-breaking—thereby choosing to be a hypocrite—he does not do so in comforting Mrs. Brattle. Although she is glad to hear him lovingly pardon Carry, "when she thought of him as a minister of God, whose duty it was to pronounce God's threats to erring human beings, she was almost alarmed," because "she could hardly understand his leniency,—his abstinence from reproof" (Trollope, *Vicar* 46). Fenwick is more liberal than "The Parson of the Parish," demanding not more, either of himself or of his parishioners, but less than either Mrs. Brattle or Jacob Brattle—a mealman himself—expects, the wife for reasons of faith and the husband for a faithless yet Old Testament worldview.

The crisis of hypocrisy and credibility comes home for Fenwick in his relationship to Carry. Carry bears the burden of beauty, and Fenwick is not quite self-reflexive enough to fully understand the complexity of his own motives or the risk that he is taking in the eyes of the community. Thus we read: "He thought for a moment that he would tell her that the

Lord loved her; but there was something human at his heart, something perhaps too human, which made him feel that were he down low upon the ground, some love that was nearer to him, some love that was more easily intelligible, which had been more palpably felt, would in his frailty and his wickedness be of more immediate avail to him than the love even of the Lord God" (Trollope, *Vicar* 175–76). Indeed. While the novel approves the Broad Church toleration that facilitates Fenwick's genuine Christian charity, it also expresses an ambivalence around that latitude, which occurs at the interface between the spiritual and the temporal, in the form of Fenwick's natural human frailty and the observance of it by his critics in the community. Fenwick's temporal frailty is a commentary on the frailty of his spiritual position, and this is one way that Trollope participates, even if indirectly, given his reticence on spiritual topics, in the general discourse of his time about spiritualism versus materialism, which is a connective thread throughout *Spirit Matters*.

The text enacts this ambivalence as an oscillation in the narrator's commentary. The narrator first observes that "perhaps it was a fault with [Fenwick] that he never hardened his heart against a sinner, unless the sin implied pretence and falsehood" (Trollope, *Vicar* 172). Then, when Fenwick says, in discussing with his wife Brattle's casting away of Carry, "It is very difficult to make crooked things straight," the narrator comments, "It is probably the case that Mr. Fenwick would have been able to do his duty better, had some harsher feelings toward the sinner been mixed with his charity" (185, 186). The narrative appears to be aligning itself with Brattle's harsh judgment, though with the qualification of "perhaps" and "probably." A hundred pages later, the same question arises: "Was it a fault in him that he was tender to her because of her prettiness, and because he had loved her as a child? We must own that it was a fault. The crooked places of the world, if they are to be made straight at all, must be made straight after a sterner and a juster fashion" (281). Yet when the narrative returns to this topic it comments, "The straight-going people of the world, in dealing with those who go crooked, are almost always unreasonable" in expecting the crooked to embrace with gratitude the harsh corrective measures sanctimoniously offered (367). This is the Trollopian dialectic, the "characteristic doubling mind" of his "subversive" or "slippery" narrator, the canny structuring through which the "narrative voices establish a dialogue between themselves while playing a teasing game with the reader, so quintessential of Trollope, [and it] feels decidedly modern" (Swingle 112; Kincaid 155; Morse, *Reforming Trollope* 7; Markwick 81).

## The "Old Shore" of Faith, the Broad Church Compromise, and Paganism

It would appear that Trollope, like his age, was divided. "Isn't the world a better place if we all live by the example of Jesus's love?" he seems to be saying, but then, in the same instant, "Wouldn't the straight path be easier to discern if God's law and the method of following it were universally clear for all to follow?" Trollope says something quite similar in *Clergymen*, referencing the clergyman who subscribed for Colenso:

> If one could stay [with nonmodernized Christianity], if one could only have a choice in the matter, if one could really believe that the old shore is best, who would leave it? Who would not wish to be secure if he knew where security lay? But this new teacher, who has come among us with his ill-defined doctrines and subrisive smile,—he and they who have taught him,—have made it impossible for us to stay. With hands outstretched towards the old place, with sorrowing hearts,—with hearts which still love the old teachings which the mind will no longer accept,—we, too, cut our ropes, and go out in our little boats, and search for a land that will be new to us. . . . Who would not stay behind if it were possible to him? (128)

There is some genuine pathos here. Trollope knew that neither he nor, ultimately, Christianity itself could remain on the old shore but rather must follow the new clergyman who "had, by the subscription, attached himself to the Broad Church with the newest broad principles, and must expect henceforth to be regarded as little better than an infidel . . . by the majority of his brethren of the day" (130). "Infidel" is the word used repeatedly by the Marquis of Trowbridge for Mr. Fenwick.

*The Vicar of Bullhampton* thus enacts the competing historical pressures inherent in what Victor Shea and William Whitla, commenting upon *Essays and Reviews*, describe as the "Broad Church compromise" (124).[19] This was the rhetorical maneuver by which first the literalness of the Bible is disproved and the necessity of accommodating it to "modern criticism" and to science is established, but then "these discrepancies are swept away and a faith position is asserted" (110, 125). That "faith position" was based upon the felt rightness of awe before God and of adherence to Christian morality. Matthew Arnold employed a very similar argument to posit the essence of Christianity as "righteousness . . . not simply *morality*, but *morality touched by emotion*," meaning in effect God's immanence verified by the common human experience of right and wrong (*Literature and Dogma* 176). The Broad Church compromise was the resolution that resulted from the "juggling of these two factors, the emotional, located in the truth of the human heart, and the rational, located in the critical faculties of the mind analyzing history and language" (Shea and Whitla 124). In *Vicar*, all three of the primary subplots—the fallen women/fallen man, religious, and romantic subplots—enact the ascendency of the "truth of the human heart" and a compromise with rationality, and Trollope's artistic mastery resides in part in his design of the implicit parallels between Fenwick's choices in the former two subplots and Mary's choices in the latter one.[20]

The Broad Church compromise actually was between three not two positions: faith, unbelief, and "morality touched by emotion." Faith, according to Broad Church proponents, was implicit in or folded into morality/emotion, but according to some Broad Church opponents, was therefore effaced and lost. For the Broad Church, morality/emotion was, to use nonphenomenological language, the deconstructing third term; it kept faith alive by not opposing it irreconcilably to the rationality or worldliness that might lead to unbelief. *The Vicar of Bullhampton* represents all three of these religious positions. Put simply, Fenwick and Mary each represent morality/emotion and faithfulness to one's deeply held emotional truths, whether in religion or in love. They demonstrate the compromise needed to balance spirituality with temporality or materialism, as do all of Trollope's sympathetic clerical characters.

The two most lionized religious figures in this novel are none of the clergymen but rather Fanny, Carry's sister, and Jacob, her father. They stand respectively for faith and unbelief of a particular kind, true spirituality and a certain type of materialistic ethics. Fanny is the unbeautiful, selfless, pious sister, but she is neither simpering nor sanctimonious. She reflects upon "the strange destiny of women" by which her beautiful sister has been ruined, and she is likely to have no lovers and continue as "a homely, household thing," but she does this without judgment or self-pity (Trollope, *Vicar* 378). She stands true to both her sister and her brother. It is she who has the will to admit Carry into the house against her father's edict. It is she who cares for Carry's physical needs for food and clothing and, when those are met, asks, "will you kneel here and say your prayers as you used to?" (377). She is emblematic of the old shore of faith, the unmodernized Christianity, pure and purely Christian spirituality, but compassionate rather than judgmental, and still free from doubt.

Jacob Brattle, working-class, almost primitive, "pagan," is more than a match for Fenwick, who, while pugnacious to robbers and noblemen alike, says that Brattle "is the only person in the world of whom I believe myself to be afraid" (Trollope, *Vicar* 185). Brattle is not reluctant to tell the vicar that "people knows well enough what's good for them to do and what isn't without being dictated to by a clergyman" (290). While he may be a nonpractitioner, he wields a rigorous but unforgiving Christian morality. Fenwick wonders whether he should be working harder to bring Brattle into the fold, but "of what use could it be to preach repentance to one who believed nothing"; "he could tell the man, no doubt, that beyond all this there might be everlasting joy not only for him, but for him and the girl together;—joy which would be sullied by no touch of disgrace. But there was a stubborn strength in the infidelity of this old Pagan which was utterly impervious" (449, 451). Nevertheless, in ways that no doubt concerned Trollope's devout readers, Brattle is the religious hero of the novel: "about the miller there was a stubborn constancy which almost amounted to heroism" (285). The novel opens and closes with Brattle, and on the last page one reads that "Death, when it came, would come without making the old man tremble" (527).

Brattle's character represented a radical religious statement that, as I said in opening this chapter, marks the boundary between the heterodox and the orthodox. It reflects Trollope's recognition of what was to come, that in the last quarter of the century "it would hardly be an exaggeration to say that it was the agnostics rather than the orthodox who had the sense of being official, an intellectual establishment more powerful than the church establishment" (Cockshut 11). It is as if Trollope foresaw that "by 1900, the question 'What do Anglicans believe?' [would] become, in any straightforward sense, impossible," that the history in which he was living would be "the story of how the unity represented by the Established Church of England gave way to religious pluralism and diversity and of how Britain adapted to this pluralistic society through the growth of religious tolerance and a more religiously neutral polity" (Parsons 62; Melnyk 155). Trollope deeply regretted this, but he was a realist, as is Fenwick when, visiting London, he reflects upon "the Sunday occupations of three millions of people not a fourth of whom attend divine service" (*Vicar* 493). He worked to ameliorate this trend and to shore up the Church as still the best platform for genuine religious practice and the best institutional structure for a civil and caring society. As Durey argues, "While wishing to entertain his readers, he was trying to inveigle the Victorian reading public, grown weary of sombre sermonizing and ecclesiastical wrangling, into a reappraisal of the complexities and function of the Church of England and its unique brand of Christianity" (175).

N. John Hall observes that the "segment of the Church of England informally denominated 'broad' suited Trollope nicely; he could pretty much dismiss the Old Testament, admire the moral teachings of Christ, and keep up an ill-defined belief in a supreme being and a vague hope of some kind of immortality" (184). While not inaccurate, this seems mildly dismissive, untrue to the complexity of Trollope's struggles over religion, and presumptive on questions of faith about which Trollope chose to remain silent. I too have argued that Trollope came down somewhere within the Broad Church, though I do not disagree with Amanda Anderson's nuanced conclusion that "it certainly cannot be claimed that Trollope unequivocally supports a liberal ideal, even one tempered by sober realism or anchored by exemplary character," because "there is a genuine tension between his liberalism and his persistent valuing of traditional forms of life in the face of what for him are the negative dimensions of modernity" (531). Trollope's upbringing and tastes predisposed him to High Church traditionalism, but he opposed both its dogmatic and elitist elements and was enough of a true Protestant to bridle at the paternal mediation of a priesthood between individual and God. Though he sometimes tarred evangelicals, it could be argued that he shared their characteristic allegiance to individual choice in questions of faith and individual responsibility for moral decisions. Yet he saw the proliferation of "brands competing in the religious marketplace" and the swelling culture of "consumer-consciousness" in religious choice as destructive to the Church, to Christianity, and to English culture and society (Melnyk 135). In contrast to a fully "modern Christianity" of Protestant persuasion, which might be said to stand on individualized faith but in a public arena (as in evangelical testimony), Trollope's Christianity, modified by a gentlemanly reticence on questions of faith, was at once private and communal, private faith within community practice, which may characterize one type of modern Anglicanism.[21] Trollope being Trollope, he famously described his political position as "an advanced, but still conservative Liberal" (*Autobiography* 291). A similar statement might apply to the religious position he fashioned for himself, which was more multifaceted and contingent than the primary categories of High, Broad, and Low. At the periphery of the center of nineteenth-century British religious discourse, Trollope occupied a position between all others. I have attempted to suggest here that he may have been more latitudinarian than he often is given credit for, though never categorically so, and that his writings indirectly address the dialectic of spiritualism versus materialism that *Spirit Matters* is tracing throughout the century.

Finally, there is and can be no singular religious hero in Trollope's fictional world, nor, he believed, in his society. His heart was with heart, the morality/emotions that he believed must serve as the mediating factor between unquestioning faith and unbelieving rationality, between spiritual commitment and mundane social realities. Morality/emotions—the faith of the Broad Church—must be the compass between individual choices and communal responsibilities, but Trollope well understood that this is a human instrument, even if created or guided by God, and so is fallible, frail, unavoidably self-interested, and influenced by desires beyond reliable control. Thus, Fenwick cannot be fully suitable as the novel's religious hero, given that he demonstrates also the natural frailty of the human heart, the precariousness of his author's own morality/emotion. This is the sign of Trollope's strain to believe even in the heart's unerring rightness or to hold any faith not based upon the ethics of morality/emotion and not monitored by rationality. Though Trollope never would have expressed it this way, God or spiritual truth is accessible only through the material manifestation of an ethically ordered society as demonstration of an ethically ordered universe. There is no absolute dichotomy between faith and works, spiritual and material. Therefore, in *The Vicar of*

*Bullhampton*, Fanny Brattle, Jacob Brattle, and Frank Fenwick (paralleled by Mary Lowther) form a trinity of partial religious heroes, each incomplete without the others, representing faith, righteous unbelief, and the morality/emotions that must balance the other two. The highly Trollope-like commentary of the narrator is required to hold this trinity in unsettling but vital community.

# 4

# The Influences of Buddhism and Comparative Religion on Matthew Arnold's Theology

> What we want to understand is, how we are to deal with this extraordinary manifestation of human nature which we call Buddhism; ... great currency has been given [to it] in a book to which I refer with the utmost respect for its author and for its motive,—I mean Mr. Matthew Arnold's "Literature and Dogma," a book which seems to me to advocate a kind of semi-Christian Buddhism.
> —The Very Reverend Henry Wace, 1874

How could Matthew Arnold's major work of biblical criticism, *Literature and Dogma: An Essay Towards a Better Apprehension of the Bible* (1873), be considered "semi-Christian Buddhism"? Matthew Arnold (1822–88), the emblematic mid-Victorian liberal intellectual, son of one of the most famous proponents of Broad Church Anglicanism,[1] who dedicated the last decade of his life to writing not the poetry for which he is most often remembered now but rather religious criticism, who wrote those works with no less an ambition than to save modern Christianity, primarily from itself—through what sources and in what ways could he have been influenced by Buddhist thought?

In order to answer these questions, we will need to consider the history of the European "discovery" of Buddhism, which only fully commenced around the time Arnold was born in 1822;[2] the roughly contemporaneous emergence of comparative religious studies as a discipline with its own practice and theory; Arnold's exposure to works of comparative religion, the primary medium through which he encountered Buddhism; and Arnold's purposes and arguments in *Literature and Dogma*, which I will argue indeed were influenced by his study of Buddhism and of comparative religion in specific ways that this chapter will delineate.

## The European Encounter with Buddhism and the Emergence of Comparative Religion

Western engagement with Buddhism reached a threshold in the 1830s after Brian Houghton Hodgson, an East India Company employee in Nepal, sent manuscripts of Buddhist sūtras in Sanskrit to the Société Asiatique in Paris, and the first major Buddhologist in Europe, Eugène Burnouf, used them as the basis for his groundbreaking work, *L'introduction à l'historie du Buddhisme Indien* (1844). One of Burnouf's several eminent students, Friedrich Max Müller, immigrated to England and to Oxford in 1846, carrying with him "German philology," the historical and comparative analysis of ancient languages and, by extension, the associated cultures and religions. At the same time, missionaries in Southeast Asia began publishing works to explain Buddhism to subsequent missionaries to aid them in gaining converts, works such as the Reverend R. Spence Hardy's *A Manual of Buddhism* (1853) and the Right Reverend P. Bigandet's *The Life or Legend of Gaudama, the Budha of the Burmese* (1858), which were widely read in England. Thus, "as late as the 1860s, but rapidly at that point, Buddhism 'hit' Europe in general and England in particular, becoming a widespread topic both in the scholarly and popular literatures that peaked in London's 'Buddhism-steeped Nineties'" (Franklin, *Lotus* 2; Caracciolo, 30). Between 1850 and 1900, the number of newspaper and journal articles with "Buddha" or "Buddhism" in their titles increased significantly on a decade-by-decade basis.[3] Popular commentators, many concerned about the encroachment of Buddhism on Christian territory, drew upon the explosion of scholarly works published especially in the 1870s–1880s, such as those listed in the bibliography of *Spirit Matters* by Henry Alabaster, Ernest J. Eitel, Monier Monier-Williams, F. Max Müller, Hermann Oldenberg, and T. W. Rhys Davids. During the second half of the century, concepts such as karma, reincarnation, and nirvana (*kamma* and *nibbana* in Pali) began to appear with increasing frequency in novels and poems, including three book-length poems in England recounting the life of the Buddha, one of which, Sir Edwin Arnold's *The Light of Asia* (1879), became an international bestseller that has never gone out of print. Thus commenced the Western romance with and struggle against the cultural counterinvasion of the West by Buddhism, which has continued up to the current popularity of His Holiness the Dalai Lama and the many recent films in the "martial-arts Buddhism" subgenre.

Comparative religious studies was a primary vehicle for Buddhism into Western thought, but it had broader ramifications than that. As a founder of it, Max Müller championed what he called "the science of religion," the first principle of which was the egalitarian application of textual rigor: that all religions—even Christianity—could be treated equally as objects of non–theologically motivated scholarship. The second principle was historicism: that religions have historically specific origins and human agents that can and should be studied using the same tools applied to secular events. Both of these principles were widely perceived as threats to the sacred, to the mystery of divine origin through revelation. For example, because David Friedrich Strauss's *Das Leben Jesu*, translated by Marian Evans (George Eliot) in 1846, portrayed Jesus as a historical man and argued that biblical miracles should be read figuratively as myths, it was widely viewed as heretical and blasphemous. But Broad Church Anglicans, such as Benjamin Jowett, F. D. Maurice, and Matthew Arnold, did not perceive this "higher criticism" of the Bible as a necessary threat to faith and so accommodated the influence of comparative religion. The Broad Church manifesto *Essays and Reviews* (1860), which was instantly infamous for its latitudinarian views, "called for a thoroughly historical and critical approach to the Bible, for recognition of the moral and spiritual worth of religious traditions outside the Bible, and for acceptance of the findings of science concerning both the age of the earth and its geological history, and the possibility (or impossibility) of miracles" (Parsons 41). Thus, comparative religion changed religious discourse in England not only by introducing foreign religions but by reframing Christianity.

The third principle of comparative religion was the primacy of textual origins: that the oldest scriptures take precedence over subsequent interpretations or additions, as well as over current-day beliefs of indigenous practitioners. Prompted by the Protestant allegiance to the primacy of the Bible as "The Word," this tenet resulted in the textual appropriation by Western scholars of authority over other religions.[4] This was at once a form of discursive violence that served imperialism and a means of preserving and honoring the ancient scriptural origins of world religions. Implicit in this principle was the belief that religions become degraded over time, losing the purity of their origins through cultural adaptation, syncretism with other practices, and the superimposition of ecclesiastical dogma. Max Müller wrote in this regard: "If there is one thing which a comparative study of religions places in the clearest light, it is the inevitable decay to which every religion is exposed. . . . No religion can continue to be what it was during the lifetime of its founder and its first apostles . . . without constant reformation, i.e. without a constant return to its fountainhead. . . . Whenever we can trace back a religion to its first beginnings, we find it free from many of the blemishes that offend us in its later phases" (*Chips* xxiii). Thus, as Christopher Clausen has argued, comparative religion came to reflect the influence of the Darwinian revolution—*On the Origin of Species* having appeared in 1859—in its view that religions (d)evolve over time and that the goal is to trace them back to their origins.

Earlier in the century, philology had traced the English language back to its origins in the Indo-European language group, which linked Britons to the "Aryans." Prior to the Nazis' appropriation and perversion of that term, it meant the ancient, Sanskrit-speaking peoples and region of what is now northern India and the adjacent countries. Siddhartha Gautama (ca. 563–ca. 483 BCE), the Buddha, had been one of those people from that region. Liberal intellectuals therefore were interested for several reasons in what Thomas Henry Huxley wrote of as "the Aryan question." As Stephen Batchelor summarizes, "by the middle of the century the term 'Aryan' had gained common currency, not merely to denote the new language group opened up through the discovery of Sanskrit, but as an ethnographic concept" linking northern Europeans racially to the Aryans, rather than to the Greeks and Romans, and religiously to the Indian or "Dharmic" religions, rather than to the "Abrahamic" religions of the biblical Holy Land (266).[5] The implications were disruptive to many foundational assumptions and beliefs.

Yet the fourth and final principle by which I will characterize comparative religion was its critical stance toward the perceived Aryan penchant for metaphysical castle-building and supernatural storytelling. These prejudices can be traced to Burnouf's seminal work. His *Introduction* is a combination of translation, analysis, and commentary on the Tripiṭaka, the oldest collection of canonical Buddhist scriptures. The "three baskets" of the Tripiṭaka are the Vinaya Piṭaka of monastic rules for monks and nuns, the Sūtra Piṭaka (Sutta in Pali) of the discourses of the Buddha and his disciples, and the Abhidharma Piṭaka (Abhidhamma) of doctrines or "higher teachings." Concentrating on the Sūtra Piṭaka, Burnouf develops a historical distinction between what he calls the "simple sūtras," the originary teachings closest to the time and words of the Buddha, and the "developed sūtras," written at later dates by various authors and recognizable by elaborateness in style and recourse to metaphysical claims and supernatural evidence or miracles. Burnouf writes that "the ordinary sūtras show us Śākyamuni Buddha preaching his doctrine," which "is above all moral; and although metaphysics is not forgotten, it certainly occupies a less grand position than the theory of virtue imposed by the law of the Buddha" (159). In the simple sūtras, "the scene . . . is India, the actors are humans and some inferior divinities; and save for the power to make miracles that Śākya [Buddha] and his foremost disciples possess, what occurs there seems natural and plausible," but in the developed sūtras "everything that the imagination can conceive as immense in space and time is still too confining for the scene of the developed sūtras" (160). By the time Burnouf's analysis reaches the Abhidharma Piṭaka, he "cannot believe that such a book . . . gives us the doctrine spread by the recluse of the Śākya race several centuries before our era" (477). Thus Burnouf ties the historical timeline of the writing of the sūtras to a scale of value judgments that privileges the earlier moral teachings based on the history of lived human experience relative to the later metaphysical dogma and appeal to miracles. These judgments became standard positions within nineteenth-century comparative religion.[6]

And those same judgments were, or came to be, more broadly shared. The two features of Buddhism that Victorians most readily approved were the saintly character of its founder and its moral tenets. Both those attracted to and those critical of the story of the Buddha's life, which was retold many times in the scholarly and popular literatures in Europe, recognized his status as a historical figure, rather than a deity, who taught an ethical way of living, rather than either divine revelation or metaphysical doctrine (contrary to the stereotypes about the Aryan penchant for both). Many who participated in the Victorian "Jesus-versus-Buddha debate" took this as obvious proof of the Buddha's inferiority to the Son of God, while others saw the Buddha's ethics of compassion and selflessness as pleasing confirmation in advance of Jesus's subsequent, similar teachings (Franklin, *Lotus* 27). Those on both sides recognized Buddhist morality, as exemplified by the Noble Eightfold Path, as a rigorous, historically tested ethical system independent of supernatural justification. One commentator in 1872 proclaimed that Buddhism "has the credit of placing morality far above everything else as a means of obtaining the blessings promised to believers," and another concluded in 1890 that "we owe much of the morality and civilization of the world to the life of renunciation and self-sacrifice of Gautama Buddha" (Amberley 316; McKerlie 225).

At the same time, others recognized that this emphasis on ethical "works" placed Buddhism in direct contradiction to the central dogma of the Protestant Reformation that "men are justified and saved without works through faith alone" (Feuerbach 258, note). As a religion whose founder refused to engage in metaphysical speculations about the origins of the universe or the existence of a creating deity on the grounds that doing so only distracted from spiritual practice, Buddhism clearly was atheistic.[7] This fact fueled the denigration of the ethics of karma and reincarnation as a "materialistic" and "selfish" system that "converts morality into a vast scheme of profit and loss" (Eitel 84). Monier Monier-Williams, a scholar who studied Buddhism in part to reveal its inferiority, described it as "no religion at all, but a mere system of morality and philosophy founded on a pessimistic theory of life" (537). Even so, its emphasis on history and morality put Buddhism in line with theoretical commitments of comparative religion—or vice versa—as well as with those that Matthew Arnold would adopt.

## Matthew Arnold's Exposure to Buddhism and Comparative Religion

It nearly is enough for my purposes simply to note that Arnold studied and quoted Burnouf's *Introduction*, as well as his translation and commentary on the Lotus Sūtra, also read *La Bouddha et sa religion* (1860) by one of Burnouf's eminent students, Jules Barthélemy-Saint-Hilaire, and at Oxford connected with Max Müller, with whom he later corresponded and whose works he undoubtedly read.[8] Even prior to Oxford, "Arnold evidenced interest in Buddhism before the majority of his contemporaries" (Whitlark 14). At Oxford, "it is clear from the evidence in the poetry and elsewhere that Arnold at the least experimented with, and in some instances embraced, heterodox religious beliefs" from Hinduism and Buddhism (Livingston, *Matthew Arnold* 16). In the 1840s and 1850s, when he was writing such poems as "Empedocles on Etna," "Resignation," "The Scholar Gypsy," and "Sohrab and Rustum," which critics have noted reflect Eastern influences,[9] in his "writings and reading-list there are many scattered references to Eastern religion and thought" (Jarrett-Kerr, "Arnold" 129). His sister Jane, whom he affectionately called "K," wrote that "Matthew has 'a good deal of the Eastern philosopher about him' and that really doesn't 'suit the European mind'" (in Honan 177). While he was working on his tragic drama *Merope* in 1857, Arnold wrote to K: "I must read Merope to you. I think and hope it will have what Buddha called—the 'character of *Fixity*—that true sign of the Law,'" as "dharma" (*dhamma*) often was translated (*Letters*, Lang, vol. 1 364). Later that year, he opened his inaugural lecture as professor of poetry at Oxford with a tribute to Buddhism, quoting from "one of those legends that illustrate the history of Buddhism," the allegory of Purna (whom he calls "Pourna") that he had read in both Burnouf and Barthélemy-Saint-Hilaire (Arnold, *Essays* 4). Significantly, he chose a sūtra the moral of which, in Burnouf's translation, concerns the righteousness of "quietude, morality, wisdom, and . . . contemplation" (267), which Arnold summarizes as the "moral deliverance, eminently, of which the great Oriental reformer spoke" (*Essays* 4). The Buddhist emphasis on ethical conduct was a primary draw for Arnold.[10]

But make no mistake, Arnold was no Buddhist. He saw himself as defending the truest form of Christianity, though he understood that it would be viewed as revolutionary, indeed hoped it would be "an inevitable revolution" comparable to the Reformation (Arnold, *Literature and Dogma* 147). Though he was decried by contemporary Low Church and High Church critics alike, and though T. S. Eliot and other modernists famously dismissed his theology, some now consider Arnold "the precursor of the Anglican modernism of the next two generations and beyond," or, "beyond doubt, the greatest influence in the last century in the direction of liberalism in religion" within the Church of England (Livingston, "Matthew Arnold's Place" 35; Gardner, in Machann 125). The fact is that Arnold read encyclopedically in several modern and several ancient languages, and so he read and was influenced by comparative religious studies and Buddhism, but he was more deeply influenced by, among others, Johann Wolfgang von Goethe, Samuel Taylor Coleridge, John Henry Newman, his father, the classical tradition, and certainly the Bible, his knowledge of which rivaled that of ministers and professors of divinity.

What is more, Arnold's understanding of Buddhism was limited to the positions of the first generation or two of Buddhologists in Europe. As C. A. F. Rhys Davids wrote near the end of the century, "Much, for that matter, in Arnold's thought is soundly Buddhist, and in pathetic contrast to his ignorance of Buddhism" (224). Arnold's relationship to Buddhism started as a young man's romantic fascination with a dimly understood exotic alternative. One glimpses this in the opening of his poem "Consolation," published in 1852:

> Mist clogs the sunshine.
> Smoky dwarf houses
> Hem me round everywhere;
> A vague dejection
> Weighs down my soul.
> . . . .
> Far hence, in Asia,
> On the smooth convent-roofs,
> On the gilt terraces,
> Of holy Lassa,
> Bright shines the sun.

"Lassa" refers to Lhasa, one of the seats of Tibetan Buddhism, idealized here relative to the smoke and dejected soul of England. Yet, by 1887, Arnold concludes his essay "Amiel," about the writings of Henri Frédéric Amiel, whom Arnold felt had been too much influenced by Buddhism, in this way: "Maïa has had her full share of space already: I will not ask for a word more about the infinite illusion, or the double zero, or the Great Wheel" (Arnold, *Complete Prose Works* 281). The "infinite illusion" and "double zero" are allusions to nirvana assumed to mean nihilism, and "the Great Wheel" is the "Wheel of the dharma" or *dharmachakra*. The shift from idealization to condemnation reflects Arnold's mature recommitment to Christianity. It also reflects his eventual subscription to Burnouf's dismissal of the more complex Buddhist doctrines, such as nirvana and the *dharmachakra*, as "Aryan metaphysics," as well as his failure to enquire beyond the misinterpretation of nirvana as stark nihilism, which was propagated by the early Buddhologists, as well as by Arthur Schopenhauer, but corrected in the later scholarship of Hermann Oldenberg and T. W. Rhys Davids.[11] While "a distant, detached admiration for oriental wisdom remained with him all his life," Arnold's serious consideration of Buddhism declined as he aged, certainly as biblical criticism became the central occupation of his writing life (Jarrett-Kerr, "Indian Religion" 101).

Thus, one finds in Arnold a split, representative of his time, between the "good Buddhism" of the founder's life and moral practice and the "bad Buddhism" associated with the common Western stereotypes of Oriental fatalism and nihilism, exacerbated by the supposed Indian penchant for metaphysical abstruseness. Arnold had learned both from Burnouf and his students in comparative religion.

## Method and Ethics in *Literature and Dogma*

In *Literature and Dogma*, Arnold "is revalidating the Bible by means of literary criticism for a society in danger of losing it" (apRoberts, *Arnold and God* 200). The Bible, Arnold felt, was at risk from (at least) three directions: (1) biblical literalism and misinterpretation by Low Church Anglican and Nonconformist (non-Anglican) Evangelicals who staked the worth of Christianity on the reality of miracles; (2) imposition by High Church Anglicans, following Catholicism, of doctrinal dogma and metaphysical overinterpretation not found in the Bible itself; and (3) discrediting of the Bible by science in an age increasingly convinced by it that truth claims must have rational, empirical proof, one result of which was "the growing discredit befalling miracles and the supernatural" (Arnold, *Literature and Dogma* 142–43). Indeed, the Bible "is attacked on all sides, and the theologians are not so successful as one might wish in defending it" (238). In part like the Puritan predecessors but even more like comparative religion scholars of Buddhism, Arnold's approach was to return through historical method to the origins of Judeo-Christian belief as found in the earliest canonical text and extract the pure teachings. In characteristically Arnoldian style, he distills those teachings down to a small number of key terms that he develops throughout an immensely complex 250-page "essay" with a large number of scriptural quotations, scholarly allusions, and examples from contemporary religious debates, the majority of which I will have to leave aside. He returned to the Bible to save it, but this time equipped with the tools of philology, comparative analysis, historicism, and literary criticism.

For Arnold, "literature" means at one level "nonliteral," recognizing that the miracles in the Bible, as well as abstract terms heavily laden with signification, are figurative expressions of spiritual truths so profound that they barely can be expressed in language, much less with "scientific" exactitude: "Terms, in short, which with St. Paul are *literary* terms, theologians have employed as if they were *scientific*," terms such as "*grace, new birth, justification*" (Arnold, *Literature and Dogma* 170). Even "the word 'God' is used in most cases as by no means a term of science or exact knowledge, but a term of poetry and eloquence, a term *thrown out*, so to speak, at a not fully grasped object of the speaker's consciousness, a *literary* term, in short" (171). "Dogma" means "a scientific and exact presentment of religious things," whether in the form of dogmatic literalism or in the form of doctrinal assertions about concepts like "the Council of the Trinity" or a "Personal First Cause" that over the course of 1,900 years had been institutionally imposed upon the Bible (202). In contrast, reading the Bible as literature would be a more rigorous method, both in terms of the level of attention to words and meanings and the level of attention to the historical process by which interpretations had been layered on top of the Bible, obscuring its meanings. This historicism starts by acknowledging Jesus as a historical human being and the writers of the Bible as fallible people writing in historically specific times, places, and languages. It is the historical accretion of what he labels "'*Aberglaube*,' extra-belief," that Arnold attempts to unpack throughout the book, all the way from the "Messianic ideas" of the ancient Hebrews to contemporary "Evangelical Protestantism's phantasmagories," such as "the 'Atoning Blood'" (212, 213, 357). Arnold summarizes: "The changes that have befallen the text show, no doubt, the constant tendency of popular Christianity to add to the element of theurgy and thaumaturgy, to increase and develop it "through a process that reveals generations of theologians at work,— men with more metaphysics than literary tact, full of the Aryan genius, of the notion that religion is a metaphysical conception" (266). The "making of religion into metaphysics is the weakening of religion," and the resulting *Aberglaube* has "pushed on one side, for very many, the saving doctrine of Jesus" (241, 275). The error "has sprung out of a false criticism of the literary records in which the doctrine is conveyed; what is called 'orthodox divinity' is, in fact, an immense literary misapprehension" (276).

"Righteousness" is the central key term in *Literature and Dogma*, especially in analyzing the Judaic prehistory of Christianity and the thesis of the Old Testament. The lead argument is that "conduct" or "righteousness" is *"Three-fourths of life"* and is "the object of Bible-religion"—not faith or miracles or metaphysical dogma about the Trinity or the afterlife, but moral feeling and behavior (Arnold, *Literature and Dogma* 175), very much like the "morality/emotion" that I delineate in Anthony Trollope's writing. Arnold argues, borrowing his approach from philology, that what has been interpreted as "God" or "Lord" is most accurately understood from the ancient languages as "the *not ourselves* by which we get a sense for *righteousness*," "*the Eternal that makes for righteousness*" (182, 250). While the figurative concepts in the Bible over which Christians throughout history have generated *Aberglaube* require well-read and trained interpretation, morality, according to Arnold, is universally experienced and recognized.

This last point is critical, because upon it Arnold hopes to build a "rational" Christianity, one that can stand up to dogma, metaphysics, and even science because it "can be verified" (*Literature and Dogma* 150). Righteousness—unlike miracle, unlike "the fairy-tale of the three supernatural persons no man can verify"—is experiential, what he calls "experimental," and "natural" (148, 240, 362). It was infused into humankind first via the natural awe before the divine: "so much is there incalculable, so much that belongs to *not ourselves*, in conduct" that it has always "struck the minds of men as they awoke to consciousness, and has inspired them with awe" (182). Therefore, "when St. Paul says, that our business is 'to serve the spirit of God,' . . . and when Epictetus says: 'What do I want?—to acquaint myself with the natural order of things, and comply with it,' they both mean, so far, the same, in that they both mean we should obey a tendency, which is *not ourselves*, but which appears in our consciousness, by which things fulfil the real law of their being" (with "law" echoing the law of the dharma) (191). This is akin to the "argument from cerebral design" as the proof of God that I discuss in the first chapter of *Spirit Matters*. Therefore, righteousness, moral feeling, is natural and God-given. This receives further verification from the fact that "Conduct brings happiness" (205); doing the right thing, sacrificing oneself for a loved one, feels good and right, and this feeling is natural proof of the divine origin of righteousness and the ethical order of the universe. This is the reason why Arnold argued, knowing he would be accused of reducing religion to morality, that "religion is thus, not simply *morality*, but *morality touched by emotion*," where "emotion" means the profoundest of which humans are capable (176).[12] That God was the "Great Personal First Cause" is unverifiable, "but that there *is* an enduring Power, not ourselves, which makes for righteousness, is verifiable, as we have seen, by experience" (243, 375). Arnold strove to free the Bible from reliance upon the unsupportable evidence of miracles and metaphysics by grounding it in something he considered verifiable, namely righteousness.

What the New Testament and Jesus added to the Hebraic genius for righteousness was "righteousness explained to have its essence in *inwardness*, *mildness*, and *self-renouncement*" (Arnold, Literature and Dogma 228). This is "the secret of Jesus"—another key term throughout *Literature and Dogma*—which is in effect the selflessness necessary for humans to choose, even against self-interest, moral conduct toward others, to choose the "whole self as opposed to a partial self, a best self to an inferior self, to a momentary self a permanent self requiring the restraint of impulses a man would naturally have indulged" (179, 296). Jesus's "method" and the way of learning "the secret" is "*metanoia*," translated as "changing one's mind," as in conversion, or "repentance" (288). For Arnold this means first a social and psychological act of opening one's mind through the self-reflection induced by wide learning and exposure to different worldviews, which in effect is "culture" as he defined it in *Culture and Anarchy* (1869). Arnold alludes to but largely eschews the hard necessity of the orthodox doctrines of sin and redemption as the enforcement of ethical behavior (288). Instead he concludes that "the conjunction of the three in

Jesus,—the method of inwardness, and the secret of self-renouncement, working in and through this element of mildness,—produced the total impression of his 'epieikeia,' or sweet reasonableness" (300). Jesus came in order to manifest and embody the "emotion," the "inwardness," the interiority of the "not ourselves" that makes for righteousness.

"The secret" and "the method" of Jesus—inwardness and renunciation—are precarious points for Arnold requiring the most delicate distinctions. He delineated what he saw as Jesus's "method of pure inwardness, individual responsibility, personal religion," but not to be confused with the inwardness of justification by faith and not the personal religion of those who claim to have a relationship with God "as if he were a man in the next street" (Arnold, *Literature and Dogma* 200, 356). Arnold's Jesus made his followers "feel that they had a best and real self as opposed to their ordinary and apparent one," but Arnold must have known that his focus on the self treaded perilously close to other discourses of self that he opposed. Among those were the "unfettered egoism" of the "Romantic obsession with self," as well as utilitarian individualism and traditional liberal individualism, not to mention the conception of self or "not self" within Buddhism (Livingston, *Matthew Arnold* 19, 175). James Whitlark argues that Arnold took his concept of the "higher self" from Burnouf and Buddhism, using it as "the rational and better self that he employs in *Culture and Anarchy*," as well as in *Literature and Dogma* (5). This claim is supported by many Victorian commentators who observed, for example, that the "Buddha's doctrine was that of 'self-redemption,' which was afterwards preached by St. Paul, as in 'Work out your own salvation,'" or that Buddhism "requires the perfecting of one's self by the accumulation of merit with the sole view of a great final self-renunciation" (McKerlie 207; Rattigan 309).

The centrality of self-renunciation to *Literature and Dogma* required the most delicate distinction relative to Buddhist self-renunciation. Arnold had baulked at the metaphysical dogmas of nirvana and *anatman* (*anatta* in Pali), the doctrine that there is no essential self or eternal soul, both of which Burnouf had dismissed as nihilistic. While some of his poetry, such as "Empedocles on Etna" or "Resignation," explores self-annihilation, Arnold ultimately turned away from it toward more optimistic self-culture. Even so, the key term that he uses for renunciation of self is "*necrosis*," death of self, an extreme concept in the age of the "self-help" movement and the Personal Savior (Arnold, *Literature and Dogma* 291). As the dying of the lower self for the rebirth of the higher self, or as the selflessness of self as an expression of the "not ourselves," necrosis was "the crux of his understanding of Christianity" (Livingston, *Matthew Arnold* 20). But it verges dangerously close to nirvana, which the dominant understanding at the time took as the extinguishing of the identity of the eternal soul, utter nihilism. This Arnold could not endorse, even while some part of him leaned toward it. He could not help but admire what he saw as the "Aryan genius" both for complex metaphysical thought and for utter self-renunciation, but, following Burnouf, he ultimately condemned the former as *Aberglaube* and the latter as entirely incompatible with Christian faith, as it was (Arnold, *Literature and Dogma* 357). While clearly identifying himself with what he saw as the Indo-European Aryan birthright, he defended Christianity as founded on Hebraic righteousness in contrast to Aryan metaphysics.[13] Thus he chose to defend a form of self-renunciation that was more profound than was comfortable for his contemporaries but that also had to be kept distinct from the even greater extreme to which Aryan metaphysics had taken it.[14] Arnold's use of *"necrosis"* is the densest trace in *Literature and Dogma* of his reasons for being attracted to Buddhism compounded with his reason for turning away from it.

The split within Victorian discourse between "good Buddhism" and "bad Buddhism" is captured in a passage near the end of *Literature and Dogma* in which Arnold links a number of his central concepts to Buddhism but then finds it unable to fulfill them: "And if [contact with other religions by Christians] carries them to Buddhism, they are carried to a religion to be saluted with respect, indeed; for it has not only the sense of righteousness, it has, even, the secret of Jesus. But it employs the secret ill, because greatly wanting in the method, because utterly wanting in the sweet reasonableness, the unerring balance, the *epieikeia*" (382). As Arnold knew, Buddhism has the righteousness and the inwardness and the self-renunciation, but it does not have Jesus's method of repentance, nor sin and redemption in a Christian sense. There is no judging deity or heavenlike eternity in most denominations of Buddhism; there is nirvana, and that was a concept considered entirely beyond "sweet reasonableness." Arnold had gained the conviction to challenge the central Protestant tenet of salvation by faith, as well as the traditional reliance on revelation through miracles, in part from the ethical focus and historicism of both Buddhism and comparative religion. However, Buddhism led to a nirvana assumed to be damnable on two counts: as a nihilism, which was much too dark for Victorian progressivism, and as a metaphysical *Aberglaube* imposed upon the original moral teachings of the Buddha, both of which Arnold had learned to condemn in part from Burnouf and comparative religion.

## Postscript

The Reverend Henry Wace had more justification than he likely knew for describing *Literature and Dogma* as "semi-Christian Buddhism." Even so, Arnold's is an important work of Christian theology, deeply dedicated to the Bible as the basis for an ethical society. Arnold brought to his subject, in addition to other more significant influences, the influence of Buddhist thought, in particular the centering upon ethical conduct, the opposition to metaphysical speculation, the Buddha's compassion and renunciation, and the emphasis on self-culture. The influence between Arnold and Buddhism came full circle when William H. Rattigan summarized Buddhism in 1899 using Arnold's key term—"It inculcates the necessity of overcoming evil by good, and teaches that there is no happiness except in righteousness" (390)—and when W. S. Lilly wrote in 1905 that Buddhism's "one sole dogma," "that the universe is under one and the self-same law of causation which is ethical," had become obscured by "superfluous beliefs—*Aberglaube*" ("Message of Buddhism" 209).[15]

More significant than the influence of Buddhism was that of philology and comparative religion, from which Arnold gleaned, above all else, a method of analysis. That method included the application of scholarly rigor to the study of all religions, historicism and a return to origins, the treatment of supernatural and miraculous scripture as figurative and mythological, the privileging of the earliest canonical texts, the position that religions "decay" from their origins and canonical texts as centuries pass, and, tied to that time frame, the higher valuation of earlier moral teachings over later doctrines, viewed suspiciously as "metaphysics" or "dogma." Donald S. Lopez, Jr., in his "Introduction to the Translation" of Burnouf's *Introduction*, summarizes its broadest points as follows:

"that Buddhism is an Indian religion, that the Buddha is a historical figure, and, perhaps of particular consequence, that the Buddha was the human teacher of a religion (or perhaps a philosophy) that preached ethics and morality, without recourse to dogma, ritual, or metaphysics" (26). It would not be inaccurate to say that the broadest points of *Literature and Dogma* are that Christianity is a religion from the Land of Israel, that Jesus is a historical figure, and, perhaps of particular consequence, that Jesus was the human teacher of a religion that preached ethics and morality, without recourse to dogma, ritual, or metaphysics.

The preceding statement would have been understood by many Britons in the nineteenth century as nothing short of sheer materialism and blasphemy, a reduction of the divinity of Christ and a denial of the power of spiritual faith. Not a few readers of Arnold felt that way, while perhaps a smaller number recognized the necessary compromises through which he strove arduously to preserve Christian faith both from dogmatic textual materialists, as he viewed biblical literalists, as well as from metaphysical materialists, with whom he held no kinship.

We have seen how Buddhism, along with its primary vehicle of comparative religious studies, first entered debates about Christianity and infiltrated thinking about traditional Protestant concerns such as faith versus works. We have gotten a glimpse of how the elements of Buddhism most foreign to the Abrahamic traditions, such as nirvana and *anatman*, came to be implicated in the European discursive struggle to rescue spirituality from materialism, because those elements were interpreted as unwanted confirmation of the most fearful forms of materialism. The counterinvasion of Christianity by Buddhism was one of the events that drove orthodoxy to the wall of heterodoxy if not heresy. The two chapters in the next section of *Spirit Matters* provide the prehistory to Arnold's exposure to Buddhism by tracing it back to the original encounters of the British Empire and Christianity with Buddhism in Sri Lanka and Thailand.

Part II

# The Interpenetration of Christianity and Buddhism

5

# Interpenetration of Religion and National Politics in Great Britain and Sri Lanka

## *William Knighton's* Forest Life in Ceylon

In the first half of the nineteenth century, Great Britain strained to manage its expanding empire in the face of multiple violent uprisings abroad, two of which occurred in Ceylon (Sri Lanka) in 1818 and 1848. It was during those decades that Europeans "discovered" Buddhism, of which Ceylon was a primary source of knowledge, and began to construct a Western Buddhism that was distinct from the practices of indigenous Buddhists for multiple complex reasons that I have analyzed previously and will illustrate further in this chapter.[1] During those decades also, one foundation for comparative religious studies, which would emerge as a scholarly discipline in the 1860s, was laid by Christian missionaries, who studied Buddhist practices and scriptures and wrote about them primarily for the purposes of conversion. Missionaries became an influential political force in London starting in the 1820s–1830s and mounted, with the support of the British government, a religious invasion of India, Ceylon, and other colonial possessions. The Sinhalese encounter with Christian missionaries, and then with Theosophists later in the century, would contribute to a transformation in the dominant indigenous Buddhist culture, the "Sinhalese Buddhist revival" starting at midcentury, and the growth of anticolonial nationalism in Ceylon in the second half of the century.[2] As a result of that encounter, as Elizabeth J. Harris observes, "the Buddhism that had emerged [in Ceylon] by the end of the nineteenth century was neither the creation of the West nor the East, but had developed through the interpenetration of the two, at a particular historical moment" (163). That "moment" stretched from the 1840s, when William Knighton (ca. 1820–1900) was in Ceylon and the Kandyan Revolt of 1848 occurred, to the 1880s, when H. S. Olcott, cofounder with H. P. Blavatsky of Theosophy, joined with Buddhist monks in Ceylon to defend against Christian missionaries and in shaping a hybrid religion, "Protestant Buddhism."[3] The other half of that story was the counterinvasion of Britain by Buddhism, as in Matthew Arnold's work, and its impact upon discourse about religion in England. The interpenetration was bidirectional, as I have shown in *The Lotus and the Lion*. Postcolonial scholarship has taught us what Peter van der Veer summarizes: "Both colonizer and colonized were intimately connected and transformed through a shared process of colonization" and a "shared imaginary of modernity" in which the ostensibly secularizing separation of church and state "gave religion a strong new impulse," both for colonizer and colonized, and it became necessary to define and defend even Christianity in relationship to other world religions (7, 8, 24).[4] This chapter explores the bidirectional interpenetration of Christianity and Buddhism in a colonial context through analysis of William Knighton's *Forest Life in Ceylon* (1854). The analysis links the debates between the two in Ceylon to debates about religion in England and to national politics in both countries, linking the British encounter with Buddhism to the cultural contests between spiritualism and materialism, Natural Theology and scientific naturalism.

While *Forest Life* generally is called a novel, it is a hybrid of a half dozen genres: the travelogue, the autobiography, the anthropological notebook, the big-game hunting story, the fable-like animal tale, and the treatise on comparative religion, as well as the novel, itself variously conceived. It exhibits some of the cataloging of social, biological, and geographic features that is characteristic of a different but related type of writing, what might be called the "colonialist's owner's manual."[5] Unlike these, *Forest Life* sustains a storyline across its two volumes. The narrative is interrupted regularly, however, by nondiegetic digressions, in particular two religious biographies "founded upon facts related to the author," one of a Parsee named Hormanjee, who does not appear in the main narrative, and one of a Buddhist "Modliar, or Kandian [sic] Colonel, named Marandhan," who is a significant character throughout (Knighton I.vii, 1:133).[6] The narrative focuses on a group of coffee plantation owners, Knighton's narrator and his friends: Marandhan, the Masseys, and Fowler, who is the protagonist. The ultimately villainous trio of Mouat, Siggins, and Vanstrut is pitted against the newly married and newly arrived Hofers, Ernest and Emma, around whom the main conflict unfolds through a confluence of financial crisis in the coffee market, which was occurring at that time, and romantic scandal of suspected infidelity. The first volume concludes with a short appendix, "History of Ceylon, 1140–1186, A.D.," and the second with a seventy-three-page appendix, "Four Dialogues Between a Budhist [sic] and a Christian," Marandhan and Knighton. This dialogue is an extension of one that begins in the narrative, with a footnote directing the reader to its continuation in the appendix. My analysis of *Forest Life* is not comprehensive; it treats only the main narrative and then the appendicized dialogue between Knighton and Mirandhan.

*Forest Life* was the first novel in English of which I am aware to be set fully in Ceylon.[7] It was among the first works in English to provide not only a portrayal that is recognizable as reasonably accurate by subsequent Sinhalese commentators but also as relatively sympathetic, if unavoidably patronizing. Yasmine Gooneratne has written that, in the character of Marandhan, "Knighton tries to present the reader with some idea of the living force of Sinhalese cultural tradition," and, though he "does not entirely succeed in his portrayal of Ceylonese character, he achieves the distinction of presenting native characters as personalities in their own right, and no longer as comic caricature or as part of a picturesque background" (*English Literature* 167, 170). *Forest Life* "becomes a searching inquiry into the shams, the inconsistencies, and the hidden weaknesses of English colonial society" (165). It was perhaps the first popular work in English to provide a relatively respectful and evenhanded portrayal of Buddhism. The Buddhism-versus-Christianity dialogues between Knighton and Marandhan consist of a civil give-and-take between equals. If it is predictable that they ultimately arrive at partial capitulation by the Buddhist—the exact terms of which will require analysis—along the way Marandhan is portrayed as holding his ground and winning points in favor of Buddhism. This would have made many of its British readers uncomfortable and would have incensed the Anglicist proponents in London and the body of missionaries in Ceylon, as I will discuss below. What is more, *Forest Life* directly incorporates Buddhist elements, including the form of the dialogue between Knighton and Marandhan, which in the Sinhalese context unavoidably points to the Buddha's primary teaching method in the suttas (sūtras, in Sanskrit).

## Orientalists versus Anglicists

The Orientalist-versus-Anglicist debate in London in the first half of the century was a disagreement concerning the best approach to colonial governance, in particular of India and then Ceylon, and specifically concerning the role of religion and the access of Christian missionaries to those two countries, among others. The father of this Orientalism was Sir William Jones (1746–94). Jones was a founder of the Asiatic Society of Bengal and of the study of comparative philology, which would provide one crucial basis for the formation of comparative religious studies, of which Buddhism was a primary object. In 1786, Jones theorized the concept of the Indo-European language group, which would prove significant in European thought about its "Aryan" links to India and then to Buddhism. This Orientalism, two centuries before Edward Said's important work, *Orientalism* (1978), meant academic cultural studies of the colonized people, their language, history, and religion. It derived in some part from respect for the colonized culture; the initial "Orientalist position that Hindus had a great civilization whose achievements could be compared to the highest ones of classical antiquity led them to argue that the East India Company had to support the natives to pursue studies in their native classical tradition, just as the British did back home" (van der Veer 114). But of course this study was wed to the mission of colonial governance and unavoidably involved assumption of superiority and the instrumental use of "intelligence" to exploit the other. Thus, Orientalists unavoidably held conflicting motivations, even in advocating for an approach to colonial rule built upon respect for and noninterference with indigenous religions. Recognizing this inherent ambivalence in Orientalism, Michael S. Dodson argues that it is best understood as "a shifting set of policy positions and localised practices, which were constantly adapted to changing circumstances in both the colonial contest, and with respect to evolutions in metropolitan British thought, rather than a static *modus operandi*" (4).

The Anglicist rebuttal of Orientalism gained political traction in the 1820s–1830s. It was informed by James Mill's anti-Indian *History of British India* (1817) and carried to political advantage by T. B. Macaulay's *Minute on Indian Education* (1835), which dismissed the value of Indian culture and recommended blanket Anglicization of colonized peoples. Although the Anglicist position cannot be reduced to a prescription for colonial rule by force, it was more compatible than Orientalism with those who advocated military response to native resistance. This can be seen, for instance, in the public debate between Thomas Carlyle and John Stuart Mill over the "Negro question," with reference to the Jamaican slave uprising of 1831, the British abolition of slavery in 1833, and, subsequently, the Morant Bay rebellion in 1865.[8] Carlyle's position was similar to Thomas De Quincey's in his essay "Ceylon" (1843), which celebrated the English as the "one race of men . . . selected and sealed for an eternal preference in this function of colonizing" and argued that in colonial contests "the power constitutes the title": might makes right (622, 623). As James H. Warren, among others, has observed, "colonization was a masculine endeavor defined by 'man's ability'" and the construction of a "white, Anglo-Saxon, Christian, and bourgeois . . . authoritative masculinity" by which British men licensed themselves to rule "over nature, the labouring class, the 'heathen,' the colonized, and 'woman'" (45, 47).[9] Carlyle, De Quincy, and likeminded others championed a form of masculine colonialism that I will call *bully masculinity* (with Victorian rugby and field hockey connotations). This form of colonial masculinity was exemplified by many legendary Victorian explorers and soldiers, among them Samuel White Baker, a colonial traveler, big-game hunter, and author of *Eight Years Wanderings in Ceylon* (1855). Baker's writings on Ceylon, in contrast to William Knighton's, as I will show, represented indigenous cultures, foreign environments, and wildlife as dangerous elements to be conquered and tamed. In contrast, J. S. Mill's position in the "Negro question" debate was based upon respect for the equitable rule of law and the example set through adherence to it in British governance. His was an "intellectual masculinity," a specific type of "colonial masculinity that was detached and more metropolitan in character" and that built a "cultural technology of rule" using Orientalist methods (J. Warren 58). I will refer to this as *liberal-intellectual masculinity*. While there was no straightforward identity between Anglicism and bully masculinity, or between Orientalism and liberal-intellectual masculinity, those parallels undeniably emerged in debates about colonial rule and thus formed a central opposition in *Forest Life in Ceylon*.

The Anglicist ideological and political position was joined by the period's evangelical revival in British Christianity. This included the formation of the missionary societies of the primary Protestant denominations in the 1790s to 1810s and the rapid influx of missionaries to India and Ceylon immediately thereafter.[10] The evangelical lobby, with powerful representatives in government, argued that the Orientalist policy of noninterference with indigenous religions constituted government interference with missionary access to potential convertees—a breach of the desired separation of church and state—and that Christianization was a moral duty that also served colonization. In India and Ceylon, the precolonial monarchies historically had supported the dominant Buddhist establishment administratively and financially, and when the colonial governments assumed some of those responsibilities for the sake of stability, evangelical interests in London labeled these practices "idolatry," as in the Anti-Idolatry Connexion League, formed in 1817. Thus, there was a "radical change in British colonial policy on Christianisation that came in the mid-1830s and early 1840s," and that change was "owing to the hostility of the Ceylon missionaries and their powerful adherents in Great Britain to the British Government's connexion with 'idolatry'" (De Silva 116; L. Mills 126).

This is not to say that Anglicism vanquished Orientalism or that the two ever were categorically distinct. Quite the contrary. In the first place, Orientalism thrived in the emerging discipline of comparative religion. The first generation of European Buddhologists, such as George Turnour (1799–1843) and Eugène Burnouf (1801–52), had been members of the Ceylon Civil Service. Second, missionaries, notably Daniel J. Gogerly (1792–1862) and R. Spence Hardy (1803–68) in Ceylon, quickly learned to adapt the methods of academic Orientalism to the purposes of instructing subsequent missionaries on the beliefs and practices of Buddhism in order to best undermine them and convert Buddhists.[11] Thus British Orientalism shifted from being a means through which "a secular Company official-cum-scholar could acquaint himself with the languages and cultural traditions of the people over whom he ruled in order (at least theoretically) to make himself a more responsive and efficient administrator"; rather, it "would become the means through which Victorian missionaries and civil servants would attempt to exert and exercise control over the ruled people," becoming "part, perhaps the most significant part, of the Evangelical Christian technology of subjectification and colonial discipline" (Scott 340–41). Third, and as part of the inherent ambivalence of Orientalism, it became difficult to distinguish academic Orientalists from missionary Orientalists, since, as Philip C. Almond's *British Discovery of Buddhism* (1988) shows, both shared key assumptions derived from centuries of Protestant culture: that authentic religion is not what the contemporary natives practice but rather what is found in the originating texts, a model that implicitly assumes a bible revealed by a transcendent God, of which Theravada Buddhism had neither. This allowed Europeans, whether in government or mission or university, to claim an expert authority over the religions of occupied countries superior even to that of indigenous practitioners.

Knighton's *Forest Life* portrays all of the ambivalences of the above context, enacting within its narrative the contemporary Orientalist-versus-Anglicist debate as a contest between competing models of colonial masculine rule, and staging that debate more directly in its "Four Dialogues between a Buddhist and a Christian."

## Missionaries, the "Buddhist Temporalities Question," and the Sinhalese Buddhist Revival

After three centuries of European occupation, first by the Portuguese and then by the Dutch, Ceylon became a British crown colony in 1802. The ancient Kingdom of Kandy, the central seat of Buddhism in that country and a primary seat of Buddhism in the world, which had remained independent through the previous occupations of the coastal regions, fell to British rule in 1815. Given the dominance of Theravada Buddhism—70 percent or more of the population—and the Kandyan resistance to British rule, Sir Robert Brownrigg, perhaps also influenced by Orientalist thought, included in the fifth article of the 1815 "Kandyan Convention" treaty this statement: "The religion of Boodhoo, professed by the chiefs and inhabitants of these provinces is declared inviolable, and its rights, ministers, and places of worship are to be maintained and protected" (in Sivasundaram 128). This clause soon became infamous among Anglicists and missionaries as the "*Magna Charta* of Buddhism" that betrayed Christianity ("Buddhism" 489). In assuming rulership of Kandy, "the British Government became the legal successor of the king of Kandy, not only in political but also in religious matters, and the Sovereign of Great Britain became the defender and protector of the Buddhist faith in Ceylon" (Evers 324). Missionary interests were inflamed by the "Idolatrous System of Religion" in the "Buddhist Temporalities Question," which concerned the legal status of the Buddhist establishment, financial support of it and oversight of its properties, and even appointment by the British governor of head "priests" (so called with unflattering allusion to Catholicism) (Evers 326).[12]

As Anglicist and missionary interests prevailed in London, the colonial governors in Ceylon in the 1830s–1840s worked to sever the government's direct relationships with Buddhism. This was one factor that spurred the 1848 uprising, "to the extent that some members of the rebel leadership articulated the widespread resentment at the British decision to abrogate the traditional association of Buddhism with the state" (De Silva 121). Another factor, in addition also to taxation issues, was Wesleyan Minister Daniel Gogerly's publication of *Kristiyāni Prajñapti* (Christian Institutes, 1848), "a trenchant and provocative critique of Buddhism based on a penetrating analysis of the Pāli Canon that galvanized the [Buddhist] revivalist leadership as well as the laity at large as no other tract or pamphlet of the Christians ever had" (Young and Somaratna 45).[13] Gogerly marshalled the "closely argued philology" of academic Orientalism to defame the monks before their followers for neglecting and perverting original "pure" Buddhism (Harris 203). Historians have observed variously that the "ingrained traditions of Buddhist tolerance afforded a courteous welcome to influences and even to religions of all kinds" from the beginning of interactions with Westerners, that signs of Buddhist resistance to evangelical Christianization are detectable as early as the 1820s, and that "it was not until the 60s and the 70s that Buddhist ranks closed at last against the aggressiveness of the missionary advances" (Gooneratne, *English Literature* xiv; Harris 203; Prothero, *White Buddhist* 95). But it was in 1848, with Gogerly's direct assault on the monastic sangha, that the missionaries' intention to sweep Buddhism out of existence and replace it with Christianity became unmistakable.

It is within this context that Knighton wrote *Forest Life*. The work draws upon events from the four years between 1843 and 1847 when Knighton was overseeing a coffee plantation and serving as the secretary to the Ceylon Branch Royal Asiatic Society, but it was published in London in 1854. This timing is crucial. Knighton left Ceylon soon after the arrival of Lord Torrington as the new governor and just before the violent rebellion and reprisal of 1848. In London, in 1850, he witnessed the recall of Torrington under charges of mismanagement and brutality—he had executed a monk in robes. In the highly publicized parliamentary inquiry, Torrington's colonial secretary, a dedicated career civil servant, Sir James Emerson Tennent, found himself in the difficult position of defending the questionable actions of his superior against criticisms brought by a fellow member of the Ceylon civil service, Philip Wodehouse. The exchange became acrimonious and inappropriately personal, Parliament was strongly divided, and the government was publically embarrassed. In censuring Torrington and dismissing Tennent and Wodehouse, Lord Grey cited in particular the men's failure to maintain "harmonious co-operation with each other and that respect towards yourself, which are indispensable to the proper administration" of a colony (in L. Mills 202). This event constituted a breaking of the ranks within colonial masculine solidarity that "shook the certainty of Britain's global colonialism," as would the subsequent Indian rebellion of 1857 (J. Warren 39). *Forest Life* stages between its male characters just this crisis within colonial masculinity.

Through the events of the 1840s and 1850s in Ceylon, the Buddhist response to the missionaries began to shift from passive tolerance to active resistance and solidarity across temple districts. In 1862, "the Sinhalese started their own Lamkopakara Press at Galle," and then one in Colombo, and "the Buddhist resistance became organized" (Prothero, *White Buddhist* 95). They too adopted the methods of academic Orientalism, turning them back upon Christianity, with some parallels to the contemporaneous "New Criticism" of the Bible. They deployed lessons from comparative religion, for instance contrasting the unerring justness of the ethics of *kamma* (karma, in Sanskrit) to inconsistencies among ethical judgments portrayed in the Bible. They adapted public oratory and rhetorical tactics from the missionaries, such that in the 1860s "the technique of the public debate, which the missionaries had used so effectively in the past, only succeeded in providing Buddhist spokesmen with a platform for a vigorous re-assertion of the virtues of their own faith" (De Silva 122). In the pivotal debate at Pānadurē in 1873, Mohoṭṭivattē Guṇānanda, "appealing meticulously to the letter of Christian scriptures—that Moses was a murderer, that the birth of Jesus was accompanied by the culling of children . . . accused Christians of worshipping a jealous, capricious, violent and demon-like god" (Harris 202). His perceived victory "gave back dignity and identity to the Buddhist spectators" (203). Buddhism in Ceylon for the first time became part of a national political identity in a modern sense. As Peter van der Veer has argued in relationship to the parallel pattern in India: "Indian religions were transformed in opposition to the state, and religion became more important in the emergent public sphere. As in Britain, religion was transformed and molded in a national form, but that form defined itself in opposition to the colonizing state" (23). This movement, as well as the movement toward the Protestantization of Buddhism, was advanced by the arrival in Ceylon of Olcott and Blavatsky, who in 1880 became the first Westerners to take Buddhist vows. Theosophy's "'scientific' critique of Christianity" and its unsupportable supernatural claims augmented the case for Buddhism, which by then many in Europe had observed was much more consistent with scientific naturalism in general and Darwinian evolutionary theory in particular than was Christianity.[14] Just "the presence in Sri Lanka of a group of Westerners openly championing Buddhism had a deeply significant psychological effect" on national religious identity, countering half a century of denigration of Buddhism (De Silva 127). There is double historical irony in the fact that the invasion of Ceylon by missionaries—and even, or especially, the resulting revision of Buddhism through that contact—ultimately stimulated a revival of Buddhism that would in turn become one foundation for national political revival and perhaps even for independence from Great Britain in the twentieth century.

### Buddhist Animal Fables and Colonial Masculinity

Elephants and monkeys (also leeches and mosquitoes) figured prominently in British descriptions of Ceylon, as they do in *Forest Life*. The Sinhalese Asian elephant was an important symbol in reference to British colonial rule, colonial masculinity, and Buddhism. It long had been an icon representing Ceylon, and then the British, having captured and tamed it, centered the colonial coat of arms of Ceylon on the image of that elephant, securely barred on each side by parallel rows of palm trees. The elephant was the largest and most dangerous animal to hunt in Ceylon, and so one of the highest marks of bully masculinity was the proper stalking and eye-to-eye shooting of elephants (as opposed to perching in trees and picking them off, as Britons claimed only natives would do). The Prince of Wales, visiting Ceylon in 1875, understood the symbolic significance when he affirmed his "imperial masculinity" by hunting wild elephants, "shooting one from ten yards 'when it was about to charge him,'" as the press reported (Hahn 179). Also, the elephant's combination of dangerousness and domesticatability made it a figure for the Sinhalese people, in particular the danger of rebellion by them, which was very present in the British mind, especially after 1848.

The elephant is such a recurring figure within Buddhist folklore and scripture that there are too many instances to cite. I will mention two sources that anyone living in Ceylon for any period of time would have encountered as the most popularized texts from the Theravada canon: the *Jatakas* and the Dhammapada. The *Jatakas*, or Buddha birth stories, contain many humorous and instructive animal parables, which were one source for Aesop's fables.[15] A number focus on elephant characters, as well as monkey characters. The Dhammapada is an ancient series of scriptural verses attributed to the Buddha.[16] Knighton cites it in volume 2, chapter 1, titled "Budhism," in which he also draws upon the Reverend Spence Hardy's *Manual of Buddhism* (1853), written in Ceylon, and George Turnour's translation of the "*Mahawanso*" (*Mahavamsa*, 1837), the Pali history of Ceylon, among other well-known sources on Buddhism. Chapter 23 of the Dhammapada is titled "The Elephant," and it begins with the following three verses, taken from the first translation published in England in 1881:

> 320. Silently shall I endure abuse as the elephant in battle endures the arrow sent from the bow: for the world is ill-natured.
> 321. They lead a tamed elephant to battle, the king mounts a tamed elephant; the tamed is the best among men, he who silently endures abuse.
> 322. Mules are good, if tamed, and noble Sindhu horses, and elephants with large tusks; but he who tames himself is better still. (Müller, *Dhammapada* 77)

Within Buddhism, the elephant often stands for perseverance, steadfastness, and quiet strength, and a mind not tamed by Buddhist practice often is compared to a raging elephant. From a Sinhalese perspective, the elephant represented Ceylon and Buddhism patiently enduring British rule and intense missionary pressure, while the unruly mind of European bully masculinity was like a raging elephant.

The several humorous and instructive animal tales that appear in *Forest Life* evidence the influence of the *Jatakas*, as well as the Dhammapada. The same source later directly shaped Rudyard Kipling's *Jungle Book* (1894) and *Just So Stories* (1902).[17] It is significant that two of the animal tales in *Forest Life* make sport of bully masculinity, revealing its weaknesses as failures to meet Ceylon on its own terms. In volume 1, Lister, a large man and the most respected elephant hunter, takes a swim in a jungle lake and has his clothing stolen by a troop of monkeys. He ends up having to dress himself at Mouat's table in the feminized garb of a gown and pajama bottoms, which threaten further humiliating exposure as the seams are split by his bulk. He then swears at his native "peons," to whom he must appear as a rogue elephant, by calling them "monkeys," thereby completing the circle of associations by which the relationship between this brand of British masculinity and native people is characterized (Knighton 2:208). It is not difficult to recognize Lister as representative of one or more Victorian masculine archetypes, such as "the rugged sportsman, the muscular Evangelical, [or] the colonial man of action" (J. Warren 54), nor is it difficult to discern that the narrative laughs with the monkeys at the great white elephant. It is true that Knighton's narrator, in his first encounter with Sinhalese people, observed that to his "unsophisticated eyes" the loin-clothed crew of a boat coming alongside his arriving ship "appeared to be tame monkeys," but part of the honesty of Knighton's account is that he traces a progression from this knee-jerk prejudice to learned tolerance (2:7). He comes to lament that his "conception of humanity [had been] mixed up with clothes and white or black skins," and in one of several addresses to the reader on the subject, he pleads, in describing Marandhan's appearance, "let us begin to judge men by other than tailors' eyes, and to think more of the furniture within the cranium than of its external ornaments" (1:7, 139). This could be the moral of the parable of the great white hunter who is stripped of his external ornaments by monkeys.

But the strongest proponents in the novel of forceful rule through bully masculinity are Mouat, Siggins, and Vanstrut. One evening when the British coffee planters are having cigars and drinks, Siggins defends the supremacy of the planter over his native workers: "Every man is a magistrate on his own estate, you know . . . and therefore, as long as the man is working for you, you have a right to do what you like with him—that is, anything short of killing" (Knighton 1:281). But Mouat is the local magistrate, and it is part of his job, under the law, to defend Sinhalese and Britons alike against violent coercion or abuse. As the narrator previously has commented: "What redress could the poor coolie, for instance, have against his European master who illtreated [sic] him, miles away in the jungle, far from a magistrate or a court, with all his fellows up in arms against him, lest they should lose their employment, and his wife and family almost at the complete mercy of his persecutor?" (1:124). He, along with the other liberal-intellectual colonial males in the novel, are aligned with John Stuart Mill's position in the hearings that followed Governor Edward John Eyre's violent suppression of the 1867 Jamaican rebellion. Mill's point, in sum, was that effective and justifiable colonial government must take its authority from, and therefore act in accordance with, an equitable rule of law.[18] The problem with Mill's logic, from the perspective of some Anglicists, was, first, that it would limit the methods available to colonialists for handling disaffected native people and, second, that it would treat people of color as equal under the law, possessing the same Millian individuality and—perhaps more fearful—the same potential claim to manhood like their own. Thus, Mouat permits if not endorses Siggins's view, and Vanstrut says, "Siggins understands the native character," that it must be checked through distrust and harsh treatment (1:282).

As the conversation progresses, Knighton's narrator and Fowler try to defend a different type of relationship with the Sinhalese and their right to fair treatment under the law. Finally, however, the whip comes out, that signature "symbol of this exercise of power" by colonial masculinity (Scott 335).[19] Siggins recounts his horsewhipping of a father who protested because Siggins had "honored the rascal's daughter with a little attention"—he wanted to keep her as a sex slave (Knighton 1:284). When the father threatened to go to the magistrate, namely Mouat, Siggins gave him another twelve lashes. Rather than applauding, the group of men falls silent. The narrator, who is morally outraged, debates whether to urge

Mouat to prosecute Siggins, but a knowing look from Hofer tells him that it is more important not to create a schism in the colonial masculine solidarity, as Knighton had witnessed in London following Torrington's response to the 1848 uprising. Mouat demurs from fulfilling his legal duty on the grounds that he has heard this story privately, not in his official capacity.

But the text and Fowler in particular will punish Mouat for this in several ways, one of which is through another animal tale. In volume 2, Lister gets even with Mouat for telling the monkey tale on him by recounting the story of Mouat's first elephant hunt. Mouat avoided the dangerous skirmish with the herd in which the other men were engaged—implying cowardice—and ended by stumbling upon and shooting a chained elephant owned by the British commissioner of roads, for which he was arrested and fined. All the men laugh at this blunder, but the laughter is uneasy because Mouat's disgrace threatens to taint their shared masculine code. Mouat has failed the test of the "pukka Sahib," as Preseeda Gopinath (205) analyzes that concept—failed to uphold the code of bully masculinity. But this tale is significant in several other ways as well. The British government employed elephants, as they had been used for centuries prior, for such heavy work as road and bridge building and jungle clearing. While the wild elephant was the most appropriate target to test the mettle of the bully male, such as Samuel White Baker, the tame elephant was the economic asset of the liberal-intellectual colonial male, for example, James Emerson Tennent. In addition, as the hunting of the wild elephant figuratively reenacted the British conquest of Ceylon, with the wild elephant continuing to signify the danger of Sinhalese rebellion, so the killing of a tame elephant might represent unjustified violence against the domesticated Sinhalese, as perpetrated by Siggins. Thus, in shooting a tamed government elephant, Mouat has enacted at once three figurative killings. The bully colonial male (or the failure of that code) figuratively kills its rival masculinity, the liberal-intellectual colonial male, which indeed nearly occurs later in the story in the duel between Fowler and Hofer, who wrongly suspects Fowler of advances toward Emma. Second, the bully colonialist figuratively kills the already subjugated native people, as from one perspective did occur in Lord Torrington's putdown of the 1848 rebellion. And, third, in light of the verse quoted above from the Dhammapada, he who has failed to tame his own mind, in this case a certain kind of British Christian man, figuratively kills he who has tamed himself, the Sinhalese Buddhist.

There is another telling adoption of a Buddhist animal parable in *Forest Life*. Hofer is the lynchpin character in that he hangs in the balance between the two groups of men. The crisis of masculinity in the novel comes to a climax near the end of volume 2 as Hofer struggles between aligning himself either with Mouat, who lies to him that Fowler has been making love to Emma Hofer, or Fowler, who indeed is in love with Emma but even so has treated her with gentlemanly forbearance, unlike Mouat. Prior to any of this, early in volume 1, the narrator describes Hofer as brilliant, perceptive, warm, benevolent, and just, but continues as follows: "yet it appeared to me that the key-stone of the arch was wanting. The mind may be compared to the horse, the will to the rider. It avails nothing that we boast of the powers of our steed, of his swiftness, of his endurance, of his sure-footed paces, if we cannot guide and control him. The animal that runs away with his rider may travel over the most ground at the swiftest rate, but the slower-paced obeyer of the rein is still the more valuable of the two. And so the mind" (Knighton 1:83). Gooneratne's commentary on this passage is relevant: "Such a depiction of character in terms of a noble but uncontrolled horse ties up with Knighton's ideal of British colonialism informed by the chivalrous aspirations of a new Round Table; but it derives from his familiarity with Buddhist imagery. The image can be traced to its origin in stanza 5 of *Arahanta vagga*, which Gooneratne goes on to quote ("In Search" 138). Fowler bridles his British masculine activism and desire; Mouat does not. Once again a Buddhist animal parable is employed to demarcate between competing models of British colonial masculinity.

Tellingly, however, Knighton's narrator appears to reverse the moral of the horse parable soon thereafter. In his first dialogue with Marandhan within the narrative, he identifies himself with the charging stallion of ceaseless progress, in contrast to the supposedly plodding, contemplative mare of the East. He says, "You surely will allow that the civilization of the West with its world-traversing ships and engines of every kind to diminish human toil, is a superior thing to that of the East, with its empty despotic shows, and stand-still-do-nothingness" (1:154). This is of a piece with one of the most common Victorian stereotypes about Asians in general and Buddhists in particular: that they are passive, tradition-bound, ruled by the masses, and, therefore, fatalistic and atheistic with no future to believe in, in contrast to Westerners, who are active, progressive, optimistic, individualistic, and guided by certain faith in the future of the Empire and the reward of heaven.[20] Marandhan counters by pointing out that this touted progress "make[s] men look to change, and not permanence, as their greatest happiness; and, that is, in my mind, a lie" (1:154–55). He notes that England is full of people living in poverty and asks what good is such progress if it is built upon exploitation of the underclasses at home and of slaves abroad. Each man remains unconvinced by the other, and it is perhaps exceptional that the text does not dismiss Marandhan's position outright.

Yet, 120 pages later, a second apparent reversal occurs. Marandhan's very argument reappears from the mouth of the narrator, again in describing Hofer's lack of "that resolute will that is necessary to success and happiness": "What greater enemy can man have, as an individual or a community, than a restless, ever-acting desire of change? The peevishness of the child who tires of one toy and cries for another, carried into the important business of life and cankering the fair buds of happiness," in this case the happiness Fowler images any man should be able to find in a marriage with Emma (Knighton 1:277–78). Hofer's restless addiction to changefulness, which characterizes the whip-handed, hell-for-imperial-leather man of action, is both the source of British progress and the reason why it does not lead to happiness. By contrast, the redeemed Hofer is the one who, dying of fever near the end of the story, identifies Fowler's liberal-intellectual masculine code as the superior model of manhood. He has been led by Fowler "to value the friendship of that inestimable man Marandhan" and lies holding hands in homosocial solidarity with Fowler and, by extension, with that Buddhist Mudaliar who shares their code of masculinity, if neither their race nor their religion (1:212). The Buddhist elements in *Forest Life* directly contribute to Hofer's conversion to Fowler's brand of masculinity, even though Buddhism itself will be shown to give way to Christianity in the appendix.

The ambivalence in the narrator's position, this switching back and forth of the inherent ambivalence of Orientalism, is a sign of the discomfort created by the incomplete correspondence between masculine code and either race or religion. In the character of Marandhan, Knighton reverses an often-repeated British stereotype about native men, in particular men in Ceylon, who were said to exhibit the "effeminate, pusillanimous dispositions of the Cingalese" (Sirr 275). As multiple descriptions of his Kandyan manliness make clear, as well as the fact that he is allowed to speak for himself as a man and as a gentleman, Marandhan could participate fully in any brand of British masculinity, if race were no bar. It is a bar in relationship to bully masculinity, but it is less of a bar in relationship to liberal-intellectual colonial masculinity. It is significant that masculine code appears here to take precedence, though uneasily, over racial and religious difference. How is this possible? Gopinath identifies an explaining variable, one superadded to loyalty to an equitable rule of law, as exemplified by the relationship between Mr. Fielding and Dr. Aziz in E. M. Forster's *A Passage to India* (1924), for instance. That cross-racial, cross-religion friendship is licensed by "Fielding's belief that the values of gentlemanliness are universally applicable, that is that they are not racially delimited" (Gopinath 209). This gentlemanly code is drawn in part from archaic "ideals of chivalry" combined with "male (homoerotic or otherwise) bonding"; it "privileges intimacy over nation, justice and fair play over race" (204, 209).[21] This puts Fielding directly at odds with the bully masculinity of the pukka Sahib. The pukka Sahib "is an imperial mediation of the domestic ideal of the gentleman, where the ethnonational or the racial/tribal code takes precedence over the personal-ethical code: race becomes the defining factor of the Englishman" (205). As in the conflict between Governor Torrington and his critics, or between Carlyle and Mill, a division between pukka Sahibs and liberal-intellectual gentlemen produces a shattering schism in colonial masculine solidarity. Such a schism compels the pukka Sahib to question his own assertions about the essentiality of racial difference, upon which the exploitation-based profits of empire depend, and places him in the untenable position of having to justify his own violence against native people in relation to the British rule of law, upon which the necessary myth of the civilizing mission of empire depends. *Forest Life in Ceylon* is centered on the eruption and resolution generated by this schism, which in the novel is mediated by Buddhist figures.

In Knighton's story, seventy years prior to Forster's, it is the white man, Fowler, who is falsely accused of sexual misconduct with the recently arrived British woman; it is Marandhan who serves Fowler while he is in jail; and it is that native gentleman who demonstrates cross-racial magnanimity by financially assisting his white friends when the coffee market crashes. In *Forest Life*, the schism in colonial masculinity is partially resolved, though certainly not healed, by three actions. First, Fowler reverses the bully trademark of the whip, as previously wielded by Siggins, by horsewhipping Mouat. He does this in the very seat of justice, the magistrate's office, the justice that Fowler presumably also is defending against Mouat's failure to uphold it, breaking the law to save the law. This reversal was forecast by a story Mouat has told in which Vanstrut's whip was wrested from him by the native upon whom he intended to use it and turned against him. Second, Fowler is compelled to duel Hofer with pistols as a result of Hofer's failure to listen to the reason characteristic of the liberal-intellectual male and by his own sense of honor. Bully masculinity and liberal-intellectual masculinity settle their differences by recourse to a more archaic masculinity, the chivalric code, to which both masculinities trace different elements of their lineages. The event must be "kept strictly private" because it is outside of the rule of law to which Fowler's preferred liberal-intellectualism subscribes (Knighton 2:202). Fowler twice holds steady while Hofer fires at him, the second shot hitting his shoulder, then discharges his two shots into the air. In this way, he demonstrates not only his innocence but the superior masculinity of the liberal-intellectual gentleman and the greater claim of that brand of masculinity to the chivalric heritage. Third, Marandhan takes it upon himself to investigate the outcome of the case of the father whose daughter Siggins was molesting and finds that the father has died under suspicious circumstances and that there has been a payoff to Mouat to turn a blind eye. Marandhan gathers sufficient evidence for the chief justice to take action against Siggins and Mouat. Thus, the equitable rule of law, the signature of liberal-intellectual colonial masculinity, is reseated on the bench of justice, from which colonial bully masculinity has been ejected. But, significantly, this is accomplished by a native man, who thereby effectively becomes the champion of the rules of the power by which he and all of his compatriots are subjugated. John Stuart Mill's liberal-intellectual colonial masculinity has been proved right.

The ambivalence that the schism within colonial masculinity generates also manifests in the fact that, even if the law reigns in the end, the ascendance of liberal-intellectual gentlemanliness is made possible through the violence of the bully masculinity that it opposes. The ends and the means do not correspond. This is a replication of the dilemma that always faces bully masculinity, which Gopinath describes as "the contradiction of the imperial matrix": "In order to contain and civilize the Other, the Englishman must use force, exceeding his own restrained views of justice, and transgress his own articulated ethical code" (214). *Forest Life* cannot fully resolve this contradiction nor fully heal the schism within colonial masculinity. That it strives to do so in part through adaptation of Buddhist animal tales and, then, a dialogue between a Christian and a Buddhist exhibits the bidirectional interpenetration of colonizer and colonized, Christianity and Buddhism.

## Dialogue between Christianity and Buddhism

The very idea of genuine dialogue between a Christian and a Buddhist about the comparative merits of the two religions was unheard of by Britons in the 1840s. That idea, as Knighton understood, might be considered by Anglicists to be counterproductive to colonial rule and by evangelical missionaries to be a slippery slope to heresy. The Orientalist-versus-Anglicist debate is not mentioned in *Forest Life*, but Knighton's speaker and the character of Fowler embody the Orientalist position and demonstrate its efficacy in inculcating the British code of the gentleman and Christian faith as the best cultural technologies of colonial rule. Marandhan points toward the missionaries several times during the dialogues, as here: "The evidence of Christian missionaries on the subject [of the morality of Buddhists] cannot be received. They must look upon all heathen creeds with a jaundiced eye. It is impossible that they can judge, either the religious system or the lives, of opponents of Christianity impartially" (Knighton 2:415). Even without these pointers, however, British and Sinhalese readers of the time would have understood that these dialogues unavoidably were a critique of the missionaries, if also of Buddhist doctrines, and a demonstration of a dialogical approach as a more effective alternative to unreasoned denigration of another's faith.

The "Prefatory Remarks" to the dialogues note that Knighton and his "Buddhist friend" met for an unspecified number of months or years one evening per week, presumably as gentlemen would, over brandy and cigars, or the Sinhalese coffee grower's equivalent (2:359). Knighton addresses his

Christian readers in this way: "To the majority of Christians the idea of entering into an elaborate discussion to prove that there is a God, and that Budhism is false, may appear to be an absurdity; not so, however, to the inquiring mind that finds itself thrown into a Budhistic stronghold, and often assailed, without chance of honourable escape, save by victory" (2:359). The final outcome will be partly predictable: Marandhan will come to admit belief in a negotiated and unorthodox understanding of God and will denounce his belief in reincarnation, though notably not his belief in Buddhism generally. But getting there is both torturous, with perhaps twenty turns in their debate overall, and suspenseful: Marandhan wins the majority of points for Buddhism in the first dialogue, winning fewer and fewer in subsequent dialogues; Knighton concedes points that undoubtedly raised strong objections among Christian readers; and the tension builds toward climactic but less than fully credible capitulations by Marandhan.

Knighton stages the dialogues with Marandhan to demonstrate a method, one built upon Orientalist inquiry, liberal-intellectual impartiality, and the code of the gentleman. From the start he figures their "combat" as martial and chivalric, setting the terms of engagement for this the second duel in the text, after the pistol duel between Hofer and Fowler (2:359). This time, superseding racial and religious difference, both knights are gentlemen—Hofer's behavior having been questionable on these grounds—and each approaches the other avowing evenhanded consideration of opposed ideas. The weapons are not to be those of physical or even emotional violence, which bully masculinity might employ, but rather ideas exchanged in dispassionate, rational discourse. Early on Marandhan says, "You want to put my religious faith upon its trial, and I am willing that it should be, for, from friendly and candid discussion such as ours, uninfluenced by passion or interest, nothing but good can result, and I should have but a poor opinion of Budhism if I feared its investigation" (2:365). He also knows that he has equal right to demand reciprocity: "The discrimination I willingly grant in reference to Christianity, I confidently ask in reference to Budhism" (2:375). The fencing therefore includes moves to display honorable acknowledgement of the other's successful "touches." When Marandhan points out that "most Christian thinkers regard Christian enlightenment, and Christian cultivation, and Christian philosophy, as the only kinds worthy of the names, oblivious of the early civilizations of China and of India, of Greece and of Rome, which were independent of Christian influence," Knighton concedes the point, acknowledging that "until we know more of the early literature of the East, that of the West will be constantly liable" to such errors (2:373). Later, in the second dialogue, after Knighton has defended Christian faith on the basis of the number of intelligent believers (implying that the West produces a higher percentage of those) who would dismiss belief in reincarnation as unthinkable, Marandhan parries and thrusts: "So far can early training prejudice us against truth we are not used to! Transmigration has been the belief of the vast majority of mankind from the remotest times to the present. . . . Pythagoras and Plato received it [from Buddhism], and introduced it into Greece, and yet you can scarcely suppose that any intelligent mind seriously holds it!" Knighton bows: "Your rebuke is just. My remark showed great want of thought, and was the result of early prejudice" (2:383). He who remains cool-headed and scores his points gallantly through rational argument rather than prejudice or dogma will emerge victorious. These are the rules of engagement of the Victorian liberal-intellectual gentleman, as will be formulated for instance by Matthew Arnold.

It is more representative of debates about religion in London than of those in Ceylon that Knighton's opening criticism of Buddhism concerns its relation to "modern science," that, as Marandhan puts it, "there may be opposition or contradiction, you would infer, between Buddhism and natural philosophy" (2:365).[22] Knighton is writing from a pre-Darwinian religious context, one in which the Anglican Church's long compromise with Natural Theology, dating from the Enlightenment, permits Knighton to state that "all truth must be harmonious" between science and religion, that the "grand harmonious *kosmos* of material science . . . will be found to form a beautiful portion of the great temple of religion" (2:363, 364). This widely shared consoling belief will be shattered five years after the publication of *Forest Life* by the appearance of Darwin's *On the Origin of Species* (1859). In the decades after that, the disjunction between religion and science of which he accuses Buddhism will fall upon Christianity, Natural Theology increasingly will be supplemented by scientific naturalism, and Buddhism will be in the early stages of its counterinvasion even of Christian discourse in England.

Both British defenders of Buddhism and defenders of Christianity against Buddhism will cite the greater compatibility of Buddhism with evolutionary science.[23] By the 1870s, Sinhalese Buddhists will realize that their best defense is to "present Buddhism as scientifically rational and positive, free from superstition and ethically superior," emphasizing its "non-theistic nature" and "the absence of a capricious, arbitrary, vengeful power on which human fate depended" (Harris 187). Writing decades prior to this, why would Knighton choose compatibility with science to be the first test of a religion's veracity? Part of the answer is that William Paley's "argument from design," which Knighton cites directly, was in its heyday and still served to make the supernatural dogmas of Christianity—the existence of God, the Virgin Birth, the Resurrection—appear supported by nature, whereas the Buddhist dogmas of reincarnation and *kamma* appeared to Westerners to be patently and "wholly unsupported in science and nature" (2:408). This was the strongest argument that Knighton could make at the time. But the main reason that he could not help but transplant these concerns to Buddhist Ceylon is because he was a subject of British culture, which was enmeshed in the cultural contest between spiritualism and materialism. Therefore, it can seem odd in retrospect—or prescient—that Marandhan becomes in these dialogues the spokesperson for the spiritualism side of that debate, citing the conflict between "geology and the Bible" and warning Knighton that wedding religion to science ultimately might undermine Christian faith, and Knighton defends what will come to appear by the 1860s as the materialist side of that argument (2:366).

Throughout the dialogues, Knighton's primary objective is to convince Marandhan of the necessity of believing in a creating, judging, and redeeming God, but he has set himself the task of doing so through rational "scientific" means. The debate therefore reveals not only contradictions within Knighton's position on spirit and matter, religion and science, but those broadly characteristic in this discourse in Britain at that time. Marandhan explains that in Buddhism there is no need or place for God, that "we believe matter to be eternal as spirit, both subject to general laws by which they are ever changing" (Knighton 2:367). This was at worst the horror of materialism or at best Deistic or pantheistic immanence, the unity of the divine and the natural. It is crucial to Knighton's argument that he convince Marandhan instead that God transcends nature, is outside of it, and this requires the traditional Western metaphysics of the separation of spirit and matter. Knighton asks, how "can you conceive of laws without a lawgiver?," and Marandhan alludes to the unifying doctrine of the *dhamma* (dharma, in Sanskrit) in responding, "I do not mean laws impressed externally, but principles inherent in matter and spirit" (2:368, 369). A corollary to such a law was scientific law, specifically pre-Darwinian evolutionary theory. Knighton pits the transcendent immortality of the soul, which attests to God's special relationship to humankind as distinguished from animals, against the Buddhist doctrines of *kamma* and reincarnation, which place humans on a natural continuum from the lowest life forms upward. Marandhan counters presciently that such an evolutionary chain can be discerned in nature, and, in terms strikingly similar to those that Darwin will use in *The Descent of Man* (1871), concludes: "Is there any cogent reason why the naked, brutal savage . . . should be possessed of a soul, and the chimpanzee, that wanders in troops, and similarly provides itself with food, and exhibits superior strength and sagacity, should not?" (2:391).[24] Monkeys and the Sinhalese continue to be a motif. Here it is Buddhism that is aligned with scientific law.

But there is another evolutionary law that Knighton will invoke to prove the existence of God, his special dispensation for the human species, and, in particular, his singling out of one race and one nation to lead the world: the law of progress. "The distinction" between the human species and all others "is between the perpetual progress and advance of the one, and the eternal immobility of the other," with the implication that the most progressive human societies are nearest to God (2:396–97). What else could progress signify but "the living soul of man urging him on to mighty deeds, and higher destinies" (2:398). Imperial manifest destiny and cultural stereotypes of the "immobile Oriental" are not very far beneath the surface here, as Marandhan observes. He also observes that progress is far from universally experienced or defined among human societies and that "it seems to me rather to be the result of language and of printing than of the soul," a canny observation that "progress" is culturally constructed and only currently monopolized by British discourse (2:399). Marandhan also notes that those who consider themselves the bearers of "civilization and improvement" not infrequently "exterminate" other peoples "with a self-satisfied consciousness of performing [their] mission on earth" (2:392, 393). The human species, in its cycles of violent inhumanity to man, is not so very far advanced above wild animals, which also seems consistent with trans-species reincarnation. But the reason behind

Knighton's recurrence to his progress argument finally comes clear here: "Admitting that there is a Deity . . . , admitting that he has shaped and fashioned the universe, is not such an idea of progress towards some consummation ultimately to be attained, a necessary consequence!" (2:406). Progress confirms the divine plan of a supreme God and, by association, British supremacy. British colonial government was simply an extension of "God's government" (2:378). God's existence then explains (tautologically) the plan behind progress, which is an upward trajectory throughout human history and continuing even after death unto heaven. And this partly explains Knighton's rejection of reincarnation, which is that it, rather than pointing ever upward, is bidirectional: humans who commit evil actions—including colonial violence—will retrogress, even to the state of "fishes and oysters" (2:390, 388). This was one of the most frightening and unthinkable prospects that Buddhism offered in the minds of Western observers. The doctrine of reincarnation threatened the central Victorian ideology of progressivism, and progressivism underwrote at once the Christian God and the British Empire.

Marandhan, however, is not easily convinced (to the credit of Knighton the author) and repeatedly drives the dialogues back to an issue that threatens to undermine convenient beliefs: how to explain human suffering and the existence of evil. Marandhan argues: "You admit a Deity of infinite power and of infinite goodness, and yet you see around you death, sorrow, disease, pain, want, suffering of every kind"; "goodness and power combined could not have constituted such a world as we inhabit" (Knighton 2:370, 379). Knighton responds by recourse to the spirit/matter dualism, as here: "Now the universe is composed of matter, which is, in its nature, imperfect; man is a compound of this imperfect matter, and of spirit, which, as being separated from the great pervading Spirit, is therefore, in so far, imperfect likewise" (2:428). The "imperfection" of matter causes suffering and evil, which in turn necessitates "a freedom of choice between good and evil"—the familiar apologetics of freewill (2:370). But Marandhan, characteristic of a Buddhist, insists on thinking nondualistically and so finds that Knighton's argument "den[ies] infinite power, for surely what man can conceive of as possible, the infinite power could effect, and man can conceive as possible the construction of a world on purely benevolent principles" (2:379–80). Knighton appears to have no rejoinder other than emphasizing God's love, the "intimate relationship between God and man," in contrast to the "cold metaphysical creed" of *kamma* and reincarnation, an argument that would be echoed in many subsequent critiques of Buddhism (2:381).[25] If religion is about the most loving deity who furnishes the most delightful afterlife, then why, Marandhan asks, should we all not convert to "Mahommedanism, which promises, not an ideal abstract heaven, but such an one as realizes material bliss, not to a few, but to all its votaries" (2:382). Knighton cannot counter this without reference to the other side of God's love—divine punishment—which would require using the language of sin and damnation, topics conspicuous by their absence from these dialogues. Thus, Marandhan succeeds throughout the first two dialogues in resisting Knighton's arguments against reincarnation and in favor of the Christian deity.

The first change in Marandhan's position comes without precedent at the beginning of the third dialogue. He says, "since our first conversation on the subject I find my mind has been gradually undergoing a revolution, which leads me by imperceptible degrees to this Supreme Architect, this great Primary Cause" (Knighton 2:401). However, he has neither surrendered belief in reincarnation and Buddhism generally nor yet accepted God as described by Knighton. Rather, he says that he is becoming "a heretic to the orthodox Budhism of Ceylon, and a member of the sect called the Aïshvarika of Nepaul, a sect who acknowledge an Abi-Budha" as the original Creator who "now leaves the universe to its fate" (2:402).[26] Invigorated by this partial capitulation, Knighton reiterates previous points about free will, progress, the argument from design, and the scientific basis of Christian doctrines. But the sticking point for Marandhan remains the contradiction between a loving God and the existence of suffering, evil, and eternal damnation.

Thus, the third dialogue shifts to consideration of the relative merits of Christian as opposed to Buddhist reward-and-punishment systems as incentives for ethical behavior. Later in the century, even critics of Buddhism would acknowledged the laudable thoroughness and rigor of its ethical tenets, though this would not occur until after Knighton.[27] Knighton insists that an ethical system should be judged not on its doctrines but rather on the lived behavior of its adherents, appealing to the then dominant British judgment, reinforced if not created by missionary reports, that Sinhalese society was rife with licentious and immoral behaviors.[28] Modeling a tactic that Buddhists in Ceylon will adopt later in the century in debates with missionaries, Marandhan marshals testimonies by eminent Orientalist scholars to the civilizing impact of Buddhist morality throughout the history of Asia. He then reverses the critique, observing that "the very vices you have named have flourished luxuriantly in England itself," and finally, pointing to the Inquisition, charges: "O Mr. Knighton, ignore not the evils of Christianity when you descant so eloquently on those of Budhism" (2:417, 421). Knighton again gallantly gives ground. One wonders if Knighton as author was not using Marandhan as a mouthpiece for his own criticisms of British society and even of Christianity. Certainly he created a dialogical exchange in which the othered voice is permitted to speak for itself, up to a point. Though the third dialogue begins with a partial capitulation, its main body consists of close combat and ends with both opponents standing and still armed.

Again, however, the final dialogue opens with an unexpected capitulation. Marandhan says, "you have opened my eyes to a great fundamental truth . . . an article of faith" in "the Deity" (Knighton 2:424). But, once again, there is a reservation: "that this Architect and Ruler is a being of infinite goodness I cannot discover" (2:424). The dialogue therefore returns to the question of suffering and evil, with divine punishment of sin lingering in the background, but Knighton evades this by insisting not only that God is infinitely good but that this goodness necessarily surrounds itself with "infinite happiness" (2:426). Marandhan again notes the abundant unhappiness in the world, asking: "Why any amount of evil at all? Why not all good? Infinite happiness, desiring happy beings only, would not surely bring into existence those whose lives must be only misery" (2:429). Not far beneath the surface lies the question of the suffering of the Sinhalese people under the rule of the British, who like their God profess concern for their subjects' well-being and promise blessings of "civilization" and "progress." From the beginning, Marandhan has been unwilling to accept a religion that leaves unexplained why the majority of (Sinhalese) human beings are expected to suffer while the (British) few live luxurious and pleasure-filled lives. To him this seems a corollary to the uncertain promise of eternal reward in heaven, in comparison with the lawfulness and justness of the system of *kamma* and reincarnation. Marandhan cannot accept what he perceives as inequity and injustice in life (under colonial rule) coupled with an indeterminate and perhaps fallible system for adjudicating reward and punishment after death.

In order finally to sway Marandhan toward conversion, Knighton must resort to an interpretation of Christian doctrine on divine judgment and eternal reward that was heterodox if not heretical to the majority of Christians in the 1840s. When it becomes clear that none of the previous arguments will bring Marandhan into the fold, Knighton offers this: "It is the belief of many Christians that all will ultimately reach that better life, and that all the expressions which imply the contrary in our Bible are to be regarded as figurative and hyperbolical" (2:430). Marandhan's final capitulation immediately follows: "The foundations of Budhism are so thoroughly shaken in my mind, that I have little difficulty in giving up the doctrine of transmigration, and looking to something nobler in another world than our unsatisfactory nirwana [sic]" (2:430). He goes on to say that if the "universalism you hint at" of equal access for all to eternal "happiness" were widely preached, "there would be little difficulty in making its way amongst Budhists" (2:430). One might suspect that here and elsewhere Knighton is speaking through Marandhan to those Low Church Anglican and Nonconformist missionaries who preached hellfire-and-brimstone atonement theologies. Indeed, sin and hell have all but vanished from the Christianity that Knighton's speaker offers to Marandhan. Christianity has become a religion of "happiness" for all, the promise of which has brought Marandhan if not to a full conversion, then, in the final words of the book, to a vow to "investigate the system with full and entire desire to arrive at the truth and a determination, when I have found it, to embrace it earnestly and unreservedly" (2:432).

No doubt this ending, and the dialogues in general, were read in multiple ways.[29] Some Christian readers would have denounced the work outright for giving such a godless, heathen religion so much consideration. Knighton's Orientalist and liberal-intellectual concessions to Buddhism would have been read by Anglicists as naive if not disloyal to the Empire. Those in London reading in the aftermath of the 1848 rebellion and the embarrassment of the Torrington hearings could not have overlooked the fact that Knighton models an approach to colonial rule and relations that was in opposition to the model exemplified by Torrington's actions. On the other hand, some Christians could have taken heart in the story of successful conversion, however partial, to the one true faith. But, then, the portrayed victory for Christianity is won at the cost of ignoring if not surrendering major portions of Christian doctrine and, in particular, effacing the figure of the judging Jehovah in favor of an all-loving Christlike God, which was a broad trend throughout the century within British Christianities away from Calvinist theology. Marandhan is permitted to offer many critical observations about Western prejudices and assumptions that apply not only to religious positions but to Westerners and colonial rule in general. He voices Knighton's critique of his own race, nationality, and religion, and this must have discomforted many of his readers. Though Knighton defended British, Christian honor valiantly, he did so too valiantly for most, allowing Marandhan and Buddhism too much quarter, too many touches.

As for the Sinhalese readers of *Forest Life*, who would have been the most Westernized, they may have been pleased by the genuinely intended consideration shown to Marandhan and to Buddhism. But it is likely that Buddhist readers would have been incredulous at Marandhan's capitulations. Any critical reader might recognize that his changes of heart occur offstage without commensurate logical or emotional motivation. Perhaps more likely, Buddhist readers would have been unconcerned about the issue of conversion, understanding that although many Sinhalese converts were claimed by missionaries the majority of those reverted to Buddhism or simply practiced both religions.[30] Buddhists, unconstrained by a "jealous God," saw no necessary contradiction in "double religious belonging," though few missionaries could appreciate this as "a sophisticated understanding of what interreligious co-existence might require" (Harris 195). While *Forest Life* presents a Buddhism that has been greatly oversimplified and rendered more vulnerable to defeat in debate than an educated Buddhist would find plausible, at the same time it presents a similarly simplified Christianity that has been revised significantly through its encounter with Buddhism.

William Knighton's *Forest Life in Ceylon* is a highly complex cultural artifact that demonstrates the interpenetration of debates occurring in London about the relationship between religion and national politics and debates occurring in Ceylon about that same relationship. Christianity in Britain was taking on a newly modern role in British national politics that in turn gave Christian missionaries a role in Sinhalese religion and politics that in turn would give Buddhism a modern role in Sri Lanka's national politics. In the process, Buddhism in Ceylon was hybridized in specific ways with Protestantism, while Buddhism was making its way into discourse about religion in England, even to the point of being given a position in the spiritualism-versus-materialism dialectic in Britain.

*Forest Life* enacts that bidirectional interpenetration first by enlisting Buddhist animal fables in the narrative as a corrective to Anglicist, bully-masculine, and evangelical colonial politics and second by staging an unprecedentedly evenhanded dialogue between a Christian and a Buddhist, granting the Buddhist full respect as a gentleman, an individual, and a faithful person of another religion. Not only does the novelistic narrative integrate Buddhism, but the appendicized dialogues continue the narrative's contests between codes of masculinity and their associated modes of colonial rule; the narrative is as much a dialogue about religions as the dialogues are a story about masculine roles and colonial politics. *Forest Life* enacted Orientalism in its full inherent ambivalence. The text was at once an Orientalist corrective to the prejudice and violence of the missionaries-versus-Buddhists standoff that was developing in Ceylon and an Orientalist lesson to Sinhalese and Buddhists concerning the rightness of British colonial rule-of-law and the ultimate superiority of Christianity.

*Forest Life* also appears to have been historically prescient in a number of remarkable ways. The Knighton–Marandhan dialogues predict by enactment the debate format that soon after Knighton's departure from Ceylon would be adopted by Buddhist monks in public debate with missionaries as a strategy of resistance. While Knighton's speaker "wins" the debate, Knighton permits Marandhan to demonstrate Buddhism's integrity as a religion and thus its status as a world religion on equal footing as such with Christianity. Marandhan also demonstrates mastery of the method, the cultural technology of the rule of law and the code of the liberal-intellectual gentleman, which by their own rules must be equitable and thus potentially reversible, applicable by the colonized upon the colonizer. In addition, *Forest Life* also prefigures, in the form of Marandhan's unconvincing capitulation, the Protestantization of Buddhism that indeed will occur before the end of the century but, also, the preservation of Buddhism's unshaken identity even within hybridization. Indeed, "an enterprising researcher could perhaps make a case that Knighton was the author of the Protestant or Reformed representation of Buddhism" (Harris 170), of which H. S. Olcott, over thirty years after Knighton, generally is credited as the author. *Forest Life* likewise prefigures in the form of Knighton's many concessions to Buddhism the counterinvasion of England by Buddhism, which will not be significantly detectable in British culture for over a decade after Knighton. In the course of the dialogues, one can observe Christianity being revised in order to make it more appealing to a Buddhist, hybridized in the direction of that for which Buddhism was most renowned (and sometimes criticized) in the West: compassion and tolerance. At the same time, as Jesus had been transformed by medieval missionaries called crusaders into the chivalric ideal and then figured by Victorians as the highest example of the perfect English gentleman, so too we observe the Buddha being translated into "an ideal Victorian gentleman, a 'verray parfit gentle knight'" (Almond 79).

Finally, in this book about heterodox religious positions in nineteenth-century Great Britain, those in between Christian orthodoxy on one side and atheistic materialism on the other, *Forest Life* charts parts of that territory. Between the orthodox (likely Broad Church Anglican) Christianity that Knighton starts out defending and the unapproachable nihilism of Buddhism, we find, in between, a Christianity revised up to the boundary between heterodoxy and heresy and a Buddhism in the process of Protestantization and in the earliest stage of translation to an approachable alternative in the West.

# 6

# Identity, Genre, and Religion in Anna Leonowens's *The English Governess at the Siamese Court*

> We put off our shoes,—my child and I,—having respect for the ancient prejudice against them; feeling not so much reverence for the place as for the hearts that worshipped there, caring to display not so much the love of wisdom as the wisdom of love.
>
> —A. H. Leonowens, "The Religion of Siam"

Anna Leonowens (1831–1915) died in Montreal as the beloved matriarch of a respected upper-middle-class family, reputedly having been born and raised in Wales of genteel lineage. She had lived in Canada—Halifax and then Montreal—for thirty-four years, during which time she worked tirelessly for women's rights, education reform, and literary and artistic organizations, speaking in public and publishing articles, while also traveling internationally and helping raise her grandchildren. She had "acquired at least eight non-European tongues," lectured widely on her travels and on world religions, and read and translated ancient Hindu and Buddhist texts in Sanskrit (S. Brown 601). Most North Americans had forgotten that it was she who wrote *The English Governess at the Siamese Court; Being Recollections of Six Years in the Royal Palace of Bangkok* (1870), upon which would be based Margaret Landon's *Anna and the King of Siam* (1944) and Rogers and Hammerstein's *The King and I* (1951), followed by multiple adaptations and movies. A 1951 retrospective proclaimed that she "had a romantic and brilliant career; and as a well read, widely travelled, brainy, queenly woman, she stands without a peer in Canada" (Blake 9).

Most remarkably, however, Leonowens while a young woman had severed herself from her family and fabricated a new family history and identity, which she unflinchingly maintained to the day of her death, even, or especially, to her children and grandchildren. She had been born Ann Edwards in Ahmadaagar, India, daughter of an English soldier and an Anglo-Indian mother, and later became the working wife of Thomas Leon Owens, a clerk, living with him in Australia, Singapore, and Penang. As a girl, "the young Ann, far from being a 'little miss' with her own pony, was instead the part-Indian stepdaughter of an abusive British Army sergeant, living in squalor in an Army camp in India" (Kepner 6). Through one of the bravest, sustained acts of self-fashioning, she reimagined her country of origin, her class, and her race, as a result of which her children and grandchildren inherited what she had performed into existence. She made herself an intellectual, a feminist activist, a linguist, and, with her first book, *The English Governess at the Siamese Court*, a famous author.

Like her life, Leonowens's books were as much imagined as reported. Her works and her identity had to endure periodic charges of fabrication and plagiarism, which, though accurate in one sense, do not adequately account for her writing or her life.[1] For one thing, her writing was subject to the same criticisms and expectations that critics applied to all women's writing and, in particular, to women's travel writing. While "travel writing as a whole has a problematic history in its relation to 'truth,'" Sara Mills notes, "women's writing is systematically judged to be exaggerated" (108). Although travel books written by women, Susan Brown observes, "differ only in degree not in kind from any other travel memoir," unequal standards have been applied (593). Thus, one finds that "the very critics who discredit Leonowens praise the works of male writers, despite their flaws"; "the works [on Siam] of . . . Crawfurd, Bowring, McCarthy, de Beauvoir and McGilvary in the 19th century and many others, are considered authoritative and valuable, despite their errors and embellishments" (Dann 102). Scholars of women's travel writing have analyzed the ways in which the question of accuracy that must be asked about all travel and autobiographical writing both has been used against women travel writers and is more complexly applicable to women's travel writing. Even, or especially, given the history of bias against women travel writers, "women critics of travel writing need to consider whether these texts are factual, whether they tell the 'truth' about the journeys" (S. Mills 30). This need is only multiplied in the case of an author whose works are banned to this day in Thailand and who, on supportable grounds, continues to be "dismissed as a meddling busybody and a liar who repaid a generous employer by representing him in her memoirs as a temperamental tyrant and crediting herself with the modernization initiatives for which he is revered in Thai history" (Smith 1060).

My purpose is not to rehash the history of critiques and defenses of Leonowens's accuracy. Rather, I am interested in pursuing several interrelated questions about how to read *The English Governess* that have not been fully answered, although Susan Morgan's excellent biography of Leonowens has done much of the groundwork. The questions to which I seek answers have been obfuscated equally by the assaults on Leonowens's veracity, by the lionizations of her as the Western woman who taught Siamese royalty about the evils of slavery, and by the adaptations of *The English Governess*, which only have compounded its misrepresentations. As Susan Kepner frames the question from which I start, "How shall we seek to understand the motives and actions of this purposefully mysterious woman who so willingly sacrificed truth and betrayed her great benefactor in the cause of her own survival and that of her children?" (27). Answering this requires addressing a second question: How shall we understand the relationship between Leonowens and her benefactor, Rama IV, King Mongkut?[2] That relationship is at the center of *The English Governess* and perhaps at the center of Leonowens's life. Finally, I will attempt to demonstrate that the key to answering these questions is a "scarcely mentioned element of *The English Governess*, . . . the curious defense of Hinduism and Buddhism by comparison with Christianity in practice" (Kepner 25). How shall we understand Leonowens's relationship to missionary Christianity and to Buddhism?

The approach I have chosen for pursuing these questions is to analyze the roles that selected generic and discursive conventions play within *The English Governess*. Leonowens's works are far from unique among travel books in mixing the conventions of multiple genres. Travel writing often combines geographical and anthropological thick descriptions with memoir and storytelling. Some Victorian writers, among them missionaries, additionally "fill[ed] their accounts of Siam with Christian righteousness, scathing criticisms, and erroneous descriptions of Buddhism, slurs on the Thai monarchy and the people themselves, generic and racist descriptions of 'Orientals' and constant references to the superiority of the European race" (Dann 102). Leonowens was more the exception than the rule in these regards, though she did mix in elements of these discourses amid genre conventions drawn from history writing, romance novel, documentary, and abolitionist tract, among others. Even readers who did not doubt the veracity of *The English Governess* could not ignore its mixing of apparently objective reporting with highly "literary" elements. Indeed, the latter is part of what attracted so many readers, as Leonowens fully understood.[3] She intended that *The English Governess* and its later companion work, *The Romance of Siamese Harem Life* (1873), should be taken as factual observation while still being, as one advocate wrote, "as 'interesting as a story from the Arabian Nights,' " casting "the inventions of our civilized romancers far into the shade" (Blake 10, 11).

Previous scholarship has situated Leonowens's works within the context of Victorian women's travel writing and the ways in which they both enlisted and resisted the stereotypes about British women and the conventions within the body of their travel writing. Frequently the focus has been on the nature of the participation of women's travel writing in one or more of the pervasive discourses of empire and British superiority, race and slavery, religious mission, and the conditions for and rights of women. Leonowens was only unequivocally dedicated to the last of these, which in her repulsion and outrage at the traditional Siamese royal *Nang Harm* or harem she conflated with the discourse of American abolitionism, drawing upon the familiar analogy between slavery and women's matrimonial and "political slavery" (Burton 304). Learning from these treatments, I propose to build upon previous work by analyzing the significant roles played in *The English Governess* by its recourse or relationship to three genres other than travel writing itself, namely memoir, Gothic romance, and comparative religious study.

## The Genres of *The English Governess*: Memoir

Because *The English Governess* begins with Leonowens's arrival in Bangkok and ends soon after she has announced her departure from it, the book gives the appearance of a chronological recounting of her six years in Siam (1861–67), but this is not necessarily so. The text is structured as a roughly alternating series of largely informational or documentarian chapters with what I will call "harem-slavery episodes." The informational chapters are on such topics as the city of Bangkok, history of the Siamese monarchy, Siamese literature and art, national history, and Buddhist ceremonies and sacred sites. The harem-slave episodes include the opening combative encounter between Leonowens and the prime minister, Chow Phya Sri Sury Wongse, and a visit to his harem; the beating, on King Mongkut's orders, of Khoon Chom Kioa, a member of the harem, while her daughter weeps at her neck; the sacrifice, on the king's orders, of six randomly selected slaves by the method of "squelch[ing]" their heads to consecrate a newly built city gate; and the final persecution of Leonowens, as part of which she and her son Louis are roughed up by palace soldiers until "the generous rescue of a crowd of the poorest slaves" (*English Governess* 220, 279). In the informational chapters, Leonowens is present largely as a removed narrator, and she could not have been present during the harem-slavery episodes, because most if not all of them either never occurred or did not occur at the extremes presented by the narrative.

The basis for this claim, even without resorting to the documented evidence of misrepresentations in *The English Governess*, is the historical record concerning King Mongkut. At the time he was made king as the result of the death of his elder half brother, he had been a Buddhist monk for twenty-seven years. His royal brother recognized his dedication to Buddhist practice and scholarship and first made him head of the Board of Pali Examinations, a chief scholar of the Pali canon, and then abbot of Wat Pavaranivesa ("Excellent Abode") monastery, an eminent national position (Griswold 15). A highly devout and deeply intellectual middle-aged monk when he became king, Mongkut "scarcely fit the role into which [Leonowens] had cast him" (Kepner 13).

More significant than these accomplishments, Mongkut was one of the sources of a Buddhist reformation in Siam toward the "pure Buddhism" of the original scriptures, and this had profound and lasting effects both doctrinally and politically.[4] Henry Alabaster, "Interpreter of Her Majesty's Consulate General in Siam," who was in the country during the same period as Leonowens and authored a noted book aimed at convincing his fellow Britons of the merits of Buddhism, *The Wheel of the Law: Buddhism Illustrated from Siamese Sources by the Modern Buddhist* (1871), observed: "Mongkut, the late King of Siam, has been called the founder of a new school of Buddhist thought, having, while himself a monk, eminent among monks for his knowledge of the Buddhist Scriptures, boldly preached against the canonicity of those of them [the scriptures] whose relations were opposed to his reason, and his knowledge of modern science. His Majesty was a man of remarkable genius and acquirements" (2). A recent history of Thailand similarly observes that "the reformed Dhammayutika sect of Buddhism founded in the mid-nineteenth century by Mongkut had, by the early twentieth century, a profound effect on religion" and had given citizens of the modern Siamese state "a common religious tradition and educational experience" (Wyatt 202, 203). Earlier, in the middle of the nineteenth century, the Dhammayutika Nikaya had served the crucial role of giving the Siamese elite the unity and confidence to withstand not only the insistent proselytizing of Western missionaries but the threat of colonization being applied by Britain and France, which was most intense during Mongkut's reign. The Siamese elite became "confident that they had found and upheld the truth of the world, *dharma*, and that this enabled them to interact with Westerners as intellectual and moral equals" (Aphornsuvan 414). Ironically, "the confrontation between the Buddhist monks and the American missionaries," rather than generating more than a negligible number of converts to Christianity, "paved the way for the Siamese to exercise their Buddhist rational thinking" (Aphornsuvan 420–21). The missionaries gave the Siamese the motivation and the approach to challenge the supernatural elements of Christianity as unsupportable and to defend the compatibility of Buddhism with modern science in contrast.

Acting in the political arena, King Mongkut was no less dedicated and accomplished. Under his stewardship, "Siam dexterously played upon rivalries among the imperial powers and even within the ranks of the powers themselves" to keep the country singular in Southeast Asia in remaining independent of colonial rule (Wyatt 169). King Mongkut rightly is viewed as one of the fathers of modern Thailand. He opened Siam to controlled Westernization, introducing many modernizing reforms in trade, education, science, and technology. He managed simultaneously to strengthen the Siamese sense of shared culture and national identity. In sum, he was "a charismatic and gifted leader, a loving and indulgent father, a brilliant scholar and religious reformer—and a notable wit" whose humor was "one of amusing self-deprecation" (Kepner 21). "Without question a great king," he was "little understood by either Anna Leonowens or Margaret Landon" (23). One of his biographers surmises that "when history adopts a more comprehensive view of the world, King Mongkut's name will rank higher than the names of the empire-builders" (Griswold 2).

One cannot leave a discussion of King Mongkut without touching on slavery and the harem. Leonowens modeled the Mongkut of *The English Governess* in part on Mr. Haley or Simon Legree from *Uncle Tom's Cabin* by Harriet Beecher Stowe, whom she idolized. But the "mild system of slavery" in Siam was hardly comparable to American slavery (Alabaster 56). In the first place, it was not based principally on race. All royal subjects not themselves part of the nobility were considered *that* or *corvée*, "slaves, freed slaves, and servants" (Aphornsuvan 425). Most slaves were paid salaries and retained the prerogative to buy themselves out at will. Sir John Bowring, who negotiated the trade treaty named after him with King Mongkut during Leonowens's stay in Siam, noted in his two-volume *Kingdom and People of Siam* (1857) that Siamese slaves are treated "better than servants are treated in England," continuing: "This is proved by the fact that whenever they are emancipated, they always sell themselves again. Masters cannot ill-treat their slaves, for they have always the remedy of paying the money they represent" (vol. 1, 193). And King Monkgut, who had spent nearly three decades in the egalitarian Buddhist monkhood, carrying his begging bowl alongside monks from all social stations, "tried, with but limited success, to ameliorate the condition of slaves and allow women some choice in marriage," without any need for prompting to do so (Wyatt 173).

Similarly, as Leonowens herself wrote in an article published in a Boston journal a decade after her departure from Siam, "the ladies of the Harem have each an annual salary and a private residence assigned to them within these walls," but, she continues, "where they live exactly in the condition of State prisoners" (Leonowens, "City" 35). Yet King Mongkut himself had put into law "specific rules by which they [the royal consorts] might resign and marry private persons" (Griswold 43). The women of the harem lived in relative safety, comfort, and luxury, and "there was scarcely a well-born woman in Siam who did not dream of becoming one of them" (Kepner 17). Leonowens believed deeply in hard work, self-determination, and the especially American concepts of "liberty" and "independence," but her insistence that the women of the *Nang Harm* should leave their cloistered comfort to work and act on their own was not shared by many of them. On the contrary, "so far as we can tell from stories remembered by their descendants, most of them were devoted to [King Mongkut]" and, "with a very few exceptions, it is clear that they were contented with their lot" (Kepner 45). As for King Mongkut, he followed the tradition of the royal harem and, after decades of celibacy, performed the expected duty of the king in fathering as many potential heirs as possible. His many marriages were politically crucial in themselves; it was through the system of elite family intermarriage that the national stability and unity necessary to resist Western encroachment was ensured. The fear or fantasy that King Mongkut "wanted to make Anna a part of his harem, either because he was lecherous or because he was parsimonious or a combination of the two, is nothing more than a completely invented projection, and a highly insulting projection, on the part of those Western commentators who have suggested it" (S. Morgan 102). From any Siamese perspective, the *Nang Harm* was a very complex social and cultural institution that many Westerners grossly oversimplified.

I do not justify or defend nineteenth-century Siamese slavery or the *Nang Harm*. I only note that the representations of them in *The English Governess* required a willed denial of the indigenous culture and society and a superimposition upon them of a projection of another culture and society's concerns fused with an Orientalist imaginary. The portrayal of King Mongkut was subject to the same willed denial and superimposition.

Where, then, are the elements of the memoir genre in *The English Governess* if they are not in the informational chapters and not in the harem-slavery episodes? Even if, as Caron Dann argues, "Leonowens's books were read as the memoirs they are, not as histories" (100), the memoir genre is primarily represented in this text by its absence. If "an autobiography is a chronological telling of one's experience, which should include phases such as childhood, adolescence, adulthood, etc., while a memoir provides a much more specific timeline and a much more intimate relationship to the writer's own memories, feelings and emotions" (Wordclay), then *The English Governess* is certainly not the former nor truly the latter. Leonowens had made a lifelong pact with herself never to reveal her actual origins, and her book includes no memories of life prior to Siam and very little self-reflection once there. *The English Governess* may be a mockumemoir, and the conspicuous absence of its author begs explanation. There are intimate thoughts and personal revelations in the text, but only indirectly, expressed in disguise through the generic conventions of Gothic romance.

## The Genres of *The English Governess*: Gothic Romance

*The English Governess* opens on the deck of the *Rainbow*, anchored in the mouth of the Meinam River at evening, with a premonition—"the gloom and mystery of the pagan land into which we were penetrating filled me with an indefinable dread"—then the approach of a "shadowy gondola, fashioned like a dragon, with flashing torches," then the arrival on deck of a Siamese official "swaying himself with an absolute air," and "to cover his audacious chest and shoulders . . . only his own brown polished skin," at whose appearance "every Asiatic on deck" drops into prostration, leaving Leonowens standing face-to-face with the lesser of her two nemeses, the prime minister (*English Governess* 7, 8–9). At the other end of the book, as Leonowens is preparing her escape, she delivers this summary assessment: "Like a troubled dream, delirious in contrast with the coherence and stability of Western life, the land and its people seem to be conjured out of a secret darkness, a wonder to the senses and a mystery to the mind" (286). Moments such as these erupt periodically throughout the book, sustaining the Gothic romantic subplot.

That subplot is set in a shadowy, labyrinthine palace, the "enchanted world within [its] walls," and our female protagonist gives "a secret shudder at the idea of sleeping within those walls," aware as she is of "the heart's darkness of those tabooed women," whom she must both resist joining and rescue (Leonowens, *English Governess* 63, 65, 94). She realizes in horror that "the palace and its spells, the impracticable despot, the impassible premier, were not the phantasms of a witching night, but the hard facts of noonday" (67). There are naked chests and breasts and all sorts of perversity and intrigue: "Here were women disguised as men, and men in the attire of women, hiding vice of every vileness and crime of every enormity,—at once the most disgusting, the most appalling, and the most unnatural that the heart of man has conceived. It was death in life, a charnel-house of quick corruption; a place of gloom and solitude indeed, wherefrom happiness, hope, courage, liberty, truth, were forever excluded, and only mother's love was left" (94). This is a medieval place with its own "inquisition,—not overtly audacious, like that of Rome, but nocturnal, invisible, subtle, ubiquitous, like that of Spain; preceding without witness or warning; kidnapping a subject, not arresting him, and then incarceration, chaining, torturing him, to extort confession or denunciation" (100). By the end, she herself is no longer safe and "comes to perceive how continually and closely [she] was watched" and hears whispers that she is considered a "proper person to behead or drown" (269, 278).

What devil is behind all this? It is the cruel father-king, and he has designs on her. It is rumored that he is seeking "an English woman of beauty and good parentage to crown the sensational collection" of his harem (even, or especially, if she is not quite English or of good parentage) (Leonowens, *English Governess* 94). In this Manichean world, he is evil, and she is good, representative of the innate superiorities of being British, Anglo-Saxon, and Christian. In the absence of a knight to slay the devilish tyrant and rescue her, she must be her own hero, a role she bravely accepts (though doing so breaks womanly decorum and casts off one genre convention whereby "women travel writers have to substitute self-effacement or self-mockery for more aggressive or positive assertiveness in order to demonstrate a true femininity" [Foster 19]).[5] Her sacred charge is to defend the enslaved women of the *Nang Harm*, who are but a synecdoche for all captive and legally subjugated women and, therefore, for all women (but thereby obscuring differences of nationality and race and so enacting what Antoinette Burton and then Susan Zlotnick analyze as "the white women's burden").[6] Unable to separate her chosen charge from the sources of her authority, she cannot avoid championing the empires of Britain and Christianity, though less her concerns than the conditions for women. On all of those grounds, then, she must show herself standing up to the raging father-king, which she does at multiple crisis moments. Her first battle is for women's sovereignty over the domestic realm, her right to have her own private dwelling outside the *Nang Harm*, in which contest she defeats the father-king's suspected plot to force her into sexual slavery. She reports that "his Golden-footed Majesty presently repented him of his arbitrary 'cantankerousness,' and in due time my ultimatum was accepted" (Leonowens, *English Governess* 66). Later, her heroic moments are rescues; "whenever the king should be dangerously enraged, and ready to let loose upon some tender culprit of the harem the monstrous lash or chain," she would fly to their aid (276). Such moments can be expressed only through the highest peaks of melodrama and overwrought emotion, other common features of Gothic romance, as here: "There indeed was a case for prayer, *any* prayer!—the prostrate woman, the hesitating lash, the tearless anguish of the Siamese child, the heart-rending cry of the English child, all those mothers with groveling brows, but hearts uplifted among the stars, on the wings of the Angel of Prayer. Who could behold so many women crouching, shuddering, stupefied, dismayed, in silence and darkness, animated, enlightened only by the deep whispering heart of maternity, and not be moved with mournful yearning?" (115). When she finally escapes, she will be able to say—and be saddled with the necessity of continuing to say for the rest of her life—that she gave ultimatums to an Asian king, teaching if not him then his son and heir, King Chulalongkorn, the evils of slavery and of the harem and thus reforming an entire nation.

The preceding renarration of the Gothic-romance subplot of *The English Governess* is not intended to mock Anna Leonowens but rather to illustrate the extreme to which she was driven in order to be able to express her most deeply buried emotions, which could not be expressed directly. These emotions were at once sociopolitical and traumatically personal. She could not have been more genuinely committed to improving conditions for women and, more broadly, to the right of self-determination for all people. At the same time, these commitments were inextricably bound to her own personal history, specifically her relationship with her abusive stepfather (and perhaps also with the Reverend Mr. Badger, an older man with whom the teenage Anna may have toured Egypt and Palestine and with whom she may have had an "indiscretion").[7] According to Susan Kepner's reading of the available biographical sources, "there are three certain and central facts about her early years: 1) she had a stepfather, 2) she loathed him, and 3) he deserved it" (5). My reading of the Gothic romantic subplot is consistent with Kepner's argument that "to Anna Leonowens, the Siamese court was one great, dazzling Rorschach blot of an institution; the closer she looked, the surer she was of what she saw: a tyrannical, omnipotent 'father' surrounded by frightened girls who lived in constant terror of his brutish advances" (12). This reading suggests that Leonowens sublimated a repressed personal trauma into a worthy social cause—abolitionism applied to the harem—that required demonizing and then correcting the abusive patriarch.

This reading also seems inline with a point Shirley Foster makes that "many women found the 'feminine' elements of travel writing appealing, especially its confessional nature which permits self-exploration under cover of response to an external reality" (19). Foster could be describing Loenowens when she continues that "on a more psychological level, the literary re-enactment can be seen as an act of self-expression, combining the urge to articulate and communicate with a desire to examine the self in an unfamiliar context," which may lead to "a more unconscious mode of articulation—there may be no evidently confessional element—which expresses otherwise inadmissible feelings" (19). For Leonowens, the unconscious imperative to confess while concealing certain inadmissible feelings to herself was of a piece with the conscious imperative to conceal her identity from others, never entirely free of the fear of disclosure. These imperatives must have placed her under tremendous psychic pressure, intensified by a situation that would have been daunting if not terrifying to any unaccompanied woman with a child entering an alien land. Even so, her response was dazzlingly inventive. Part of that inventiveness is that her text does indeed confess while concealing. Though there is no overt confessing, nor the self-reflection typical of the memoir genre, the text even so bears everything she could not afford to feel or to reveal in the form of the Gothic-romance genre.

There is one other way in which *The English Governess* manifests the psychic pressure under which its author wrote. The last third of the book is structured as a series of violent oscillations between chapters and sections of chapters that are very respectful, even reverential, about Buddhism and about King Mongkut's achievements in the public realm and, interspersed in counterpoint, harem-slave episodes and other examples of the supposedly jealous, hypocritical, murderous, and petty sides of King Mongkut's character in the private realm. At the center of this section of the book is the chapter "The Supreme King: His Character and Administration," which internally reproduces this same oscillating pattern. The first sentence of the chapter sets the pattern, stating of King Mongkut that "it may safely be said (for all his capricious provocations of temper and his snappish greed of power) that he was, in the best sense of the epithet, the most remarkable of the Oriental princes of the present century" (Leonowens, *English Governess* 237). It "may safely be said," but actually it is anything but safe. The chapter first gives an admiring summary of Mongkut's life as a monk and his commitment to Buddhism, then cuts suddenly to his "deplorable example of the degrading influence on the human mind of the greed of possessions and power," then back to a cataloging of his achievements, his ability "to rule with wisdom, to consult the welfare of his subjects, to be concerned for the integrity of justice and . . . by a prudent administration, to confirm his power at home and his prestige abroad" as "an able and virtuous ruler" (242, 243). This pattern continues throughout the thirty-page chapter. It is as if every time Leonowens begins to slip too near loving and admiring King Mongkut she must pull herself, and her reader, up short with a sharp reminder that he still was that evil Oriental devil. This pattern enacts the intensity of her ambivalence and the violence of her struggle to maintain certain claims that at some level she must have known were not wholly true while concealing truths that she did not want known. She desperately wanted King Mongkut to be her good father, and I will argue that she was able to allow him to approach being such through his Buddhism, which *The English Governess* represents by employing some of the conventions of the genre of comparative religious study.

## The Genres of *The English Governess*: Comparative Religious Study

Anna Leonowens does not appear to have been a devout Christian, though she likely would have claimed to be a "good Christian." She had grown up in India in the midst of Hindus and Muslims, and she never believed that Christians were inherently superior to them. Her granddaughter and biographer Anna Fyshe reported: "Grandmama was not religious in the sense of being a churchgoer; in fact she hardly ever took us to church except to listen to a Bach cantata. . . . Often she spoke with resentment about missionaries in India trying to convince deeply religious Hindus or Buddhists that Christianity was the only hope of salvation" (in S. Morgan 199). She never fully subscribed to the discourse of Christian mission that was common among British and American travelers, even though it provided a position "particularly useful to women travelers who desired to reconcile their actions with conventional gender discourse" (S. Brown 595). At the same time, however, her Western community in Siam consisted largely of missionaries, she modeled her writing in part on the moral and emotional power of the Christian rhetoric that pervades *Uncle Tom's Cabin*, and she knew that her intended American market for *The English Governess* would expect support for a Protestant reading. *The English Governess* therefore includes several commendations for the hard work of missionaries she knew and periodic statements of allegiance to the supremacy of Christianity. These read variously as sincere homage and faith, as less theological imitations of Stowe's religious melodrama, and as correctives, for the sake of expected readers, in passages that otherwise might appear too favorable toward Buddhism. While we do not know how much time Leonowens spent reading the Bible, we know from her account that King Mongkut spent time studying it and querying her about certain passages. Those instances show that the king respected Christianity and the missionaries but that he was a skeptical reader of the Bible whose critiques of it illustrated its incompatibility with modern science. The text allows King Mongkut's criticisms of the Bible to stand largely without rejoinder. In sum, Leonowens's "texts stage circuitous but persuasive critiques of Christianity, through 'dialogues' with Mongkut and other Buddhists" (S. Brown 600). Her representations of Christianity were ambivalent, falling far short of Stowe's example and eschewing the dogmatism of those missionaries who, according to one Siamese witness, "spare[ed] little sarcasm or insult in their never-ceasing endeavours to bring [our] religion into contempt" (Alabaster 18). Leonowens was much closer to the example for which King Mongkut, and Buddhism in general, was famous of extending tolerance to other religions, even if they denigrated one's own.

However much or little time Leonowens spent reading the Bible, we know that she spent a significant amount of time reading comparative religious studies about Buddhism and studying Hindu and Buddhist myths and scriptures in Sanskrit. We know this in the first place because she cites and quotes some of the major early contributors to comparative religious studies (and, according to one critic, "her best passages on Buddhism are slyly plagiarized from earlier writers" [Griswold 44]). In introducing her readers to Buddhism early in the book, she cites the work of Eugène Burnouf, the first major Buddhologist in Europe whose *Introduction to the History of Indian Buddhism* (*L'introduction à l'historie du Buddhisme*

*Indien*, 1844) laid the foundation for the formation of the field. She quotes the Reverend R. Spence Hardy, a missionary in Ceylon (Sri Lanka) and author of *A Manual of Buddhism* (1853), praising the "Buddhist Moral Code," "which in the purity of its ethics could hardly be equaled from any other heathen author" (Leonowens, *English Governess* 79). On the character of the Buddha, she quotes one of Burnouf's students, Jules Barthélemy-Saint-Hilaire, author of the widely read *Buddha and His Religion* (*La Bouddha et sa religion*, 1860), who writes, "save the Christ alone, there is not among the founders of religion a figure more pure, more touching, than that of the Buddha" (Leonowens, *English Governess* 80). These were common positive responses to Buddhism in Europe, conditioned by comparative religious studies. Also as part of establishing her credibility on the subject, Leonowens cites a dozen canonical works of Buddhism, though surprisingly they range across the Theravada, Mahayana, and Vajrayana traditions, indicating either her ignorance of the distinctions (which would not have made her unusual) or the ecumenical reading list of Siamese Theravada monks.

As her six years in Siam and her chapters progress, Leonowens's treatment of Buddhism becomes both increasingly sympathetic and more documentarian. She describes Buddhist ceremonies with a scholarly neutrality and specificity of detail. This too reflects the influence of comparative religious studies. Friedrich Max Müller, another of Burnouf's students who spent his career at Oxford, influentially championed "the science of religion, . . . the first principle of which was the egalitarian application of textual rigor: that all religions—even Christianity—could be treated equally as objects of non-theologically-motivated scholarship" (Franklin, "Influences" 814). Leonowens articulates this view late in the book in a lengthy chapter titled "Buddhist Doctrine, Priests, and Worship." She observes that Westerners "are prone to ignore or to condemn that which we do not clearly understand; and thus it is, and on no better ground, that we deny that there are influences in the religions of the East to render their followers wiser, nobler, purer" (*English Governess* 184). She continues:

> Many have missed seeing what is true and wise in the doctrine of Buddha because they preferred to observe it from the standpoint and in the attitude of an antagonist, rather than of an inquirer. To understand aright the earnest creed and hope of any man, one must be at least sympathetically *en*

*rapport* with him,—must be willing to feel, and to confess within one's self, the germs of those errors whose growth seems so rank in him. In the humble spirit of this fellowship of fallibility let us draw as near as we may to the hearts of these devotees and the heart of their mystery. (186)

This view, in sharp contrast to that of most missionaries, combines a comparative religious commitment to open inquiry with a Buddhist (or Christlike) ethic. This passage feels more reflective and emotionally honest—closer to memoir—than any part of *The English Governess* that purports to be autobiographical. The chapter then becomes directly comparative, suggesting ways in which Buddhism is like Christianity and that "the doctrines of the Buddha were eminently fitted to elucidate the doctrines of Christ, and therefore worthy to engage the interests of Christian writers" (191). She also adopts a view that was another of the tenets of comparative religion, namely "the primacy of textual origins: that the oldest scriptures take precedence over subsequent interpretations or additions, as well as over current-day beliefs of indigenous practitioners" (Franklin, "Influences" 815). She writes that over the more recent history of Buddhism "errors, that in time crept in, corrupted the pure doctrine" (Leonowens, *English Governess* 191). This could have come from Burnouf (or Martin Luther), but it is most likely that it came directly from the "pure Buddhism" of King Mongkut's Dhammayutika Nikaya.[8]

The religion in which Leonowens demonstrated the most interest was not Christianity but Buddhism. I estimate that a quarter of the pages of the book are dedicated to investigation and description of Buddhist doctrines, ceremonies, and temples. In the course of its pages, the text provides a list of the ten "divine attributes" of the Buddha translated from the Pali; summaries of the life of the Buddha; several attempts to explain the concept of God in Buddhism (within most denominations of which there is no creating or judging deity); rich descriptions of the Buddhist coronation ceremony and the ceremonial hair-cutting of Prince Chulalongkorn; a listing of the Buddha's "Decalogue" as a corollary to the Ten Commandments; sketches of the doctrines of *kamma* (karma), reincarnation, and *nibbana* (nirvana); detailed descriptions of multiple artifacts, shrines, and monasteries; a narration of the dying of old age of the high priest of Siam, with chanted liturgy transcribed in Pali and then translated, followed by the cremation ceremony; and a listing of "Common Maxims of the Priests of Siam," taken from the Vinaya Piṭaka (Leonowens, *English Governess* 50, 185, 203). *The English Governess* charts a progression in its author's attitude toward Buddhism from initial dismissal to Orientalist curiosity to fascination and deep respect. In several later chapters that begin as neutral observation, with an obligatory nod toward the superiority of Christianity, Leonowens's narrative then "embarks upon a breathtaking, seemingly uncontrollable slide into the camp of Hinduism and Buddhism that all but posits self-righteous Christianity, with its hypocritical posture on matters of morality, as her own private definition of a 'religious Other'" (Kepner 25). Leonowens chose to make the final two chapters of *The English Governess* a detailed description of a visit to the ancient Naghkon Wat holy site in Cambodia (now world-renowned as Angkor Wat) and a recounting of the "Legend of the Maha Naghkon." Coming after the apparent ending of her narrative with departure from Siam, these chapters take on the significance of a closing Buddhist last word and benediction.

In the decades following her departure from Siam, Leonowens continued to develop herself as a linguist in Sanskrit, an amateur scholar of comparative religion, and a public expert on world religions. In New York and Boston, prior to moving to Canada, she supported herself with her lectures and publications, as well as continuing to work as a teacher. After the success of *The English Governess*, she was in demand, having achieved the notoriety to gain entré into the society of the most famous American authors of the day, including Nathaniel Hawthorne, Ralph Waldo Emerson, and even her hero, Harriet Beecher Stowe. She was "thrilled to be able to present herself to American audiences as a scholarly authority not only on Siam but also on subjects such as Buddhism and Hinduism" (S. Morgan 178). She developed a series of seven lectures, one of which was titled "Buddha and Buddhism in Siam." The *Boston Daily Globe* reported in 1874 on a "Lecture by Mrs. Leonowens on 'Buddha' in the Free Religious Course," in which the Buddha's "principal religious doctrines appear to have been that a life of personal rectitude and of benefaction to the needy and suffering is essential to our future welfare, that no mediator is needed between God and man, and that introspection and meditation on religious themes are productive of spiritual peace and rest" (n.p.). "The processes of nature through which spiritual emancipation is perfected," Mrs. Leonowens had said, "lie at the root of all Buddhistic art, and Buddhistic art symbolizes and demonstrates the gradual evolution of the perfect being." A year later, a Chicago-based newspaper reported that she "appears to have a thorough and comprehensive knowledge" of Buddhism and that "a good deal of the conversation turned upon the subject of Buddhism, and it was perhaps the most instructive portion of the evening" ("Siam"). Nearly a decade later, she lectured on "Buddhistic Art and Art Ideas—The Significance of the Chinese Emblems and Colors," having by then published dozens of short pieces in periodicals with titles such as "The Siamese Christmas," "A Visit from a Siamese Princess," "The City of Forbidden Women," and "The Religion of Siam." Perhaps the highest praise in her own estimation that Leonowens could have given to Buddhism is attributed to her by a reviewer of one of her lectures: "The lecturer said that he [Buddha] anticipated in many particulars the thought and philosophy of the nineteenth century.... Early in his missionary work the woman question came up, and the lecturer was happy to be able to say that he decided it rightly and recognized women as equals and appointed priestesses as well as priests. The lecturer also took occasion to say that, although he lived, so many years ago, if he were now to reappear he could give the Boston School Board some valuable advice" ("Lecture by Mrs. Leonowens"). Here Leonowens combines her admiration for the Buddha with her activism both for women's rights and for improved education, having campaigned for years for the right of women to run for and sit on school boards.

But Leonowens's primary source on Buddhism and the strongest influence upon her was not comparative religious studies; it was King Mongkut. The evidence for this claim is scattered throughout *The English Governess*, though Leonowens made it easy to overlook, relegating it to footnotes and adumbrating it with the harem-slave episodes that more dramatically demonized King Mongkut. Not until page 148 does this author's footnote appear in reference to an antiphonal prayer chanted between the priesthood and King Mongkut: "For these translations I am indebted to his Majesty, Maha Mongkut; as well as for the interpretation of the several symbols used in this and other solemn rites of the Buddhists" (Leonowens, *English Governess* 148, note). At this point one might reflect that throughout the book Leonowens offers doctrines and scripture that are most likely to have come from Pali sources and have been translated for her either by King Mongkut or at his instruction. The multiple "solemn rites" that Leonowens recounts—and there would have been many more that she did not recount—would have been attended in the presence if not the company of King Mongkut. Either he used some of those occasions as opportunities to instruct her in Buddhism or she solicited that instruction. One telling moment occurs at the end of chapter 5 as an unexpectedly reminiscent and intimate, almost nostalgic and affectionate, statement: "At a later period, visiting this temple in company with the king and his family, I called his Majesty's attention to the statue at the Beautiful Gate, as that of a Christian saint with whose story he was not unfamiliar. Turning quickly to his children, and addressing them gently, he bade them salute it reverently. 'It is Mam's P'hra [saint],' he said; whereupon the tribe of little ones folded their hands devoutly, and made obeisance before the effigy of Saint Peter" (52). Whether the king intended to provide Leonowens with a lesson in the open-mindedness and respectfulness of Buddhism, she received and appreciated his teaching.

There are very good general reasons why Leonowens would have turned to King Mongkut as her teacher. As she wrote in retrospect, "The late king was an authority on all questions of religion, law, and custom, and was familiar with the writings of Pythagoras and Aristotle" (*English Governess* 82). He was "more systematically educated, and a more capacious devourer of books and news, than perhaps any man of equal rank in our day," and he was "an authority among Oriental linguists" (97, 238). He also had a library in multiple languages to which Leonowens had access. She was young, intellectually acute, eager for further education and self-improvement, and especially interested in languages and non-Christian religions, and this was the first time in her life that she had regular access to such a mind and such resources. In the qualities that Leonowens most valued, perhaps even when she arrived in Siam—rigorous ethics, compassion for others, intellectual achievement, discipline and hard work, belief in the value of education, and love of children—King Mongkut was more experienced and more accomplished than she. Further, he was a model of religious devotion, which he and his court demonstrated daily in ritual and meditation that Leonowens sometimes attended. It would have been surprising if someone of her capabilities and interests had not taken King

Mongkut as a teacher. For decades after her departure from Siam, she would lecture, write, and apply what she had learned of Buddhism in Siam, at least in part from King Mongkut.

The Buddhist concept that most appealed to Leonowens was *maitrî*, *mettā* in Pali, which is unconditional friendship or loving-kindness for all beings, but that Leonowens followed other Westerns in translating as charity. She gives it special attention in her initial discussion of Buddhism, quoting a definition from Burnouf: "that universal feeling which inspires us with good-will toward all men and constant willingness to help them" (*English Governess* 80). Leonowens took something akin to this as one of her life's guiding principles. She returns in the latter part of the book to this subject after attending a temple service in which the monks chant to inculcate "the strictest practice of charity [*maitrî*] in a manner so pathetic and so gentle as might be wisely imitated by the most orthodox of Christian priests" (189). This is followed by a dialogue initiated by King Mongkut, who asks, "Do you understand the word 'charity,' or *maitrî*, as your apostle St. Paul explains it in the thirteenth chapter of his First Epistle to the Corinthians?" (196). He is interested in the verse, "Even if I give my body to be burned, and have not charity, it profiteth me nothing." He and Leonowens concur that self-sacrifice is truly virtuous only if done for the purest motives, not to appear generous or brave or earn merit, for instance, but to serve others before one's self. To illustrate the purest motives, the king tells the story of the spiritual progress of a young man who became a monk and is now the ninety-five-year-old high priest of Siam. Having previously passed through being "great in the Christian sense," he is now "great in the Buddhist sense also,—not loving life or fearing death, desiring nothing the world can give, beyond the peace of a beatified spirit" (198–99). The narrative then leaps forward eighteen months, when King Mongkut calls Leonowens to join him in the cell of that high priest, now dying. There are candles and chanting and solemn watching, but neither grief nor fear. The old monk's last words are that he gives his body to be burned. "I can imagine no spectacle more worthy," comments Leonowens, "to excite a compassionate emotion, to impart an abiding impression of reverence" (202). She accompanies the king to the cemetery where the body is burned, after which he turns to her and says, "This is what your St. Paul had in his mind,—this custom of our Buddhist ancestors, this complete self-abnegation in life and in death" (202). This is not a Westerner teaching the "pagan" about Christianity or how to read the Bible; this is a long-serving Buddhist master teaching his young Western pupil that the most illuminating way of reading the Bible is through the example of Buddhism, which she accepts without challenge. Most tellingly, at the death of the high priest, Leonowens's narrator finally receives release and comfort: "My heart and eyes were full of tears, yet I was comforted. By what hope? I know not, for I dared not question it" (202). If here she had approached an emotion-driven conversion to Buddhism, she knew in writing that she "dared not" say more explicitly which faith it was that had given her comfort and hope.

*The English Governess* is a deeply conflicted text. Upon first reading it might appear as an episodic hodgepodge of styles, but closer inspection reveals a systematic pattern of oscillation between two genres, Gothic romance and comparative religious studies, with elements of other genres and discourses mixed in. This pattern coincides in part with what I defined as a rough alternation between harem-slave episodes and documentarian segments. The text forces together two largely incompatible genres that then clash with one another and compete for the reader's sympathy. Although the genres of Gothic romance, (mocku)memoir, and travel writing attracted and entertained Leonowens's many readers, what they in fact most received was a lesson in Buddhism informed by comparative religion. A greater portion of *The English Governess* is written in what I have outlined as the comparative religion genre than in either memoir or Gothic romance. More important is that the oscillation between contradictory genres generates tremendous tension, which threatens to tear the text into pieces. The oscillation between genres represents, and the tension enacts, the almost irresolvable psychic schism that Leonowens experienced in her life between the bad-father Mongkut, which she projected from the emotional imperative to exorcise abusive patriarchy, and the good-father Mongkut, which she longed to heal and guide her. The ultimate meaning of *The English Governess* is this violent oscillation and this tension; it resides in the gap between genres, in the violence of a juxtaposition that is at once formal and thematic. It also enacts the oscillation that many Westerners experienced between "bad Buddhism," the nihilistic opponent of Christian faith, and the "good Buddhism" by which even Christianity might be instructed.

Buddhism was the vehicle by which Leonowens could accept, at least in part, King Mongkut as the good father. We cannot know if Leonowens gained increasing sympathy for Buddhism through her teacher–pupil relationship with King Mongkut or whether she gained increasing acceptance of King Mongkut through her growing interest in Buddhism. I have tried to demonstrate that both occurred. If one is a good father by providing one's daughter with the example and instruction upon which she will draw for the rest of her life, professionally and personally, and if one is a good father by additionally providing the discipline and authority against which the daughter needs to rebel in order to form her own discipline and authority without further need of the father, then King Mongkut was a good father to Anna Leonowens. She went on to live a very long, full, productive, and loving life. She did this both because of and despite the silent anxiety she lived with unceasingly of having to maintain an identity that relied upon a story she had told about King Mongkut when she was young. She could not have revised her story of King Mongkut if she had wanted to do so, because that would have undone her life's labor of making a better life for her children and grandchildren. I believe that Leonowens eventually knew and understood all of this. At the same time that she carried the necessary burden of betraying her good father, she demonstrated over and over again through her active dissemination of Buddhism in the West that King Mongkut had given her what she needed.

The preceding reading provides a basis for understanding Leonowens's purposes in ending *The English Governess* with "The Legend of the Maha Naghkon." The story is about a mythic King Sudarsana and his Princess Thawadee. The ruler of highest heaven, P'hra Indara, plants a child in the womb of Princess Thawadee. The king's elder council suspects the pregnancy and tries to move the king to kill or drive her away. She goes into exile after giving birth to Prince Somannass, whom P'hra Indara informs her will "bring peace and happiness to earth" (Leonowens, *English Governess* 318). After many years in exile, in which P'hra Indara blesses Somannass with a bounty of spiritual and earthly gifts, the mother and son return to their kingdom, and Princess Thawadee is reunited with King Sudarsana, who "took up his abode with her, and they lived together in love" (320). Prince Somannass then "built temples, and preached, and taught the people, and healed their infirmities, and led them in the paths of virtue and truth" (320). Here is a story in which the family fails, the woman is abandoned or betrayed, she nevertheless has the courage and faith to become the heroine of the story, motherhood proves triumphant over patriarchal doubt, the son will be God's gift to humankind, the marital bond is healed as a result, and the ruptured family is happily reunited. One can see why Leonowens might have found this story attractive. Here also is a story that provides confirmation for the Christ story and the supremacy of God (under the name Indara), perhaps pleasing Christian readers, but in the same motion demonstrates that this story is not unique to Christianity but rather has predecessors in other religions that greatly antedate Christianity, giving precedence to Hinduism and Buddhism over Christianity, as we will see Helena Blavatsky likewise do in building Theosophy. In this, one finds Leonowens indirectly displaying her self-training in comparative religion. And here, finally, is a story in which the bad father-king is recuperated though the efforts of the good mother-queen and becomes a good father-king. One reads in Leonowens's footnote that the story was "translated from a MS. presented to the author by the Supreme King of Siam" (314, note), the gift of Buddhism to the West.

# Part III

# The Turn to Occultism

# 7

# Ancient Egyptian Religion in Late Victorian England

> "O! dear land of Kehm [Egypt], as in a dream I see thee! I see Nation after Nation set its standard on thy shores, and its yoke upon thy neck! I see new religions without end calling out their truths on the banks of Sihor and summoning thy people to their worship! I see thy temples—thy holy temples—crumbling in the dust: a wonder to the sight of men unborn, who shall peer into thy tombs and desecrate the great ones of thy glory! I see thy mysteries a mockery to the unlearned, and thy wisdom wasted like waters on the desert sands! I see the Roman Eagles stoop and perish, their beaks yet red with the blood of men, and the long lights dancing down the barbarian spears that follow in their wake! And then, at last, I see Thee once more great, once more free, and having once more a knowledge of thy Gods—ay, thy Gods with a changed countenance, and called by other names, but still thy Gods!"
>
> H. Rider Haggard, *Cleopatra*

This penultimate section of *Spirit Matters* analyzes the contexts and writings of H. Rider Haggard and Bram Stoker as representative of the late century culmination of the cultural contest between spirit and matter with which this book opened. They portray, through the horrifying images and cathartic melodrama that only the Gothic-romance subgenre could render, the religious/spiritual crisis of the fin de siècle. That crisis was the result of the perceived, increasing irreconcilability between the truth-telling authority of orthodox Christianity and that of scientific naturalism. We have witnessed how Edward Bulwer-Lytton responded to this crisis by invoking a highly ambivalent third term, Spirit. His novels show how contact with esoteric and occult spirituality could reinvigorate traditional Christianity's genuine spirituality and its power to stand up to materialism but how it then was necessary to deny that catalytic spirituality as dangerous and damnable in comparison with Christian faith. For Bulwer-Lytton, writing in the first half of the century, that worked. The Church of England still was the unshakable national religion, Buddhism (and the ancient Egyptian monotheism analyzed in the current chapter) was virtually unknown and beneath consideration, and the Spiritualism movement had not yet fully arrived. Forty years later, what Haggard and Stoker show is that Bulwer-Lytton's solution no longer convincingly worked and that the stakes had become frighteningly higher. Science had become only more authoritative and institutionalized, Spirit had become a more widespread and powerful alternative, and institutional Christianity had become more embattled, if still widely attended and evolving. In Bulwer-Lytton, these contests had been acted out between eccentric individuals, lone outliers. In Haggard and Stoker, the scale has shifted dramatically upward; nothing less is at stake than the sovereignty of nations, Christianity's claims to divine origin and global preeminence, and the continued existence of the human species. Although they show that the British Empire and Christianity are still standing at the end, the texts that I analyze must strain against themselves in order to arrive at less than fully convincing happy endings. The two chapters in the current section anatomize this crisis and prepare the way for understanding the solution to it offered by the founders of late-century hybrid religions, which was to dissolve the centuries-old dualisms.

## From Egyptomania to Egyptology

The epigraph with which this chapter opens, taken from H. Rider Haggard's *Cleopatra, Being an Account of the Fall and Vengeance of Harmachis, the Royal Egyptian, as Set Forth by His Own Hand* (1889), is spoken at the penultimate moment of the novel as Harmachis awaits gruesome execution, to be followed by more fearful punishment in the afterlife, for the betrayal of his royal pharaoh's blood and its birthright of high priesthood to Isis, whom he forsook for love of Cleopatra. This passage contains in miniature a map of late Victorian discourse about ancient Egypt. It contains empire and occupation, with allusion to the occupation of ancient Egypt by England's imperial forbearers, unavoidably implicating Britain's occupation of Egypt starting in 1882. It speaks to the "heroic age" of Egyptian archaeology, 1870–1900, when Haggard wrote, when "men unborn" transformed Egyptomania, which had been perennial in Europe since the Renaissance, into the science of Egyptology, while others took voyeuristic thrills in desecrating tombs to unwrap the "craze for this creature of imperial fantasy," the mummy, which haunted nineteenth-century Europe, especially through Gothic-romance fiction such as Haggard's (Gange, "Religion" 1083; Deane 384). It references the "mysteries" and "wisdom" by which two millennia of Westerners have mythologized Egypt as "the profound source of all esoteric law," the law invoked in the occult spirituality of the Theosophical Society and H. P. Blavatsky's *Isis Unveiled: A Master-Key to the Mysteries of Ancient and Modern Science and Theology* (1877), as well as in the more masculine, self-willed mysticism of the Hermetic Order of the Golden Dawn, founded in London in 1887 (Hornung 3).[1] The passage emphasizes the supplanting of religions by other religions, a theme in keeping with Victorian historicist criticism of the Bible, potentially throwing into question the divine revelation upon which Western monotheisms depend for their claims to historically unique authenticity. As part of this, there is oblique reference in the biblical place-marker Sihor to what Jan Assmann describes as the "Mosaic distinction . . . between true and false in religion," the latter thereafter called "idolatry" and "paganism," by which Egypt became the necessarily evil "inverted image of Israel" in the justifying "Grand Narrative" of Judaism and then Christianity: "the myth of the Exodus" (1, 7).[2] This narrative is perhaps the primary reference to Egypt throughout Western discourse. It is all the more surprising, then—perhaps even shocking—as the last in a list of events that readers recognized as historical facts, when Haggard's speaker foresees a modern world in which the ancient Egyptian gods once more will be in ascendency. This smacks of prophecy. One argument of this chapter is that this prophecy already had come true, that Haggard understood this and intended the point, and that some of his contemporaries shared that recognition. What Haggard and others understood is that Egypt's own "Gods with a changed countenance, and called by other names," while also once again invoked in heterodox theologies by some of the original names—Isis, Osiris, Horus—had been worshiped for nineteen centuries by the "other names" of Virgin Mary, God the Father, and Jesus Christ the Lord.

The period 1880–1910 was a culminating moment in the history of European engagement with its idea of Egypt and with modern Egypt itself. In those decades, political-colonial, scientific-archaeological, literary, and religious and spiritual discourses about ancient Egypt all came to a head in conjunction with one another with unprecedented intensity. The historian David Gange gives a sense of this when he writes: "Every great figure of the nineteenth century—from Gladstone, Carlyle, and Ruskin, to Byron, Tennyson, and Yeats, or Lyell, Darwin and Huxley—read histories of ancient Egypt and argued about their content. They recognised Egypt as a focal point in disputes over human origins, patterns underlying human history, the status and purpose of the Bible and the cultural roles of the classics. Egyptian archaeology ingrained its influence everywhere from the lecture halls of the ancient universities, to the devotional aids of rural Sunday schools and the plots of cheap sensation fiction" (*Dialogues* 1). After England unofficially occupied Egypt in 1882, controlling the Suez Canal, which had opened in 1869, "the burning issue of Britain's ambitious relationship with Egypt became popularly known as the 'Egyptian Question,'" until the beginning of the First World War, when Britain could settle the question by openly claiming Egypt as a protectorate (Bulfin 412). This political context of imperialism unavoidably colored all other British thought about Egypt at the fin de siècle, but it is not a primary concern here. Neither are race, gender, and sexuality, travel in Egypt, mummy unwrappings and the "curse of the mummy," nor the outpouring of Gothic romances with Egyptian elements that swelled from the 1860s through the end of the century, all of which have received considerable critical attention.[3] The primary focus here is the less-treated topic of the effect of ancient Egyptian religion on mainstream Christian thought in England. In the process, I will situate the orthodox religious responses in relationship to the other half of the constellation of religious responses, namely the heterodox ones of Theosophy and the Hermetic Order of the

Golden Dawn. This chapter will use an analysis of Haggard's *Cleopatra* to chart the configuration of religious/spiritual discourses that the late Victorian period produced in its encounter with ancient Egyptian religion.

## The Mosaic Distinction and Ancient Egyptian Monotheism

Scholarly attention to issues of religion has not been commensurate with its level of significance in shaping late Victorian responses to Egypt. To an extent greater than generally recognized, a primary interest in the 1880s to the 1910s was in the authentification of modern Christianity, in a period of crisis, through reference to ancient Egyptian religion, but in an utterly new way. Ancient Egyptian religion always had been the negative proof of the authenticity of the Judeo-Christian God. The Mosaic distinction was the mytho-historical event by which Judaism and then Christianity marked what claimed to be the first and only true monotheistic deity's revelation, the demonstration of the authenticity of which required the contrasting falsity of Egyptian polytheism (followed by Grecian and Roman polytheisms). Ancient polytheism had functioned as a "technique of translation" between national religions in which "the gods were international because they were cosmic," immanent in the natural universe and so available to all; thus, while "different peoples worshipped different gods . . . nobody contested the reality of foreign gods" (Assmann 3). In dramatic contrast, the national God of the ancient Hebrews, prior to the formation of Judaism, constituted a world-changing " 'counter-religion' because it reject[ed] and repudiate[d] everything that went before and what is outside itself as 'paganism' " (3). Judaism and Christianity emerged from within Mediterranean cultures permeated by Egyptian polytheism. To oversimplify large pieces of ancient history, Isis had become the "universal goddess" by the Egyptian Late Period (664–332 BCE) and was the "supreme foreign god of Rome" from Claudius to Caligula, and Isis worship persisted "into the sixth century CE in Italy and Egypt" as Christianity was achieving dominance (Gabriel 139; Parramore 7). The contest that had started with the Mosaic distinction was not convincingly settled until the fourth century CE, starting with the massacre of Egyptian priests by Theophilus, the patriarch of Alexandria, in 319, only six years before the Council of Nicaea, and then the declaration of

Christianity as the state religion of the Roman Empire with the Edict of Thessalonica in 380, during which the "institutional structure of Egyptian Religion, then more than four millennia old, was violently demolished" in a matter of decades (Gabriel 195). Egypt's ancient cosmotheism remained largely suppressed in European historical consciousness, although retained in texts such as Herodotus's *An Account of Egypt* and Plutarch's *On Isis and Osiris*, until it reemerged in the Renaissance, that "Golden Age of Egyptophilia," as a crucial element in Enlightenment Deism, and then in German Romanticism, when "European Egyptomania reached its climax," inspiring Napoleon's expedition to Egypt (Assmann 17, 143). One significant heir of this cosmotheistic historical lineage was H. P. Blavatsky, who, as I will show, staged a violent counterattack upon orthodox Christianity in the name of Isis and was paralleled in this by the Egyptian mysticism of the Hermetic Order of the Golden Dawn. These were heterodox responses, in effect on behalf of the defeated other from the fourth century, but starting in the 1880s there was, in addition, a new and extraordinary marshaling of ancient Egyptian religion not as the defining counterexample but rather on behalf of orthodox Christianity.

How did it come about that nineteen centuries of bad press were in part reversed in the 1880s such that "associations of ancient Egypt with ancient oppression and modern irreligion" (e.g., Theosophy and the Golden Dawn) were "abandoned and replaced with extraordinary attempts to write Egypt into the most highly valued traditions of the Christian West" (Gange, *Dialogues* 236)? To take a representative example, when the Reverend J. Nilan, writing in *Catholic World* in 1884, looks back at ancient Egypt, he finds a useful rejoinder to the Darwinists and historicists: "To the Christian student wishing to arm himself against the false theories and superficial learning of some modern unbelievers an acquaintance with the true nature and characteristics of the earliest historic religious creeds of man, outside of Biblical records, are of substantial service" (558).[4] He finds in the ancient Egyptian "wisdom literature" a precedent for the "Christian virtues" of piety, charity, and chastity, among other middle-class moral tenets, including "respect for property" (562).[5] After all, "Moses was instructed in all the wisdom of the Egyptians, and was mighty in his words and deeds" (Acts 7:22). Nilan also finds that "the Egyptians are derived from the same stock—the Aryan—as the Indo-European, whose original seat is traced to central Asia," not Africa, participating in the periodic eugenics debates concerning the racial features of exhumed pharaoh mummies (561).[6] Most importantly, Nilan finds that "it is now clearly established that the form of religion prevalent in Egypt some centuries before, and at the beginning of, the Christian era was but the latest and basest corruption of a far more ancient and supremely purer doctrine of perfect monotheism" (558). This is a move familiar within nineteenth-century comparative religious studies: the claim that the more recent or contemporary religious practice of a colonized people is "degenerated" from the earlier, purer doctrines and that, while indigenous practitioners are now untrue to their religious heritage, the scientific scholarship of Westerners has retrieved the originary sources, the textual and archival preservation of which is now a necessary guardianship on the part of the colonial authorities. This of course was a primary argument of European archeologists throughout the century. It figuratively justified occupation of Egypt, now considered part of the birthright of Christianity, and, therefore, violence against the current, "degenerated" religion, Islam, in the name of the purer religion. The most crucial point, however, which generally is overlooked in the context I have just sketched, is that the late Victorians discovered a confirming monotheism underneath the counter-example of polytheism. Thus Nilan concludes: "From the musty resting-places of the mummies, beneath the immovable guardianship of sphinx and pyramid, comes forth the venerable voice of antiquity to fortify the basis of Christian faith and hope—a resurrection of the natural religious spirit of man, to testify to the truth of his present sublime, revealed doctrine" (560).

Nilan's concluding five words raise a number of questions that one might expect would have been extremely troubling to Christians in the late nineteenth century but appear not to have been. Why were they not?—this question demands an answer. How can religious truth be both natural and revealed within the tradition of Western modernity that had defined itself upon the irreconcilable dichotomies of nature versus scripture, immanence versus revelation, material versus spiritual? How can a doctrine be revealed, originated by unique divine action at a singular historical moment, and yet also have a historical precedent? How can one use the findings of archaeology to document the historicity of the Mosaic distinction, which is what late Victorian Christians hoped to do, without acknowledging that this likewise places "Moses the Egyptian" within a much longer history of influences that cannot but throw into question the originality and uniqueness of the Mosaic distinction? Somehow despite— or perhaps because of —these contradictions, the " 'critical' Egypt of mid century [was] displaced by an attempt to develop Egyptology as a science that could challenge unbiblical claims made in the name of biological, anthropological, and philological scholarship" (Gange, *Dialogues* 236).

Where did Nilan and other contemporary Christian apologists get the idea of an ancient Egyptian monotheism that somehow validated Christianity in advance, prior to its historical existence but, crucially, without at the same time throwing the authenticity of the Judeo-Christian revelation into question? They got it, at least in part, from archaeologists in Egypt, or rather their associated Egyptologists in England. Archaeology was the vehicle upon which ancient Egyptian religion arrived at the orthodox center, not only the heterodox periphery, of late Victorian fascination. The advent of the modern study of Egypt is generally traced to the Napoleonic campaigns of 1798 to 1801 and the resulting *Description de l'Égypte*, the thirty-eight volumes and 909 plates of which were produced by 160 scholars from 1809 to 1829 and included, in 1822, the landmark event of Jean-François Champollian's decipherment of Egyptian hieroglyphics. However, "it was in the 1870s and 1880s, not in the 1820s or 1830s, that the impact of decipherment really began to make its presence felt and it was in the 1870s, not in the Napoleonic era, that Egyptologists found ways to communicate directly with the public and began to gain sustained interest and support from numerous reading Britons" (Gange, *Dialogues* 1–2). British archaeology accelerated especially after the launching in 1882 of the Egyptian Exploration Fund by a partnership led by Amelia Edwards, author of the best-selling *A Thousand Miles up the Nile* (1877). Edwards penned a series of articles with titles such as "Was Rameses II the Pharaoh of the Exodus?," inviting the British Christian community—beleaguered by Darwinism, higher criticism, schism, and loss of congregation—to join in a "sudden quest for biblical verification," historical evidence to counter the geologists and historicists (Gange, "Religion" 1089). Egyptologists and Christians found each other to be useful allies for their respective purposes, which is not to say they did not genuinely hold and share those purposes. Indeed, "late Victorian Egyptologists, painfully aware of the challenges facing contemporary religion, held up this aspect of ancient Egyptian culture as an ideal for Victorian Britain to aspire to" (1092).

The most successful popularizer of Egyptology, if not H. Rider Haggard, was Haggard's friend Sir E. A. Wallis Budge, Keeper of the Department of Egyptian and Assyrian Antiquities at the British Museum from 1894 to1924. In his diary of 1910, Haggard observes that "there is nothing that I enjoy more than a talk with Budge and a solitary walk in the Museum" (in Luckhurst 195). Writing as if in parallel to Haggard's Egyptian novels, Budge published many popular-scholarly books, such as *Easy Lessons in Egyptian Hieroglyphics with Sign List* (1889), *The Mummy: A Handbook of Egyptian Funerary Archaeology* (1894), and *Egyptian Religion: Egyptian Ideas of the Future Life* (1900). He opens the latter of these stating, "The Egyptians possessed, some six thousand years ago, a religion and system of morality which, when stripped of all corrupt accretions, stand second to none among those which have been developed by the greatest nations of the world" (W. Budge 12). Far from being the negative counterexample of idolatrous paganism, this religion is now worthy of deepest respect and study. This reversal is accompanied by a more momentous one, since it might undermine the Mosaic distinction by replacing the traditional scapegoat of polytheism with a monotheism remarkably like the Judeo-Christian one. Budge argues throughout that "it is certain that from the earliest times one of the greatest tendencies of the Egyptian religion was towards monotheism," though—now as if an afterthought—"it is also certain that a kind of polytheism existed in Egypt side by side with monotheism from very early times" (30). In his examination of Osirian mythology, Budge concludes: "for thousands of years men and women died believing that, inasmuch as all that was done for Osiris would be done for them symbolically, they like him would rise again and inherit life everlasting. However far back we trace religious ideas in Egypt, we never approach a time when it can be said that there did not exist a belief in the Resurrection," with a capital "R" (81). Regardless of the archaeological and historical support for these claims, it is evident in his overemphases that he was determined to produce an ancient Egyptian religion in the image of late nineteenth-century (Protestant, Anglican)

Christianity. His reliance upon recognizably King Jamesian diction, such as "God Almighty," "ascended into heaven," and "attained unto everlasting life," unmistakably signals his purpose (13, 104).

Two other points concerning Budge's work are crucial. First, he describes the strong analogy between Egyptian religious figures and the subsequent Christian ones, as when he notes that "in Osiris the Christian Egyptians found the prototype of Christ, and in the pictures and statues of Isis suckling her son Horus, they perceived the prototypes of the Virgin Mary and her Child," but he avoids critically examining the unavoidable implication concerning influence and originality, even while stating that "when the Egyptians declared their god to be One . . . they meant precisely what the Hebrews and Arabs meant when they declared their God to be One" (105, 133). Second, Budge eschews the fact that for millennia Egyptian religion(s) was unmistakably polytheistic with the explanation that while that may have been true for the masses "the educated classes in Egypt at all times never placed the 'gods' on the same high level as God" (108). A question that remains to be answered is why monotheism was repeatedly the most emphasized point, not only for Budge but for an apparent majority on the orthodox religious side (while the opposite was true for those on the heterodox side). As Gange summarizes the mainstream impact: "In terms of popularity traditional Christian approaches to ancient Egypt eclipsed all rivals, every major practising Egyptologist of the 1880s employing them and publications receiving large, demonstrably enthusiastic, audiences. Support for biblical Egyptologists demonstrates that, in Egyptology, the fin de siècle enjoyed a little-noticed but widely supported revival of Old-Testament-based Christianity amidst a flowering of diverse beliefs" (Gange, "Religion" 1083).

The watershed event in this confluence of discourses about ancient Egyptian religion was the archaeological discovery at Tell el Amarna of the writings by and about Pharaoh Akhenaten. Amarna was the capital newly built by Akhenaten, who ruled between 1378 and 1359 BCE, and "until its rediscovery in the nineteenth century, there was virtually no memory of Akhenaten," no written historical record, though the finds at Amarna established his historicity beyond question (Assmann 21). Amarna was excavated by Sir W. M. Flinders Petrie, the most significant Egyptian archaeologist of the nineteenth century and author in 1894 of *Tell el Amarna*. He was partly funded by contributions from Christian supporters to the Egyptian Exploration Fund. As a result of "Petrie's excavations, Akhenaten's capital burst into British culture in all its glory in the early 1890s . . . [and] Amarna art was popularized as an achievement to match Athenian sculpture" (Gange, *Dialogues* 232). What Petrie and others revealed is that Akhenaten had come to rulership as Amenhotep IV but had changed his name to incorporate that of his new deity, Aten, whom he enforced as the one true god with whom he intended to replace the polytheistic pantheon that had been worshipped in Egypt for millennia. As Rosalie David, historian of ancient Egypt, summarizes, "having systematically destroyed the old gods and theologies and the priestly infrastructure that had given them expression in Egyptian life, Akhenaten spent the next 12 years imposing a new god and theology upon the country" (48). The pharaohs who followed Akhenaten, in particular Tutankhaten/Tutankhamun, returned Egypt to its popular, traditional gods, centered on Amun or Amun-Ra (or Amon, or Amen), and attempted to eradicate Amarna and all memory of Akhenaten and Aten.

Even so, the cultural memory of Aten worship would have world-changing ramifications through the figure of Moses. The finds at Amarna revealed to the late Victorians that "the monotheistic revolution of Akhenaten was not only the first but also the most radical and violent eruption of a counter-religion in the history of humankind," preceding and setting the pattern for the God of Moses (Assmann 25). Later research would show that the "identification of Moses with a dislocated memory of Akhenaten had already been made in antiquity" (24). James Henry Breasted, the foremost American Egyptologist at the turn of the century, whose 1894 Amarna thesis was "the first appraisal of the Amarna hymns and their religious content," argued that "the description of the *Habiru* [Hebrews] contained in the Amarna letters date [sic] from the fourteenth century B.C.E. and suggest that the period of the Israelite arrival was probably some time during the reign of Amenhotep III, Akhenaten's father" (Assmann 152; Gabriel 67).[7] Moses the Hebrew Egyptian, for whom, in contrast to Akhenaten, there is no historical verification other than the Bible, is thus difficult to date, but the consensus among historians, both in the nineteenth century and now, locates him during the reign of Ramesses II (1279–1213 BCE), between 1250 and 1200 BCE.[8] In that case, historical evidence suggests that "Moses would have been readily aware of Egyptian religious practices and of the story of Akhenaten as almost all educated

Egyptians of his time would have been" (Gabriel 80). Thus it should not be surprising to find, as does the historian Richard A. Gabriel, that "the theological precepts of Akhenaten's radically new Egyptian religion and the Mosaic Yahwehism of the Israelites, the forbearers of modern Judaism, are substantially the same in content and even form" (97).[9] Specifically, "both share the following precepts: (1) a monotheism that rejects all other gods as false; (2) the role of religious leader as prophet, not priest, who alone communicates with god [i.e., Akhenaten, then Moses]; (3) a hatred of idols and rejection of the notion of indwelling; (4) the rejection of a transcendent or cosmological destiny for human beings; (5) denial of the existence of an immortal human soul; (6) denial of the possibility of resurrection after death; (7) rejection of a moral judgment of the deceased; and (8) denial of the possibility of an eternal life" (97–98).

These latter points are among the reasons why the ancient Egyptian people and the pharaohs who succeeded Akhenaten not only did not subscribe to Atenism but attempted to wipe it from the face of the earth. Atenism held none of the comfort in the face of mortality provided by Isis and Osiris, the resurrected man-god who promised life after death to all who followed him; "the cult was destined to fail because it did not address people's most basic fears and uncertainties, which are common to all mankind; by denying the very existence of evil and death, Atenism could not hope to provide either comfort or inspiration for Egyptians" (David 245). Aten was nonanthropomorphic, represented by a sun disk (Ra), immanent not revealed, and therefore both invisible and everywhere visible because omnipresent in the natural universe.[10] Atenism was an immanent monotheism and, as such, perhaps unique in human history. Thus, although it was cosmotheistic, its impersonal singularity did not describe a cosmos that embodied the story of humankind, its suffering and hope for eternal life, as did the polytheistic pantheon and trinitarian formation most characteristic of ancient Egyptian religion.

Indeed, "from beginning to end, except for the period of Akhenaten, Egyptian religion remained centered on the following principles: (1) a single trinitarian god; (2) a cosmology in which all things, man, god, and nature, have a place that can be comprehended by man; (3) man's possession of an immortal soul; (4) resurrection of the dead and life beyond the grave; (5) a final judgement beyond the grave where man's ethical life is weighed; and (6) an eternal life for the deceased" (Gabriel 105). The trinity was a persistent formation, whether of Ptah, Sokaris, and Osiris in the Old Kingdom (twenty-fifth–twentieth centuries BCE), or of Amun, Re, and Ptah in the New Kingdom (sixteenth–eleventh centuries BCE), or, finally, of Osiris, Isis, and Horus. There is no other historical source in the ancient world from which Jesus and the early Christians could have derived the Holy Trinity and the Resurrection than from ancient Egyptian trinitarian resurrectionism. That theological tradition and the Osirian myth "had existed without major interruption for more than three millennia by the time Christ was born and, as a consequence of the Ptolemies and Hellenism, was thriving as a theological system with a wide following inside Egypt and throughout the Mediterranean world, including the Palestine in which Christ was born and raised" (Gabriel 147). While frequently hyperbolic, Madame Blavatsky had a basis for arguing that "the foundation of the fierce hatred of the [early] Christians toward the 'Pagans'" was because "too much had been *borrowed*" from ancient Egyptian religion; "had not the ancient creeds been speedily obliterated, it would have been found impossible to preach the Christian religion as a New Dispensation, or the direct Revelation from God the Father" (Blavatsky, *Isis Unveiled* vol. 2, 51, 635). It appears that in order to maintain that Jesus of Nazareth was the one true Son of God whose divinity in the Holy Trinity was demonstrated by the Resurrection, the early Christian bishops found it necessary to deny the entire historical context of ancient Egyptian religion.

## Orthodox and Heterodox Responses to Atenism

Europeans around the end of the nineteenth century came face to face with the historical context of ancient Egyptian religion with an immediacy that had not occurred since the fourth century, before the ancient creeds were "speedily obliterated." One might expect that this would have created a terrible dilemma for late Victorians, because, in theory, there can be no historical precedent for a revealed monotheism. As Assmann puts the point, "there is no natural or evolutionary way leading from the error of idolatry to the truth of monotheism"; "this truth can come only from outside, by way of revelation" (7). This dilemma was literally doubled, because there was at once proof that the Judeo-Christian God had been adapted from Atenism and, if this first conclusion were granted, the accompanying acknowledgement that the Jesus story was simply the latest expression of Osirian mythology. I have attempted to demonstrate that the constellation of religious/spiritual positions in relationship to Egypt between 1880 and 1910 enacted this dual dilemma by splitting between what I have called the orthodox and the heterodox responses to ancient Egyptian religion. The heterodox responses, as in Theosophy and the Golden Dawn, were cosmotheistic and therefore more than prepared to exchange revealed monotheism for immanence, scripture for nature. Rather than defending Jesus's revealed divinity, they embraced Osirian mythology, even celebrating Jesus's membership in that lineage, and also reinstated the divine feminine.

The orthodox response was more complex. Their dilemma could have been much more dire, because "if the space of religious truth is constructed by the distinction between 'Israel in truth' and 'Egypt in error,' any discoveries of Egyptian truths will necessarily invalidate the Mosaic distinction and deconstruct the space separated by this distinction" (Assmann 8). It appears, although more historical research would be required to confirm this hypothesis, that mainstream Christians, in partnership with Egyptologists, chose to do both: acknowledge an Egyptian truth but without allowing it to deconstruct the Mosaic distinction. It would appear that they chose to channel the discoveries of Egyptian archaeology toward reinforcing, rather than questioning, the Mosaic distinction. One interpretation, which certainly may not be the only one available, is that this required a combination of the courage of their convictions and denial. They made ancient Egyptian monotheism into the validation of the God of Moses, which one might interpret as requiring a willed nonrecognition of the implications of the accompanying historical precedence. Had they acknowledged the anxiety of influence, how could that not have undermined defining metaphysical dichotomies of "Western Civilization"—revelation versus immanence, scripture versus nature, spiritualism versus materialism—that had in part originated from the Mosaic distinction and were original to that event as monotheism in fact was not? Perhaps for mainstream Christians, that God might not be God, according to the definition of scripture, was literally unthinkable, nonsensical, beyond the boundary of the comprehensible because unassimilable to mainstream Christian culture.[11]

Even though now enlisting ancient Egyptian religion positively for that purpose, the late Victorian orthodox response of reinforcing the Mosaic distinction can be interpreted as if not a replication of the strategy of the fourth-century church fathers in constructing Christianity then at least as analogous to it. The fourth-century strategy had been to reaffirm the essential partnership of Christianity with Judaism, welding together what some have considered an uneasy unity of the Old Testament and the New Testament. This hinged upon reaffirming the Mosaic distinction, which I suggest reinscribed the erasure of the historical debt to ancient Egyptian monotheism. And this, finally, obscured the second and even more crucial erasure for Christianity, that of the debt of the Holy Trinity and the Resurrection to ancient Egyptian trinitarian resurrectionism. If one were to acknowledge the historicity of the Hebrew God in Aten, then one would invite the accompanying second acknowledgment of the historicity of Jesus Christ in Osiris. This line of thought suggests a hypothesis, substantiation of which would require more thorough historical scholarship, that Judaism and Christianity, while of course sharing a common history, had developed from two opposed strands of ancient Egyptian religion. While Christianity was two steps removed from Atenism, separated by the intermediary of Judaism, it only was one step removed from Osiris worship and trinitarian resurrectionism. Perhaps Christianity had emerged as a partial return to Egyptian paganism, or rather as a syncretic fusion of those two opposed strands of ancient Egyptian religion with Hebraic Yahwehism, but in any case it required the imprimatur of God the Father that came only from the Mosaic distinction in order to establish the divinity of Christ. If the above hypothesis is correct, then in effect choosing Judaism over Egyptianism, both in the fourth century and in the nineteenth century, was necessary to maintain divine revelation in both cases. Thus it may be that late Victorian orthodox Christians had no alternative but to turn proof of the unfoundedness of the Mosaic distinction into the proof of that distinction. As I conceive of them, either of the alternatives would have been unacceptable: on the one hand, surrendering faith to join the materialists, or, on the other hand, joining the pantheistic celebrants of Jesus as one figure of rebirth within the lineage of Egyptian trinitarian resurrectionism.

There was one other alternative available: to recognize Aten, the immanent monotheistic god, as a key to unlocking the long-stalemated foundational oppositions between immanence and revelation, materialism and spiritualism, over which Victorians were so deeply troubled. The "dream of early modernity was reconciliation of nature and Scripture," "the idea of Nature as the deity of an original, nonrevealed monotheism" (Assman 20, 103). One finds elements of this dream in Enlightenment Deism, German Romanticism, American Transcendentalism, late Victorian hybrid religions, and New Age spiritualities. These are traceable back to Akhenaten's Amarna hymn, in which "the unity of God is realized as neither pre-existence nor a (counter-religious) monotheistic concept, but as latency, as a 'hidden unity,' in which all living plurality on earth has it origin" (206). Such cosmotheistic formations bear the promise of unity where there was divisiveness and resolution of the violence that is inherent in monotheism's distinction between the chosen and the infidel, the true and the false religion, which produces "the great catastrophe of monotheism, that is, religious wars of genocide and extermination" (Gabriel 89). However, the late Victorians were less likely to view "The Temple of Nature" (1808) as did Erasmus Darwin than to consider nature, after Charles Darwin, as either indifferent or inimical to humankind. This in part explains why issues of materialism versus spiritualism were so hotly contested in nineteenth-century British culture. The violent response of the ancient Egyptian populace against Atenism sheds light upon the broad late-Victorian preference for their caring anthropomorphic god and the promised rebirth of their trinitarian resurrectionism.

## Haggard's Ancient Egyptian Religion

To what extent and in what ways does Haggard's *Cleopatra* capture the multiple, conflicting religious and spiritual discourses of its time in response to ancient Egyptian religion? Where does this text come down, finally, in relation to ancient Egyptian religion and its relevance to late Victorian religious and spiritual thought? Haggard is a fitting author to choose for these purposes. As he recounts in *The Days of My Life* (1926), "From a boy ancient Egypt had fascinated me, . . . I venerate Isis, and always feel inclined to bow to the moon!" (1:254–55). He traveled in Egypt four times, in 1887, 1904, 1912, and 1924, and began writing *Cleopatra* after returning from his first visit. He was a collector of Egyptian antiques, including a signet ring with a cartouche of Akhenaten, the character of whom appears in *The Way of the Spirit* (1906) and *Smith and the Pharaohs* (1920) (Luckhurst 193–94).[12] He considered himself to be a friend of both Budge and Petrie (though those two were rivals) and dedicated *Morning Star* (1910) to Budge. As his novels demonstrate, he was fascinated by reincarnation and claimed himself to have been an Egyptian in previous lifetimes. He famously drew upon Egyptian figures and themes in both the Quartermain and Ayesha novels, which moved the young Rudyard Kipling, in a letter to Haggard in 1889, to give him the appellation of " 'the King of Egypt' " (in Luckhurst 190). While many critics have read Haggard in relationship to empire, race, or sexuality, few have given due consideration to the fact that his "occult and religious interest, [was] the subject of a lifetime's reading and reflection" and that understanding his religious references is essential to a complete reading of many of his novels (J. D. Coates 54).

*Cleopatra* is Haggard's most extensive engagement with Egyptian religion, and it portrays the demise of the glory of that ancient nation and its religion. Harmachis, who would be the last truly Egyptian pharaoh, fails to wrest the throne from Cleopatra, the last active pharaoh of the Grecian Ptolemaic dynasty (from 69 to 30 BCE), and she in turn cedes Egypt to the Roman Empire, which stands also for the Western, Christian, British imperial supremacy to come. The novel draws heavily upon the history of that moment of transition between civilizations, as well as upon contemporary archaeology and religious studies, and it is because of the narrative's frequent contextualizing exposition that many readers have not thought it one of Haggard's best, even though he claimed it was his masterpiece. The entire first book of the novel consists largely of religious staging, which is why in a preface Haggard "instructs 'such students as seek a story only, and are not interested in the faith, ceremonies, or customs of the Mother of Religion and Civilisation, ancient Egypt,' to skip the first of the three books which is not intended as a narrative" (in Gange, *Dialogues* 217). Many readers have ignored the first book and its significance as an earnest exposition of ancient Egyptian religion, reading instead for the romance and the revenge, which Haggard also well understood.

*Cleopatra* indeed offers trials of combat for Harmachis, lavish street and court scenes, betrayals in the name of love and elided sex scenes between Harmachis and Cleopatra and then Cleopatra and Antony, off-stage battles with casts of thousands, and the final revenge by Harmachis on Antony and Cleopatra. The most sensationally Gothic part of the novel occurs when Harmachis, having succumbed to Cleopatra and believing her promise to be a champion on behalf of Egypt against Roman encroachment, leads her into the secret labyrinthine pyramid of the ancient pharaoh Menka-Ra to rob it of its treasure for the sake of financing Cleopatra's army. This is permitted as long as the purpose is to save Egypt, but, if not: "On thee be the curse that shall smite him who breaks in upon the dead! On thee be the curse that follows the traitor! On thee be the curse that smites him who outrages the majesty of the Gods!" (Haggard, *Cleopatra* 93). This is the proverbial "curse of the mummy," with which the Victorians were fascinated.[13] The crypt scene includes the lantern-lit unwrapping of the mummy, Cleopatra clawing priceless jewels from the chest cavity of Menka-Ra, and a preternaturally gigantic black bat, which will reappear to claim its own when Harmachis calls down the curse in the penultimate scene. These are of a piece with "the magic art of the Egyptians and the reading of the stars" that Harmachis learns in order to pose as a "magician or astrologer" to gain admittance to Cleopatra's court (37, 48). They are not to be confused with the genuine religious rituals and spiritual phenomena the novel portrays; while adding sensation, they afford Haggard the opportunity to comment negatively perhaps on the Hermetic Order of the Golden Dawn, such as Harmachis views "with no small shame, for I love not such play, and hold this common magic in contempt" (48). Even so, the outcomes of the magic are real enough, as when Harmachis turns a rod into snakes, with obvious allusion to Moses.

The curse of Menka-Ra is linked to the more significant curse in the novel, the curse upon Harmachis if he should fail to complete the holy mission to "deliver Egypt" from foreign occupation and religion (by killing Cleopatra, as it turns out) (Haggard, *Cleopatra* 2). Amenemhat, Harmachis's father, becomes the voice of this curse throughout the novel, though it first is delivered as prophecy through Harmachis's mother, who is dying at his childbirth. Amenemhat, in partial parallel to Abraham, had a first wife who was barren and required a second wife to produce a son in old age. The curse is "the curse of thy Royal forefathers," by which Harmachis will suffer, if he fails, "even until such time as [his] sin is purged, and the Gods of Egypt, called by strange names, once more are worshipped in the temples of Egypt" (2, 3). This curse bears the especially Judeo-Christian concept of "sin." Appropriate to the judging father, Amenemhat's name contains that of the patriarchal Egyptian god, Amen (Amun, Amon), to whom Harmachis prays as "the Godhead, who is called by many names, and in many forms made manifest": "O Amen . . . God of gods who hast been from the beginning; Lord of Truth, who art, and of whom all are, who givest out thy Godhead and gatherest it up again, in the circle of whom the divine ones move and are, who wast from all time the Self-begot, and who shalt be till all time—hearken unto me. O Amen" (13–14). As Amenemhat periodically reiterates the curse—"then, my curse be on thee . . . the curse of Egypt's broken gods!"—he ties it to the sins of "the flesh" and the temptation of women (12, 24). He warns that "there is danger in thy path, and it comes in the form of woman" (38). In a pattern familiar throughout Haggard's fiction, a fierce oscillation between gynophobia and gynomancy is ever present, and Haggard's male protagonists never can either resist or possess the divine feminine.[14] As Harmachis reflects, "And thus, while woman, that great surprise of Nature, is, Good and Evil can never grow apart" (56). Cleopatra, whom we first see in the novel costumed as the goddess Isis, is of course the negative side of this duality, though she also is portrayed as intelligent, politically savvy, stronger willed than Harmachis, and, ultimately, at one with Isis as part of the divine feminine.[15] After Harmachis's fall to Cleopatra, Amenemhat becomes the voice of divine vengeance. He charges his son as "his murderer," he who "gaveth all the dower of Khem as the price of a wanton's arms!" and exhorts him, "Harmachis, atone!—atone! Vengeance can still be wreaked—forgiveness can still be won" (130). Even after his death, Amenemhat speaks to Harmachis in dream, saying "Arise, my son!—the hour of vengeance is at hand!" (138). This vengeance is at once that of Menka-Ra, the revenge of the mummy, not only upon Cleopatra but on the invading Romans and, by extension, on the nineteenth-century British tomb raiders and colonial occupiers, and at the same time the vengeance of the patriarchal god, with reference by Haggard to the God of the Old Testament.

Though Amenemhat is the high priest of Isis, his character and religion appear antithetical to the loving voice of "The Divine Mother (Isis)" (Haggard, *Cleopatra* 8). The first book of the novel recounts a seven-day holy festival of Isis, though the emphasis is the death and resurrection of Osiris, as ceremonially sung in the temple: "We sing Osiris risen, / We sing the child that Nout conceived and bore" (22). This is a spring ceremony of rebirth: Easter. The hymn ends with, "Sing we the Trinity, / Sing we the Holy Three" (23). Isis, her brother/husband Osiris, and her son Horus are the figures of forgiveness and resurrection in the novel. But it is not Osiris or Horus to whom Harmachis regularly prays but Isis, "the Holy Mother suckl[ing] the Holy Child" (25). She appears or speaks directly to him several times, as here during the initiation for his divine mission: "I am She whom thou dost know as Isis of the Egyptians; but what else I am strive not thou to learn—it is beyond thy strength. For I am all things, all Life is my spirit, all Nature is my raiment. . . . I am the Child and Servant of the Invisible that is Law, that is Fate—though myself I be not God and Fate and Law. . . . For I am nature's self, and all her shapes are shapes of Me" (30). Isis is accountable to a higher power, "the Invisible," which as invoked throughout the novel seems above even Amen, but is herself immanently divine, embodied in the natural universe. She refuses to tell Harmachis if he will be successful in his mission or not, but she tellingly says: "Yet this for thy comfort: shame and agony shall not be eternal. For, however deep the fall from righteousness, if but repentance holds the heart, there is a path—a stony and cruel path—whereby the height may be climbed again" (31). In the last interview she permits him, after which, because of the demise of Isis worship that Harmachis's betrayal precipitates, she ascends to disappear into the stars, Isis tells him: "no more shall I come face to face with thee till, cycles hence, the last fruit of thy sin hath ceased to be upon this earth! Yet, through the vastness of the unnumbered years, remember thou this: that love Divine is love eternal, which cannot be extinguished. . . . Repent, my servant: repent and do well while there is yet time, that at the dim end of ages once more thou mayest be gathered unto Me. . . . If thou wilt but atone and forget Me no more, I shall be with thee, waiting thine hour of redemption" (132–33). Repentance, forgiveness, and redemption—these are the blessings that Isis and the Egyptian holy trinity offer.

*Cleopatra* juxtaposes these two religious orders: the vengeance of the father versus the forgiveness of the mother with redemption through the son. Haggard's novel enacts a contest between these two streams of influence from ancient Egyptian religion that sprung with new force upon European religious thought in the late nineteenth century: the monotheism of Akhenaten, translated to the Mosaic distinction of Judaism, and the promise of traditional Egyptian trinitarian resurrectionism, translated to the Christian Holy Trinity. There is little doubt which is presented more appealingly in *Cleopatra*, and for that reason one might expect the novel to end with Isis's forgiveness, but this is not the case. The novel ends with penance and vengeance. This occurs despite the Christlike figuration of Harmachis. He becomes the subject of a myth that "*When Harmachis comes again Egypt shall be free*," an allusion to the Resurrection, and in crossing the Mediterranean back to Egypt he appears to walk on the water (he surfs on a piece of driftwood), but his return to Egypt brings freedom neither to himself nor to his country (Haggard, *Cleopatra* 126, 127). Instead, he spends eight years living in a burial cave, to "work out my penance and make atonement for my sin," plotting murder of the conquering pair all the time; reenters the court unrecognized and regains access to the royals; and plays a game of cat-and-mouse intrigue that eventually leads to victory: his murder of Anthony and Cleopatra, revealing his identity to them as they die (136). This should be cause for celebration, a happy ending, but instead it is not only anticlimactic but feels petty and pointless. The vengeance tastes bitter and is too late: the majesty of ancient Egypt is lost, at least until some far distant future of its resurrection. Harmachis then turns himself over to the remaining priests of Isis, who enact their vengeance upon him—the end. How are we to read this conflicted ending?

The text, perhaps reflecting the ideological imperative placed upon late Victorian Christianity when faced with the claims of precedence on behalf of ancient Egyptian religion, which threatened to undermine revelation, is compelled to reassert the Mosaic distinction, the righteousness of God the Father, the justification of vengeance upon idolatry and the sins of the flesh. But the text does not in truth believe its own conviction. It believes in the healing love of the holy mother, the goddess, and takes as truth, as Haggard did, the promise of forgiveness and resurrection (if perhaps as reincarnation). Thus the text gives the reader the orthodoxy-prescribed ending, but robbed of any satisfaction, thereby throwing the reader back upon the conclusion that the text favors but is not sanctioned to deliver more directly. For Haggard to allow the text to become a celebration of Isis's forgiveness would be to reveal and endorse the unity of Christianity with Egyptian trinitarian resurrectionism and, in that moment, surrender claim to revelation in favor of divine immanence, dissolving foundational

Western metaphysical oppositions to embrace the material in the spiritual and the spiritual in the material. That is what Haggard wanted but could not allow himself to fully embrace.

What makes *Cleopatra* a fascinating cultural document is the extent to which it captures the conflict between the orthodox and the heterodox religious positions, as I have theorized them, in response to ancient Egyptian religion. It would seem to confirm the orthodox while subversively forwarding the heterodox, ending finally with a still deeply conflicted synthesis of the two. In the process, it catalogs and draws upon the entire spectrum of late Victorian cultural responses to ancient Egyptian religion and to contemporary Egypt discussed in the preceding sections of this chapter. On what I have called the orthodox side, there is the order of God the Father, the affiliated science of Egyptology with a crypt scene informed by contemporary archaeology, and the politics of justified colonial occupation that was indeed aligned with those. But this ruling order is shadowed by the imperialist's guilt in the figure of the "curse of the mummy" upon the northern invaders, but then that is rendered nothing more than a voyeuristic shiver by the historical inevitability of Rome's and then Britain's imperial preeminence. Yet that ruling order is tormented by the irreconcilabilities between its Christianity and its rational, scientific, and capitalist materialisms, which threaten to negate the scriptural, the revealed, and the spiritual.

This is where the heterodox uses of ancient Egyptian religion enter. The Theosophical Society will appear as Egyptian Isis worship and "the bright spirit of Good, who is of us called Osiris, but who hath many names, offer[ing] himself up for the evil-doing of the race that had dethroned him" (Haggard, *Cleopatra* 26). The "Holy Spirit" is present but is more consonant with Blavatsky's use of "Spirit," or even that by the Spiritualism movement, than with the Christian Trinity (8). The mysticism and "black" magic associated by some with the Hermetic Order of the Golden Dawn also marks the periphery. Implicit if not explicit in these heterodox positions and reaching back to Enlightenment Deism's uses of ancient Egyptian cosmotheism is the natural immanence of Haggard's and Blavatsky's Isis and, especially, of the "substance of the Invisible," at once material and spiritual (12). Haggard, like many on both the orthodox and the heterodox sides, longed deeply to heal these divisions and rescue the spiritual from the material, but the replacement of revelation by immanence was ultimately inassimilable. Thus while straining to write an ending that confirms, as it must, the victory of Europe over Egypt and the necessity of the precedence of the Mosaic distinction over polytheistic paganism, Haggard offers an ending that cannot but mourn the demise of ancient Egyptian spirituality and the advent of Roman/British materialism that he, like most other late Victorians, knew was destined to rule, at least until some far-distant second coming of the feminine divine.

# 8

## The Economics of Immortality

### *The Demi-immortal Oriental, Enlightenment Vitalism, and Political Economy in Bram Stoker's* Dracula

Dracula is the most infamous representative of that especially nineteenth-century character type, the "demi-immortal Oriental." Demi-immortal characters proliferated in the cultural imagination of late nineteenth-century Britons for reasons that this chapter will explore. They featured in multiple novels by Bram Stoker (1847–1912), H. Rider Haggard, and Marie Corelli, as well as in works by Oscar Wilde, Guy Boothby, and Richard Marsh, among others. The definitive feature of this character type is the inversion of the traditional Christian body/soul dichotomy. Demi-immortal characters possess bodily immortality at the cost of spiritual immortality. In other words, this character type embodies the spiritual-versus-material dialectic that I have traced throughout this book, of which it may be the ultimate figure. It represented the most dire threat imaginable to Christian faith—namely, a type of eternal life in competition with the traditional Christian afterlife and the potential negation of the human soul—but, as we shall see, it also could signify the recuperation of genuine spirituality. Earlier in the century in Bulwer-Lytton's *A Strange Story*

(1862), this figure was fantastical and disturbing; almost half a century later in *Dracula* (1897), the figure had become not only more horrifying but also a more genuinely terrifying threat not merely to individual lives but to the material and spiritual well-being of the nation, the civilization, and the species.[1] This progression represented the accelerating cultural crisis generated by the ascendency of materialism relative to spiritualism. *Dracula* also made explicit the parallel between metaphysical materialism and the materialism of capital, which was especially disturbing, since the former was for many the devil and the latter was becoming the privileged ideology of modern Western society. This is one example of what Judith Halberstam calls the "thrifty metaphoricity" of the Gothic: "A Gothic economy may be described in terms of a thrifty metaphoricity, one which, rather than simply scapegoating, constructs a monster out of the traits which ideologies of race, class, gender, sexuality, and capital want to disavow" (102).[2] This figurative multivalence of the Gothic in general and vampirism in particular has invited diverse interpretations of Dracula as "a figure for perversion, menstruation, venereal disease, female sexuality, male homosexuality, feudal aristocracy, monopoly capitalism, the proletariat, the Jew, the primal father, the Antichrist, and the typewriter," among many others (Ellmann xxviii). To these two lists my reading here will add religion and spirituality. As the preceding chapter did in regards to H. Rider Haggard's fiction, this chapter reads *Dracula* in order to capture and characterize the climax of the century-long historical crisis of spirituality in the modern age of materialism.

## The Demi-immortal Oriental and Enlightenment Vitalism

The demi-immortal Oriental is a character type predominantly within romance and Gothic fiction. It may have been prefigured in both Faustian and Wandering Jew mythologies. It began to become a more common literary figure in the first half of the nineteenth century. As I have discussed, Bulwer-Lytton's novels *Zanoni* (1842) and *A Strange Story* portray characters who possess, through a combination of occult spirituality and alchemy, "earthly immortality," living as young men indefinitely, which in the case of Zanoni has meant for five thousand years (*Zanoni* 175). They have mastered an ancient "art" that "recruits animal vigour and arrests the progress of decay," scientifically isolated the "primordial principle of life," which endows them with preternatural vitality and the clairvoyant power to read the minds and control the wills of others (215). Margrave in *A Strange Story* has stolen the "elixir of life," "the great Principle of Animal Life," from an ancient adept, "Haroun of Aleppo," while traveling in "the East" (230, 463). The majority of subsequent characters of this type likewise have origins in "the Orient," as very loosely defined by nineteenth-century Europeans. Thus on the first page of *Dracula* Jonathan Harker has the impression that in crossing into Transylvania he is "leaving the West and entering the East" (Stoker 1). But, demi-immortality always comes with a price, if not a curse. Margrave embodies animality; he has become "the image of sensuous, soulless Nature, such as the Materialist had conceived it" (Bulwer-Lytton, *Strange Story* 9). A precursor to Dracula, he is "devoid of a soul," and so states: "I count on no life beyond the grave. I would defy the grave, and live on" (241, 349). A central moral of these novels is that one must either resist or surrender the magnetic powers of demi-immortality in order to merit the more genuine because soul-based eternal life after death promised by Christianity. This, too, is the moral of subsequent demi-immortal-Oriental novels, including Marie Corelli's *A Romance of Two Worlds* (1886) and *The Life Everlasting* (1911).[3] Prior to the endings of all of these novels, however, living perpetually as a beautiful and vigorous youth cannot but appear to have undeniable attractions. Convincing readers that doing so is undesirable is a tough sell, requiring no small amount of logical and theological contortion to recuperate sufficiently Christian endings.

Precisely because bodily immortality is an easier sell than is bodily death, novels with demi-immortal characters must marshal additional arguments against it. One of those is the violent immorality of demi-immortals. Margrave, like Dracula and Dorian Gray, has scant regard for harm done to others or for the sanctity of human life (though Dracula might be said to observe a vampire's moral and religious code). Their sociopathic and homicidal tendencies pose a threat to social order and make a point about the undesirability of their powers. Additionally, because demi-immortality often takes its origin from an ancient as well as an Eastern source, it was tied to a conception of the past as archaic, tradition-ridden, aristocratic, and now decadent. Demi-immortality often appears to be antiprogressive, both in a secular sense and in a spiritual sense. In the secular sense, demi-immortals generally are tied to a prior age and are reactionary in relationship to the progress associated with science, technology, and market growth. In the spiritual sense, demi-immortality may be contrary to the idea of spiritual progression, which became a common theme as the Spiritualism movement encountered Darwinian evolutionary theory and then fed into the formation of hybrid religions such as Theosophy.[4] Most demi-immortal characters find themselves athwart one or both of these types of progress, secular and spiritual. For example, Ayesha, the title character in Haggard's *She* series of novels, is emotionally and spiritually fixated on a period two thousand years previous when she concurrently achieved demi-immortality and, in a fit of passion, murdered her soul mate.[5] Hers is a demi-immortal's dilemma: while her beautiful body does not age, her wretched soul is stuck in a perpetual feedback loop, not unlike the Nietzschean "eternal recurrence of the same." In similar situations, Margrave and Dorian Gray are happily stalled in perpetual, adolescent decadence. And then, most victimized by the technologies of progress, there is Dracula, who, despite his careful preparations, cannot adapt quickly enough to modern progress to avoid being defeated by its acolytes and whose spiritual condition suggests not merely a lack of progress but the far worse prospect of spiritual de-evolution.[6] Thus the demi-immortal not only threatened the Christian soul but also a belief that in the nineteenth century had become perhaps equally as crucial to the dominant social order, namely progressive ideology.

One reason that demi-immortal characters began to appear with greater frequency after the eighteenth century is because they were derived in part from Enlightenment vitalism. One prevalent debate among natural philosophers in the eighteenth century was between the vitalists and the mechanists. Hans Driesch's *History and Theory of Vitalism* (1914) traces the roots of Enlightenment vitalism to Aristotle's *De generatione animalium* and *De anima* (ca. 350 BCE). Aristotle focused on explaining what takes place at conception or at that moment when the union of gametes in the "germ" becomes infused with life (Driesch 17). Why, when, and how does matter become more than matter; what is the spark or force of life? The word used by Aristotle was "soul," though, significantly, his is not identical to the more dualistic conception of the Christian soul/body. Rather, spirit and matter find complete union or "entelechy," and "the question whether soul and body are one has as little sense as in the case of wax and its form" (Driesch 18). Enlightenment natural philosophers such as Georg Ernest Stahl (1660–1734), Caspar Friedrich Wolff (1733–94), Charles Bonnet (1720–93), and Lorenz Oken (1779–1851) defended a "dynamic teleology" that recognized the "autonomy of vital processes" from mechanical or deterministic systems (Driesch 6). Mechanists, among whom Driesch includes René Descartes (1596–1650) and Gottfried Wilhelm Leibnitz (1646–1716), defended a "static teleology" according to which "Nature as a whole, including the physical processes of life in the broadest sense, is . . . a mechanical system, [if still] arranged by God," in short, materialism (23). As Peter Hanns Reill summarizes the debate: "Enlightenment vitalists sought to dissolve this dichotomy [between the spiritual and the material, God and nature] . . . by positing the existence in living matter of active or self-activating forces, which had a teleological character. Living matter was seen as containing an immanent principle of self-movement whose sources lay in the active powers which resided in matter itself" (365). Vitalistic natural philosophers therefore set about "vitalizing the world with living forces such as elective affinities, vital principles, sympathies and formative drives" (365). Driesch's history follows this debate into the second half of the nineteenth century when Darwinian evolutionary theory has become the primary nemesis of vitalism, by then more often expressed as spiritualism. The mechanical randomness of "natural selection" appeared to remove from the universe the orderly purposiveness of divine oversight, which is in part what the proponents of Natural Theology, for example, were working to preserve. The vitalist-mechanist debate was the expression largely within the scientific community of a broader, culture-wide dialectic between spiritualism and materialism.

Demi-immortal characters arose as an expression of Enlightenment vitalism, or of the form that it took in the early nineteenth century: Mesmerism. Mesmerism's new science of "animal magnetism" or "electrobiology" hit London in the 1830s, became a subject of intense public and scientific interest in the 1840s, and peaked in the "mesmeric mania" of the 1850s.[7] Demi-immortals embody and channel the "imponderable fluid permeating the universe," the "vital fluid" or "life force" (Tartar 4; Fulford 62). They direct it at will to heal, read minds, hypnotize, physically overpower without touch, or even shape-shift or transport themselves. In Bulwer-Lytton's *A Strange Story*, for example, Dr. Fenwick, whose own book manuscript is titled *The Vital Principle; its Waste and Supply*, practices mesmeric medicine, according to which the body possesses its own natural-vital healing powers that often are hindered by medication, but at the same time he denies the existence of the type of magical "vital power" exercised by the demi-immortal Margrave (103, 371). The novel struggles to reconcile mechanist science with spiritualist vitalism, as do most novels with demi-immortal characters. In Corelli's *Romance of Two Worlds*, the female protagonist is healed by vitalistic medicine that works by stimulating natural "human electricity," but one's physical vitality is contingent upon the health of one's "electric Germ of the Soul," understood as both an atom of the divine and a natural life-force (72, 249). Demi-immortal characters all struggle to reconcile the contradiction of vitalism, which they themselves embody, that it is at once spiritual and scientific, supernatural and natural. Thus, they oscillate between manifesting evidence of Spirit and the divine order of the universe and revealing the specter of a Godless and mechanically random universe. They channel Spirit but are spiritually alienated, their souls in jeopardy. The tie to the body that is the origin of their natural, organic vitalism is also the form of the materialism that prevents spiritual realization. This produces the contradiction, to which I will return, by which Dracula can be at once a numinous figure and utterly evil.

In *Dracula*, "the mesmeric and hypnotic world of Charcot is an open intertext of the novel"—referring to Jean-Martin Charcot, who along with Sigmund Freud introduced hypnotism into the repertoire of scientifically sanctioned psychoanalytic techniques (Wicke 485). The cliché of Dracula saying, in a heavy Bela Lugosi accent, "Look into my eyes" is grounded in Mesmerism and the hypnosis that it spawned. But then his opponent, Professor van Helsing, also uses hypnosis. One might argue that Dracula's much more potent powers are tied to an archaic occultism while van Helsing's is a modern scientific technique, but van Helsing himself collapses this distinction as he strives to convince his fellow scientist, Dr. Seward, that vampirism exists: "Ah, it is the fault of our science that it wants to explain all; and if it explain not, then it says there is nothing to explain. But yet we see around us every day the growth of new beliefs. . . . I suppose now you do not believe in corporeal transference. No? Nor in materialization. No? Nor in astral bodies. No? Nor in the reading of thought. No. Nor in hypnotism" (Stoker 191). After then praising Charcot's work on hypnosis, van Helsing continues: "Then tell me—for I am student of the brain—how you accept the hypnotism and reject the thought-reading. Let me tell you, my friend, that there are things done to-day in electrical science which would have been deemed unholy by the very men who discovered electricity—who would themselves not so long before have been burned as wizards" (191). Here van Helsing straddles the very divide between mechanism and vitalism, materialism and spiritualism, that Bulwer-Lytton, along with thousands of others of his time, did in thinking, "if electricity and telegraphy had recently come within the notice of science, perhaps telepathy and mesmerism would be next" (Mitchell 140). After all, "the electric telegraphy, invented in 1837, started the spread of metal nerves to transport thought electrically from one part of the country to another," and this appeared little less magical than mesmeric thought-transference (Winter 17). Thus, Jennifer Wicke has argued, "vampirism [was] a stand-in for the uncanny procedures of modern life"; Dracula's occult and vitalistic mesmeric powers in part mirror the modern, mechanistic powers of telegraphy, typewriting, and the phonograph that are instrumental in defeating him (473). But a crucial difference remains, which will require further analysis: Dracula's power is vitalistic and so spiritually infused, while that of his Christian opponents is, in specific ways, mechanically soulless.

## The Economics of Immortality in *Dracula*

What are the sources of Dracula's evilness? Though many others could and have been mentioned, at base there are two, one spiritual and one economic. Thus, as Franco Moretti argues, "other things are needed" besides modern, Western individualism to defeat Dracula: "in effect two: money and religion" (93). A good deal has been written about Dracula and economics, vampirism as consumption, and the circulation of blood and money, often drawing upon Adam Smith's "invisible hand" as itself a Gothic figure and Karl Marx's use of vampire metaphors in describing the extraction of surplus capital from labor.[8] Many have observed that Dracula is tied to—and tied down by—an archaic, aristocratic economy based on landed wealth, as signified by his incursion into the English homeland with fifty "great earth chests" of sanctified Transylvanian soil, and based on gold, as signified by the "great heap of gold" in his castle and the "'ting' of the gold" that has fallen from his slashed coat (Stoker 251, 47, 306). Dracula is "a true monopolist: solitary and despotic, he will not brook competition"; he is "gold brought to life and animated within monopoly capitalism" (Moretti 92; Halberstam 103). In contrast, his pursuers depend upon the fungibility and portability of paper money. As Mina Harker writes: "And, too, it made me think of the wonderful power of money! What can it not do when it is properly applied; and what might it do when basely used! I felt so thankful that Lord Godalming is rich, and that both he and Mr. Morris, who also has plenty of money, are willing to spend it freely" (Stoker 356). Rather than hoarding, which many have argued is Dracula's signature relationship to wealth, they put it back into circulation by spending and consuming. While he is an invasive foreign monopoly, they, especially the middle-class professionals among them, stand for the British free-market system. Dracula is "an image of monstrous anticapitalism" because he is a hoarder, and hoarding is evil to the extent that it signifies an older model of political economy that is antithetical to the free-market economics that was perceived as the especially British model and the primary source of present and future national prosperity (Halberstam 102).

Wealth is of course not the only thing that vampires hoard. They hoard life-force, vitalism, the pervasiveness of which in this novel signals Bram Stoker's debt to Mesmerism. Renfield, Dr. Seward's mental patient, as he begins to fall under Dracula's influence, becomes a "zoophagous (life-eating) maniac" (70). In one of his lucid moments, he says, "The doctor here will bear me out that on one occasion I tried to kill him for the purpose of strengthening my vital power by the assimilation with my own body of his life through the medium of his blood—relying, of course, upon the Scriptural phrase, 'For the blood is the life'" (234). He reveals a literalist naivety about what it would mean to be a vampire, although later, when he begs Dr. Seward to remove him from the hospital where Dracula knows to find him, he has come to understand that what is at stake is his soul. Seward unknowingly touches on this point about the soul when, earlier, the band of men are preparing to liberate Lucy from her vampiric state by driving a stake through her heart and he remarks about her tomb that it "conveyed irresistibly the idea that life—animal life—was not the only thing which could pass away" (197). In truth, the body, "animal life," does not pass away in vampirism; rather, it is endowed with demi-immortality, while it is the soul that in some unspecified manner passes away, or perhaps goes into unholy suspension. Dracula feeds on "animal magnetism" without exactly killing either the body or the soul of those who will become vampires. He hoards the vitalism of his victims, removing both life and, in a sense, eternal afterlife from progression. As a result, he is supercharged with magnetism. The vampire hunters realize, for instance, that "he can even grow younger; that his vital faculties grow strenuous, and seem as though they refresh themselves when his special pabulum is plenty" (239). Later, in trying to explain to his cohort how Dracula got to be as powerful as he is, Professor van Helsing uses a mesmeric explanation: "Doubtless, there is something magnetic or electric in some of these combinations of occult forces which work for physical life in strange way. . . . In him some vital principles have in strange way found their utmost" (319–20). Dracula is a vitalist, in the eighteenth-century sense, while his human pursuers are mechanists.

Dracula's vitalism also is the sign of his status as a numinous figure. Though it may sound perverse, he is the most deeply religious figure in the novel. His very being is tied to the history of Christian symbology—crucifixes, the Host, holy water, sanctified ground. His existence motivates his human opponents, the majority of whom appear to be Broad Church Anglicans, into archaic and largely Catholic behaviors and expressions. Van Helsing, who the text intimates is Catholic, recognizes Dracula's numinous status when he remarks, "For it is not the least of its terrors that this evil thing is rooted deep in all good; in soil barren of holy memories it cannot rest" (Stoker 241). Thus Dracula invokes the Eucharist when he says to Mina, before forcing her to drink blood (Lucy's and her own, indirectly) from an incision he has made in his chest, "And you, their best beloved one, are now to me flesh of my flesh; blood of my blood" (288). This is the "terrible baptism of blood" that creates a mesmeric connection by which she is "free to go to him in spirit" and he is able to read her thoughts from afar (343). Dracula, like Satan, is an evil indissolubly part of Christianity.

The second half of *Dracula* becomes increasingly religious. A pivotal speech by van Helsing ends in this way: "Thus we are ministers of God's own wish: that the world, and men for whom His Son die, will not be given over to monsters, whose very existence would defame Him. He have allowed us to redeem one soul already [Lucy's], and we go out as the old knights of the Cross to redeem more" (Stoker 320). The contest has become at once a Darwinian race between competing species and a trial between two forms of immortality: the vampire's vitalistic demi-immortality and the Christian death-and-rebirth. Van Helsing becomes impassioned enough to make the above speech by the fact that Mina, who is "infected" by vampirism, might live to old age in her own "sweet way" and find, upon death, which is "God's sanction," that she is not reborn in the Christian sense but rather rises from the grave as one of the undead (320). Vampirism observes traditional Western soul-theory, according to which death is the trigger for the separation of body and soul, though which of the two will partake of immortality is the question. And even vampires are not utterly damned; they still possess souls that might be redeemed. After Lucy has been staked, her betrothed, Arthur Holmwood, Lord Goldalming, says to van Helsing, "God bless you that you have given my dear one her soul again" (217). One might ask in what location and in what state of limbo has it been residing, outside of her body and outside of the gates of either heaven or hell? The Spiritualism movement perhaps had furnished an alternative location, the Spirit World. Mina says to her husband, Jonathan, trying to convince him that he should have Christian compassion even for Dracula, "Just think what will be his joy when he too is destroyed in his worser part that his better part may have spiritual immortality" (308). Indeed, as the stake is being driven through his heart, Dracula smiles beatifically. Until that moment, however, he has been the fierce disseminator and defender of demi-immortality, which, as a rival to Christian "spiritual immortality," could be nothing other than evil incarnate.

There is a parallel between the evil that Dracula represents in the economic realm and the evil that he represents in the spiritual realm. In both, he is a hoarder, whether of wealth or of vitalism. In both, he prevents a free circulation, prevents continued currency and progression, since either capital or spiritual capital, the soul, is held hostage. This suggests that the two evils are in fact one: Dracula's threat to spirituality *is* his threat to political economy, and vice versa. In classical economic terms, Dracula represents use value over exchange value. Whether in relationship to the continuous exchange of spending and consuming, which certainly by the nineteenth century had become a primary engine of prosperity, or whether in relationship to the exchange of mortal life for eternal spiritual life, Dracula represents the stasis of nonexchange. He is consumption without spending, withdrawal without depositing, which only depletes the market and violates its first, self-regulating principle of free exchange. As Gordon Bigelow observes in this regard, discussing John Stuart Mill's defense of individual-centered capitalism, the "point is that the progress from the feudal society described here to the wage labor system of industrial capital will obliterate the Count Draculas of every country, abolishing the tyrannical rule enabled by concentrated wealth and securing the power of all individuals to hold and increase their property" (50). Indeed, progress toward securing the power of all individuals to hold and increase property may be what is at stake ultimately, since in both the economic and the spiritual realms Dracula represents the demi-immortal's antiprogressivism, while his opponents might be said to stand for modern Western progress toward common human, as opposed to vampire, prosperity.

It follows from the above that there is a corresponding parallel between the two goods that the vampire hunters seek to preserve, the free-market system and the Christian soul—a point familiar at least since Max Weber. What is it, one must ask, that the band of vampire hunters most stands for and defends? There is no single answer, but determining which answer takes precedence has important implications in relationship to the novel's religious message. One answer made obvious by the heightened religious discourse in the latter part of the novel is that they are defending Christianity against an unholy alternative, which undeniably is true. Having acknowledged that, I now argue that this in fact is not their foremost motivation. I agree with Judith Halberstam that the "monster itself is an economic form in that it condenses various racial and secular threats to nation, capital, and the bourgeoisie in one body" (3). Responding in kind, the vampire hunters' primary concerns are first racial or species-based, saving the human race from a competing one; then national, protecting Dracula's "dear new country of England" from his invasion of it; then economic and social, protecting a British middle-class way of life (Stoker 25). Thus Jonathan comments to himself in horror: "This was the being I was helping to transfer to London, where, perhaps for centuries to come, he might, amongst its teeming millions, satiate his lust for blood, and create a new and ever widening circle of semi-demons to batten on the helpless. The very thought drove me mad. A terrible desire came upon me to rid the world of such a monster" (51). The first obligation is to stanch the spread of the economy of vampirism. The "unselfish" duty for which Dr. Seward hungers, the "solemn duty" sworn between Mina and Jonathan, the "grave duty" of van Helsing to violate Lucy's grave, and even the "men's duty" pledged to Mina to kill her should she turn vampire have more to do with these secular values than with sacred ones, though I do not mean thereby to deny the spiritual imperative as well (61, 104, 206, 331).

The conjunction of these secular motivations appears especially in the form of (British) masculinity protecting British womanhood. All of the above concerns converge into these two figures, the union of which signifies British middle-class society and its values of marriage, progress, and prosperity, as well as the future propagation of the species. Mina in particular becomes the idealized figure into which all other motivations are condensed, and that is why protecting her becomes the paramount objective for the men. They make their most solemn vow kneeling around her: "Then without a word we all knelt down together, and, all holding hands, swore to be true to each other. We pledge ourselves to raise the veil of sorrow from the head of her whom, each in his own way, we loved; and we prayed for help and guidance in the terrible task" (Stoker 297). With this in mind, it is interesting to note that as the climactic finale approaches both the technological innovations that have so preoccupied the novel as the signs of progress and the religious fervor that had seemed so important at certain earlier points fade from view, giving way to a domestic ending. Seven years after the defeat of Dracula, Jonathan focuses on Mina and their son: "His mother holds, I know, the secret belief that some of our brave friend's spirit has passed into him. His bundle of names links all our little band of men together; but we call him Quincey," the one of the men who died in the fray (378). Mina's belief in spirit is vitalistic or occult or spiritualist, not Christian. The male child, who signifies the triumph of human reproduction over the vampiric economy, has become the repository for all the men's vitality. This parallels the previous union of the men in one woman when they all become "bigamists" by joining with Lucy through collective transfusion to her (176). Dracula's blood at first defeated their collective blood, but in the end their blood wins out in Mina. The novel suggests that "the test of history's progress, or regress, . . . is the vitality of a masculine essence, expressed through the capacity for violence" (Bigelow 47). The men have saved human progress finally neither through technological sophistication nor through free-market economic principles nor even through Christian righteousness but rather through the animal vitality of violence. Dracula may be well-and-truly dead, but his vitality lives on in the men. Dracula's vitalism has served as a necessary transfusion for British masculinity.

## A Counterinterpretation

Dracula also has been a transfusion of vitality in the two spheres in which he appeared to pose the greatest threat, free-market capitalism and Christian faith. Countering my own previous argument and that most common among economic criticisms of *Dracula*, I now suggest that Dracula may be the truest capitalist and most independent businessman in the novel. He demonstrates how astute he is in business in his early questioning about the practices in England of employing multiple solicitors in different locations in order to ensure that one's operations remain unknown to any one other individual and entirely under one's own control. He asks his solicitor, Jonathan, "I could be at liberty to direct myself. Is it not so?" (Stoker 31). He is sophisticated in the way in which multiple times he arranges the delivery and offloading of his cargo (one might say "product") and manages to purchase houses (one might say "franchises") in strategically dispersed locations throughout London. Jonathan later remarks, "Everything had been carefully thought out, and done systematically and with precision" (226).

This reading of *Dracula* derives support from Catherine Packham's history of the derivation of Adam Smith's economic theory in *The Wealth of Nations* (1776). Packham demonstrates that Smith was influenced by "the new physiological theories of his scientific contemporaries," namely "vitalist physiology" (466–67). Smith thus theorized the economy as an organically unified natural system impelled by its own internal principle—the "invisible hand"—according to which "such actions, of adjustment and response to economic reality, operate like the self-regulatory efforts of the vitalist's animal economy" (Packham 476). Recalling, then, that the humans in the novel are the mechanists and that Dracula is the vitalist, perhaps the true representative of Adam Smith's "system of natural liberty" and individual competition in the novel is Dracula. Perhaps his human opponents condemn his economics less because they are aristocratic or monopolistic than because they are foreign and too fiercely competitive. The vampire hunters' economics are in this sense protectionist, the Corn Law of immortality. They would not and cannot compete with Dracula head-to-head, as Franco Moretti notes: "Yet so long as the conflict is one between human 'individualism' and vampirical 'totalization,' things do not go at all well for the humans. Just as a system of perfect competition cannot do other than give way to monopoly, so a handful of isolated individuals cannot oppose the concentrated force of the vampire" (97). But it is the humans who must be corporatist, and perhaps the novel predicts not a future of laissez-faire economic individualism but rather what was in fact the coming dominant order of monopolistic corporate-state capitalism. If *Dracula*'s humans in effect preach the free-market economics that was and is heralded as the true British form of political economy, they practice the monopoly capitalism for which they scapegoat Dracula. Dracula thus serves a dual function: as a vital stimulant to the masculine competitive forces of British free-market economy and as a straw figure for the monopoly capitalism that typically is blamed by national governments upon foreign markets while remaining unacknowledged as a domestic practice.

Dracula similarly serves as both a vital stimulant to Christian faith and as a scapegoat for its failure of spirituality. In the novel's first half, the faith of the human characters in the technologies of modern progress, the telegraph and the phonograph, supersedes their faith in the numinous, as represented within the discourses of the time by the spiritual corollaries to the telegraph and the phonograph, namely "spirit communications" and the human-to-human "communication without embodiment" of Mesmerism (Owen, *Place of Enchantment* 121; Peters 94). In order that the humans may come to believe that such vital forms of communication might still exist, they require Dracula. They require faith in the occult spiritual phenomena that Dracula embodies in order to see beyond their mechanist worldview. The first job of van Helsing, the Catholic among Protestants, is to convince his colleagues—and the reader—of the reality of vampirism. He says to Dr. Seward, the most skeptical because most scientific, "I want you to believe," and then defines "faith" as "that which enables us to believe things which we know to be untrue" (Stoker 193).

Truly untrue, Dracula is the vehicle for faith in the novel. As Beth E. McDonald puts the point, as they "confront the numinousness of Dracula, they must also confront their apathetic faith in God," and "the dread that the forces of the sacred feel at the numinous experience of the vampires reaffirms their need for faith in a spiritual existence" (90, 127). Thus, it is after coming to believe in Dracula that the characters explicitly reembrace their Christian faith. This is the cycle, as I discussed it in relation to Bulwer Lytton's writing, according to which the occult is invoked to revitalize the spiritualism of institutional Christianity, then must be denied as too far outside orthodox belief and ultimately too materialistic itself, as a result of which Christianity has been recharged to carry on the battle against materialism without further need for the occult. The difference between Bulwer-Lytton's and Stoker's time periods is that in the former this formula appeared to produce the desired outcome, the reestablishment of confidence in Christian supremacy, whereas in the latter the formula no longer seems fully convincing. The crisis in Spirit now seems possibly beyond the strength of orthodox Christian faith to heal, and the role of heterodox religion, occultism, seems more fiercely vital than orthodoxy can deny or do without.

As a result, the vampire killers appear to invoke Christianity most often in self-defense and in conjunction with secular interests, and the novel concludes by reinforcing its secular more than its spiritual values. The vampire hunters learn to be "a force of the sacred" only in response to Dracula, but then they "create their own brand of sacredness based on social, economic, and political values and draw on the occult only to reestablish that world in the face of the vampire's threat to their society and to themselves" (McDonald 119, 127). Not only is *Dracula* more concerned with belief in vampires than with belief in God, but even that belief also must succumb in the end to materialist concerns about the species, the nation, and the economy. Thus, the presence of Dracula functions like an antibody: it stimulates society's body's own vital healing power of Christian spirituality, but once the virus of vampirism is defeated that spiritual immune system once again recedes into the taken-for-granted background of the day-to-day economy of living. In the 1890s to 1910s, when church attendance "had fallen dramatically to 27 per cent" of the population and the "general *consciousness* of religious crisis" had become widespread and undeniable, British Christianity may have needed whatever revitalizing scare it might receive from occult spirituality (McLeod 172, 222). Vampirism provided that stimulus while at the same time serving as a scapegoat on which to blame what some considered to be the anemic state of Christian spirituality. It functioned as a straw figure drawing attention away from the fact that it is modern society's own mechanistic progress and materialistic prosperity that has drained the spiritual vitality from the corporate body.

At one level, then, the high-stakes drama in *Dracula* has nothing to do with vampirism. Rather, it concerns the relationship within modern Western society between Christianity and capitalism. Christianity appears to be given precedence, but closer analysis reveals the ideology of the preeminence of Christian faith as it rolls like a masking but semitransparent screen in front of the actual preeminence of mechanistic science, secular progressivism, and an economics based more on consumption than production. Spiritualism is made to justify materialism precisely by appearing to take precedence over it. Meanwhile, in the foreground, the dramatics of vampirism claim our attention like the magician's hands, or rather mesmerizes us like the hypnotist's hands. Through *Dracula*, the vampire becomes essential to Western modernity, serving, in its "thrifty metaphoricity," manifold contradictory ideological functions. It simultaneously throws into question and reaffirms both Christian faith and corporate-state capitalism. It appears to threaten both of those two primary sources of value, while what it really does is enact the apparent incompatibility that exists between Christianity and capitalism, indicating the ultimate hegemony of the latter. It expresses a shared human longing for a vital universe that is ecologically unified by a divine Spirit, and, at the same moment, it expresses the feared truth that such a universe now has been replaced by a humanistic vitalistic system, that of Smithian free-market economics, itself a screen for corporate-state capitalism.[9] What vampirism ultimately reflects back to its readers is the justified and inevitable necessity of their own middle-class, progressive, Christian, consumption-based society. As Gordon Bigelow argues in a related vein: "If vampirism is a way of thinking about life in an emerging market society, then it encodes the pleasure and terrors of this new market. For if a consumer economy seems to offer the satisfaction of self-expression through endless purchasing, to offer commodities with which to adorn the times and spaces of life, it also brings the risk of confinement and constraint in the workplace, the limitation of life's time and space," the price to middle-class citizens of the comforts of corporate-state capitalism (57).

Perhaps, then, the clichés suggested by the upsurge in consumption of vampire-series novels and films at the end of the twentieth and beginning of the twenty-first century speaks an uncomfortable truth: we have completed the trajectory outlined in *Dracula* and become soulless consumers, vampires of vampirism (and, even more recently, of zombies, another type of the undead).[10] Perhaps it is true, as is suggested in postmodern characterizations of vampires that no longer are concerned with the state of their souls, only with their eternally youthful and animally magnetic bodies, that the vital and the spiritual truly have been overshadowed by a mechanistic and material world that hypnotizes us with endless consumption of artificially eternal youth.

Perhaps, but I would rather end with the observation that it is the vitalism of the demi-immortal that gives vampirism its multivalent power and its attractiveness. At once perhaps more vitally numinous than modern Christianity and more vitally animalistic than the human body, the vampire continuously oscillates between being numinous and materialistic, spiritual and evil. The figure of the demi-immortal, rather than being either/or, is both/and.[11] It thus always threatens to dismantle the foundational metaphysics of body/soul, which, though immensely disruptive to certain established beliefs, might also, or therefore, be desirable. Embodied soul and spiritualized body, vitalism is what we crave. This is why vampiric vitalism continues to live with demi-immortal longevity among both the humans within *Dracula* and the humans who read *Dracula* and the plethora of spin-off vampire novels and films. Postmodern Western culture still hungers for that vitalism, whether it be the vitalism of demi-immortality or the vitalism underlying individualistic economic freedom. Dracula may be the figure of vitalism in both realms, spiritual and economic. No wonder so many twenty-first-century teenagers think they want to be vampires. Their hunger contradicts the ostensible moral of *Dracula*: that Christian spiritual immortality and pseudo-free-market economics must win out in the end over demi-immortality and supposed monopolistic economics. They have not won out. If recent sales of vampire novels and films is any indication, demi-immortality might yet attract more followers than Christianity, but, then, as I have tried to show, the two are indissolubly linked. Monopolistic corporate-state capitalism continues to use the ideology of the "naturalness" of free-market economics to mask its domination. Its vampirism, not that for which Dracula actually stands, has consumed us and attempted to turn us into insatiable consumers. If, as the analysis here could suggest, the human heroes of *Dracula* stand for a Christianity that has lost its spiritual vitalism and for a corporate-state capitalism that robs individuals of their self-determination, and if it is Dracula who stands for a living rather than a mechanistic universe and for individual freedom in the exchange of life energies, then I think I am inclined to side with the teenagers and the vampires.

In the late nineteenth century, however, vampires could not yet be both/and, not yet resolve the spirit/matter dualism that they embodied. Spiritual materialism was not a possibility in mainstream religion and culture, only in the heterodox and the occult. We have seen how fiercely the texts of Haggard's *Cleopatra* and Stoker's *Dracula* strove to realize that resolution and failed. They enact the intensity that had been reached by the end of the century in the struggle between spiritualism and materialism. Their texts reflect the intensity with which they strained to resist the attraction of naturally divine immanence, cosmotheism, or vitalism—all varieties of physicotheologies, as I analyzed them in the first chapter of *Spirit Matters*. That strain is signaled by how hard these texts have to work to reach the prescribed "happy endings" of orthodox belief and dominant social order. That those endings cannot contain their own unconvincing elements is the sign of how deeply late-Victorian culture longed to retain spiritualism within materialism and, at long last, to resolve that age-old dichotomy.

Part IV

# The Origins of Alternative Religion in Victorian Britain

Conclusion

# From Victorian Occultism to New Age Spiritualities

The issues and topics treated in the preceding chapters of *Spirit Matters* culminated at the end of the nineteenth century in the formation of a "new occultism, . . . the widespread emergence of a new esoteric spirituality and a proliferation of spiritual groups and identities that together constituted what contemporaries called the new 'spiritual movement of the age'" (Owen, *Place* 4). This book has studied heterodox religious and spiritual discourses throughout the century that, though perhaps diverse enough to appear unconnected, all shared in the formation of that "new occultism." The primary form that occultism took was as syncretic or "hybrid religions," such as the Church of Christ, Scientist (1879), The Hermetic Order of the Golden Dawn (1887), the Anthroposophical Society (1912), and most important in terms of its impact on other hybrid religions and on New Age spiritualities in the twentieth century, the Theosophical Society (1875).[1] Theosophy, more than any of these, gathered the strands of heterodox thought that I have been charting in this book, and so it will serve here as the exemplary case.

There were multiple reasons why the occultism that emerged at the Victorian fin de siècle was "new." In the first place, it proliferated new alternative religions that bridged Victorianism to modernism by defining themselves in opposition to tradition and orthodoxy, as alternative to "positivism, uniformity, bourgeois master-narratives, materialist progress and the Westernization of the earth," and thus newly modernist (Bramble 3). Hybrid religions defined themselves in opposition both to traditional institutional Christianity and to scientific naturalism while at the same time claiming key elements of each as foundational to them. They built upon the foundation of the physicotheologies that had arisen in Europe from Enlightenment Deism forward, as discussed in chapter 1, but the outcome was the emergence of a uniquely modern, Western immanentism, the belief that the divine is not transcendent of nature but rather is coterminous with nature. All hybrid religions drew upon the spiritual movements of the early nineteenth century—Mesmerism and Spiritualism (and, before them, Swedenborgianism)—but then superseded them by formalizing, to varying degrees, genealogies, doctrines, and institutional structures. All synthesized elements drawn from other world religions, ancient and modern, in particular the Hindu and Buddhist doctrines of reincarnation. In this, all learned from the discipline of comparative religious studies, which had formed around the 1860s, applying its historical and critical methods equally to orthodox Christianity as to other world religions. All responded to the profound impact of the Darwinian revolution, adapting to it in fashioning various adaptations of it, whether as progressive spiritual development in this life or as spiritual evolution over the course of multiple lifetimes.

At the broadest level, two central elements of the "new occultism" were most crucial in forming hybrid religions and in shaping the New Age spiritualities that followed. The first of these was the dissolution of the spiritualism-versus-materialism dialectic from which this book started. Theosophy and subsequent hybrid religions appeared to succeed, where two centuries of continuous theological and philosophical debates had failed—or because of them—in dismantling the perennial Western dualism of spirit and matter, soul and body. This was accomplished by positing, theorizing, and working thereafter to substantiate the idea of "spiritual science," work that continues in Theosophy, Anthroposophy, Scientology, and others in the twenty-first century. The way to this resolution had been prepared by multiple preceding events, including the following:

- the "science" of mesmeric medicine, healing the body by healing the "vital Spirit";
- the argument sustained throughout the Spiritualism movement that it was grounded in empirically observable phenomena, which launched the Society for Psychical Research in 1882;
- the theorization by F. Max Müller of comparative religious studies as a "science of religion";
- the observation common in the second half of the century that Buddhism was a religion and an ethical system compatible with empirical method and evolutionary science;
- the formation of modern psychology from William James to Carl Jung such that as it became increasingly scientific it even so never ceased being a "science of the soul" and a set of techniques for spiritual "self-help";
- and centuries of justifications of religious faith on scientific or Natural Theological grounds, which only increased with the advent at the fin de siècle of areas of scientific investigation that lent themselves to mesmeric or spiritual interpretations, such as electromagnetism and modern physics.

Even given these events, Victorian culture struggled mightily from start to finish but was incapable of resolving the spiritual/material dualism. That came only with the "new occultism" and its adaptations of what I have discussed variously as monism, immanentism, or cosmotheism, forms of holism according to which all things physical and spiritual are unified and interconnected in the divine–natural continuum of the universe, what Oliver Lodge summarized in 1905 as the "ultimate identity of matter and spirit" (4).

The second crucial element of the "new occultism" was the formation of a spiritually self-determining modernist subjectivity, an occult self. The historical origins of this type of modern selfhood are daunting to summarize, given that they include the histories of Protestant individualism and the liberal individualism associated with laissez-faire capitalism. Without attempting a genealogy, one can observe that a number of significant discourses concerning subjectivity culminated in the second half of the century. I already have alluded to several of them. One was the Victorian "self-help" movement, often associated with Samuel Smiles's *Self Help* (1859), which set the stage for the subsequent formation of Christian Science, followed by the American New Thought movement. This "religion of healthy mindedness," as William James dubbed it, would in turn provide part of the context for the formation of one major strand of New Age practice (and products), "Healing and Personal Growth" (James in Wessinger et al. 757; Hanegraaff 19). Another related discourse was that of the self within the new discipline of psychology. By the 1880s, the "new psychology" began to replace what had been called "moral philosophy" as the new "science of the soul," and by 1900 "the unconscious" had eclipsed "vital fluid" as a way of talking scientifically about the soul (Hanegraaff 491; Reed 82). The pioneers of modern psychoanalysis, all of whom had explored occultism, theorized models of the psyche as split and multiplied, as in Sigmund Freud's model of id-ego-superego. The dissection and classification of the psyche or self into technical-sounding components provided one model for the fragmentation of identity and existential alienation of modernist subjectivity. The founders of Theosophy in fact had preceded psychology in this, already having theorized a seven-layered model of the self, with levels ranked from the lowest, the purely material body ("rupa"), up to a three-tiered grouping that replaced the traditional soul and was crowned by "Atma" or "Spirit."[2] Theosophy's more general distinction between one's lower, mundane self and one's "Higher SELF," at "one with the Universal Soul or Mind" (Blavatsky, *Key to Theosophy* 132–33) became a standard feature within subsequent hybrid religions and, in the next century, within New Age belief.

These are among the discourses that conditioned the formation of the "radically privatized . . . self-spirituality" of the "new occultism" and then of the New Age, "a new spirituality that was intrinsically bound up with the self-conscious exploration of personal interiority and the modern drive towards self-realization" (Dixon, *Divine Feminine* 229; Owen, *Place* 13). This modern occult self was defined by contradictions. It was individualistic and self-determining in choice of spiritual beliefs and practices but also now a citizen of a new global spirituality that equalized and syncretized all religious traditions. It was powerfully capable of directing intention and practice to enhance its own health and spiritual well-being but thereby also subject to atomized isolation and alienation in a disenchanted modern world. It was purposefully evolutionary, motivated by a "vision of personal transformation" and progressive self-realization, and yet spiritual progress also was defined as surrendering one's self in order to realize collective advancement, both social and spiritual (Melton 46). The occult self was at once human and divine. As Annie Besant, a leader of Theosophy, put it in 1898, "Only as the Self that is god is unfolded within you, will the Self that is the God without you manifest to you the full glory" (*Evolution of Life* 15). If, as I suggested in chapter 1, a master narrative of Christianity is the story of the triangular relationship between the divine, the human, and the natural in which the extent that each is unified with, divided from, transcendent of, or immanent within each of the other two never can be resolved, then the immanentism of the "new occultism" settled this question by flattening that triangle to make each of the three identical to the other: human = divine = nature. This, however, left unresolved the tension endemic to modern occult subjectivity between maximizing the individual self and realizing the ultimate insignificance of that individual self as part of the interdependently unified divine universe, an issue to which I will return.

Within the context provided above, this chapter has two purposes. The first is to demonstrate the causal relationship of all of the issues and themes explored in the preceding chapters of *Spirit Matters* to the late century formation of the "new occultism." I will do this by showing that the primary leaders of Theosophy, Helena Petrovna Blavatsky (1831–91) and then her successor as the president of the Theosophical Society, Annie Besant (1847–1933), intentionally designed and built their new religion by drawing on precisely the elements that the chapters in this book illustrate.[3] The second purpose is then to sketch in closing where all of this led, tracing the causal chain linking those elements, their combination in hybrid religions, and the specific types of modernist syncretism and subjectivity that followed from them, one expression of which was the twentieth-century "New Age movement."[4]

## The Sensationalism of Theosophy in Contrast to its Real Purpose

H. P. Blavatsky, born in the Ukraine in 1831, was by the end of her life in 1891 a true international celebrity, of which there were not yet a large number. Her past was famously exotic and mysterious, in part kept intentionally so, with wide travel on nearly every continent and wide study in all things esoteric and occult, including claimed tutelage under spiritual masters in Egypt and Tibet. Initially an investigator and practitioner of Spiritualism, she recognized its limitations as a vehicle for her ambition and so cofounded the Theosophical Society with H. S. Olcott in New York, soon spreading it to London and the Continent and then settling it in India, its home office to this day. She was a driven, complex, and fascinating person whose life deserves and has received autobiographical treatment well beyond what I will offer here.[5] I also will not provide anything like a full history of Theosophy, for which I refer readers to the existing histories, nor provide full readings of Blavatsky's major works, though I will draw examples from them.[6] However, two preparatory points are necessary.

First, I am not concerned either with the several sensationalizing scandals that surrounded Blavatsky or with the question of the authenticity of the supernatural figures and paranormal events on the basis of which she claimed a transcendental origin for Theosophy. I refer primarily to "The Masters" or "The Mahatmas," the ageless spiritual teachers in Tibet from whom Blavatsky received the "ancient wisdom-doctrine" underlying Theosophy and from whom she persisted throughout the last fifteen years of her life to claim she received letters of instruction via psychic transmission and materialization (*Isis Unveiled* 2:99). In 1882 the Society for Psychical Research investigated the authenticity of the Mahatma letters and publicly declared them fraudulent.[7] This did not deter Blavatsky, or Besant and Theosophists to this day, from citing the imprimatur of the Mahatma letters.[8]

In Blavatsky's own spiritual journey, in which she moved from participation in the Spiritualism movement to the creation of Theosophy, she "traded up." She traded the table rappings of deceased family members for esoteric instruction by "demi-immortal Oriental" masters. She traded a democratically available spiritual experience for "the secret doctrine" passed down over millennia only by and to "adepts," such as Buddha, Plato, Jesus, the Mahatmas, and now herself. She traded a popular cultural movement without formalized doctrine or institution for a religion organized around the "study of occult science" as the ur-theology from which all world religions had descended (Sinnett, *Early Days* 12). On that basis, she claimed for Theosophy a historical precedence over all other religions. But she also understood that the competing religions (even Buddhism, in her inaccurate construction of it) relied less on history than on what most world religions claim transcends history: divine revelation. She therefore welcomed or invoked the Mahatmas as Theosophy's verifying miraculous origin. I would argue that she also understood the publicity value of both miracles and scandal, and that she used those among other strategies to promote a religion that she and her colleagues constructed less from divine revelation than upon the immanence of the divine in nature and in humanity, as I will show. The Mahatma letters are in one sense irrelevant to the extent that Blavatsky succeeded, whether despite or because of them, in her real work of founding a new world religion.

Second, Blavatsky's life's work, as she fully understood, was to found a new hybrid religion that could stand up to the patriarchal institutions of Christianity, on the one hand, and to the threat of materialism and the authority of scientific naturalism on the other. She, with a series of collaborators, designed and built Theosophy's historical narrative, spiritual doctrine, ethical tenets, social commitments, and cultural appeal. Her major works, *Isis Unveiled* (1877), *The Secret Doctrine* (1888), and *The Key to Theosophy* (1889), which constitute over three thousand pages, are the bibles of Theosophy. She launched theosophical journals in New York, London, Paris, and Bombay, and published, over the course of her career, an estimated one thousand articles in English, French, and her native Russian in these and other national periodicals (Zirkoff ix). Annie Besant followed her example in delivering hundreds of public lectures on Theosophy in England, American, the Continent, and India, many of them subsequently published, and publishing at least 654 works.[9] Most importantly, Blavatsky lived to the full the charismatic dedication that only a true believer can sustain, as did Besant after her. As a result of their work, in 1925, at the time of the society's jubilee, over fifteen thousand theosophical "lodges" were reported across forty-one nations ("Early History").[10] Today, at the Theosophical Society headquarters in Adyar, India, the American Society headquarters in Pasadena, California, or the headquarters at 50 Gloucester Place, London, large portraits of Madame Blavatsky peer imposingly from the walls. Few other Victorians, or people of any period, can be said to have founded a religion that continues to be observed by thousands of followers around the world nearly a century and a half later.

## Hybridity, Ancient Origin, Spiritual Science

I am not arguing here that Blavatsky or the other founders of hybrid religions drew ideas directly from the specific authors and works analyzed in the chapters of *Spirit Matters*. Rather, I argue that those authors and works participated in and contributed to social contexts and cultural discourses that directly shaped fin de siècle hybrid religions, most importantly Theosophy.

That having been said, Blavatsky undoubtedly had read the popular metaphysical novels by Edward Bulwer-Lytton, whom I analyze in chapter 2, and it is certain that she had studied all of the ancient and contemporary works of alchemy, esoteric philosophy, Rosicrucianism, Swedenborgianism, Mesmerism, séance narratives, etc., upon which Bulwer-Lytton had drawn in his writings, as well as those that postdated him.[11] Bulwer-Lytton provided a synthesizing methodology and a model, though fictional, for the religious hybridity that Blavatsky carried to realization as Theosophy.

Blavatsky additionally was fueled by the European encounters with non-Christian religions, which fully arrived in England only after Bulwer-Lytton. Thus, one finds in Blavatsky's books samplings not only from esoteric Christianity, Gnosticism, the Kabala, Hermetic mystery religion, alchemy, Masonicism, Egyptian polytheism, astrology, Norse mythology, and Celtic lore but also from Hinduism, Daoism, Confucianism, and Buddhism. This intentional synthesizing is evident in the global variety of the between 3,000 and 4,000 quotations and over 2,400 footnotes in *Isis Unveiled*.[12] The flavor of them is suggested by these few examples: F. Max Müller's *Chips from a German Workshop*, vol. 1, *Essays on the Science of Religion* (1867, a seminal work of comparative religion focused upon Buddhism), Louis Jacolliot's *The Bible in India: Hindoo Origins of Hebrew and Christian Revelation* (1870), Kashinath Timbak Telang's *The Bhagavadgita with the Sanatsugatiya and the Anugita* (1882), and Anna Kingsford's *The Virgin of the World of Hermes Mercurius Trismegistus* (1885). Theosophy took Bulwer-Lytton's syncretism to an unmatched extreme, and in this it is representative of late nineteenth-century and subsequent Western hybrid religions.

Blavatsky's purpose in presenting what appeared to be an encyclopedic genealogy of all religions and spiritual practices in human history was to substantiate her central claim that Theosophy was the modern transmission of the "once universal religion, which antedated the Vadaic ages" (*Isis Unveiled* 2:123). This armed her to claim that Theosophy represented the original spirituality foundational to all world religions: "What we desire to prove is, that underlying every ancient popular religion was the same ancient wisdom-doctrine, one and identical, professed and practiced by the initiates of every country, who alone were aware of its existence and importance" (2:99). This impulse to find the aboriginal source of all faiths had been modeled earlier in the century by Bulwer-Lytton and, more importantly, by the recently formed discipline of comparative religious studies, the works of which Blavatsky studied and quoted.

The final way that I will mention in which Bulwer-Lytton and others who shared his esoteric fascinations set the stage for Blavatsky concerns antimaterialism and the contest in the name of Spirit with scientific naturalism, as I have traced it throughout *Spirit Matters*. Bulwer-Lytton's mission had been to anatomize and critique the materialisms of his age as he saw them—aesthetic, economic, political, and religious. His novels demonstrate the efficacy of "esoteric science" while showing it to be profane when allied only to materialist ends. In this same tradition, Blavatsky wrote early in her career: "Our Theosophical Society should really have called itself—in the name of Truth—'Society of Those Dissatisfied with Contemporary Materialistic Sciences.' We are the living protest against the gross materialism of our day" (in Gomes, *Dawning* 6).

Following the examples of Mesmerism and Spiritualism, each of which claimed a "scientific" basis in empirically experienced contact with the Spirit World, Blavatsky opened *Isis Unveiled* thusly: "The work now submitted to public judgment is the fruit of somewhat intimate acquaintance with Eastern adepts and study of their science" (1:v). Those adepts had showed her "that by combining science with religion, the existence of God and immortality of man's spirit may be demonstrated like a problem of Euclid" (1:vi). Modern physics, psychology, and psychical research had failed to account for paranormal phenomena not because they are inexplicable but because modern science, blinded by centuries of religious prejudice, had fallen short of ancient science. Blavatsky concludes the preface, "*We wish to show how inevitable were their innumerable failures, and how they must continue until these pretended authorities of the West go to the Brahmans and Lamaists of the far Orient, and respectfully ask them to impart the alphabet of true science"* (1:xlv). The first volume then sets about showing how psychic phenomena and spiritual practices were codified in an "alphabet of true science" that was shared by adepts across the ancient world, ranging from Indian Brahmanists to Babylonian Chaldeans to Greek Gnostics to Jewish Kabalists to Egyptian occultists. Examples of such adepts had appeared as characters in Bulwer-Lytton's novels, as they do later in the century in novels by Marie Corelli, H. Rider Haggard, and others.

As Bulwer-Lytton wrote that supernaturalism is natural, that "magic (or science that violates Nature) exists not,—it is but the science by which Nature can be controlled" (*Zanoni* 225), so Blavatsky likewise wrote: "There is no miracle. Everything that happens is the result of law," and "MAGIC is an ultimate practical knowledge of magnetism and electricity" (*Isis Unveiled* 2:587, 589).

## Comparative Religion, Christism, Dharma

One might think, with reason, that Anthony Trollope and Matthew Arnold could have nothing in common with Helena Blavatsky, that their Broad Church Anglicanism could share no commonality with Theosophy, but this would be an incomplete understanding. It is true that Trollope and Arnold stoutly defended the Church of England and the Bible and that Blavatsky in one sense built Theosophy upon "hatred of Christianity," but the Bible of Trollope and Arnold was a far cry from that of the majority of practicing Christians of their day, Theosophy also championed Jesus Christ, and Broad Church Anglicanism participated in trends, which I will identify, that Theosophy then carried to an extreme (Prothero, *White Buddhist* 58).

I chose to include Trollope and Arnold in *Spirit Matters* because they mark the boundary at which orthodox Christianity turned to heterodoxy and approached heresy. They locate the interface at which devout Christians struggled to assimilate biblical historicism and Darwinian science without destroying their faith. Arnold also represents the home front of the world-historical encounter between domestic Christian culture and Buddhism. The latitudinarian Broad Church of Trollope and Arnold (which is not to claim that the two of them shared identical beliefs, far from it) accepted the historicity of the Bible, the science of evolution, and the legitimacy of foreign religions. Thus, some readers of Trollope found him "evidently more at home among the phenomena of unbelief, than among those of undoubting faith and obedience," and many of Arnold's readers found him to have betrayed Protestantism by putting ethics above faith and betrayed Christianity itself by adopting a " 'semi-Christian Buddhism' " (Alford in apRoberts, *Arnold and God* 42; Wace in Claughton 159).

Blavatsky carried these same trends to their extremes. She applied that historicism to critique the Old Testament and undermine its claim to originality, adapted evolutionary science to a theory of spiritual evolution, and not only accepted Hinduism and Buddhism but emphasized their historical precedence and influence over Christianity and co-opted their doctrines in building Theosophy.

Blavatsky followed Arnold's example in adopting the methodology of comparative religious studies. The founding tenets of Theosophy, summarized here by Olcott in 1889, reflect an egalitarian, global, and academic approach to religion: (1) "To form the nucleus of a Universal Brotherhood of Humanity, without distinction of race, creed, sex, cast or colour"; (2) "To promote the study of Aryan and other Eastern literatures, religions, philosophies, and sciences"; and (3) "To investigate unexplained laws of nature and the psychic powers of man" ("Genesis" 210).[13] Sinnett phrased the second of these as, "To encourage the study of Comparative Religions, Philosophy and Science" (*Early Days* 13). Blavatsky, like Arnold, had studied the writings of the pioneers of comparative religion, frequently quoting and citing works by well-known practitioners such as F. Max Müller. A primary strategy of *Isis Unveiled* is to use comparative analysis to demonstrate the debts of Christianity to preceding religions, with phrases throughout such as, "Let us begin by once more comparing the myths of the *Bible* with those of the sacred books of other nations, to see which is the original, which copies" (Blavatsky, *Isis Unveiled* 2:405).[14] Theosophy, setting the example for all other hybrid religions, drew upon the by then mammoth archive of religious scriptures and artifacts from across the globe that European empires had amassed as the source from which to select elements to amalgamate into its hybrid religion.

Trollope and Arnold, as participants in trends that characterized latitudinarian Protestantism at large, prepared a cultural opening for Blavatsky in opposing dogmatic theology and foregrounding the ethical behavior and example of Jesus's love and compassion. In this they participated in a broad nineteenth-century "shift of emphasis" across Christian denominations "from the death of Christ to the life of Christ—from a theology centred on the Atonement to one centred on the Incarnation—and a shift from the wrath and judgement of God to the love and Fatherhood of God" (Parsons 109). Blavatsky also took this trend to its extreme. She deeply resented the theology of atonement—sin and damnation/redemption—which she felt had been too much a part of the history of Christianity, especially in the Inquisition, and too frequently wielded against women. She blamed the God of the Old Testament as violently intolerant of the ancient paganisms that she intended to resurrect, and so she traced the genealogy of Theosophy to before the time when that patriarchal figure had been used to silence the divine feminine principle, the Goddess, Isis.

At the same time, however, she opens the "Preface to Part II" of *Isis Unveiled* by praising "the glorious example of that Prophet of Nazareth," then acknowledges that "this volume is in particular directed against theological Christianity, the chief opponent of free thought," but "contains not one word against the pure teachings of Jesus" (2:iii, iv). Though Blavatsky's Theosophy is unique among late Victorian hybrid religions in being overtly anti-Christian, it is like all others in being defined explicitly in relationship to Christianity and directed "toward the Western and particularly Christian World" (Neufeldt 235). It upholds the Christ figure, if construed as one with the true esoteric teachings underlying the ancient wisdom religion, which Blavatsky argued the institutions and dogmas of Christianity had suppressed.

Broad Church Anglicanism also de-emphasized an anthropomorphic conception of God and reliance upon miracles as proof of his existence in favor of a continuing strain of Natural Theology: an understanding of the presence of God in the order of the universe as evidenced by the natural, experienced rightness of conscience and moral sense—what I call "morality/emotion" in Trollope and what Arnold labelled "righteousness." This position, carried to its extreme, pointed to the conception of the divine as coterminous with the natural universe that is itself an inherently ethical order. This is the direction in which Blavatsky went, all the way to pantheist immanentism, which would have been anathema to Trollope or Arnold, though Arnold's ethical model pointed that way. One of the insurmountable differences between Blavatsky and Trollope or Arnold is that for them the natural moral order still issued from the Abrahamic source, God the Father, while for Blavatsky the Judeo-Christian tradition was indicted upon its own history and so could no longer claim that righteousness.

Blavatsky therefore turned Eastward to dharmic sources, championing as the moral system of Theosophy the Hindu-Buddhist "laws" of karma and reincarnation. "Law" was a crucial term that intentionally enlisted two registers of meaning: it at once signaled the "scientific" nature of Theosophy's moral system, its empirically validated basis, and its roots in a source more authoritative because more ancient, the dharma, which many in the nineteenth century translated as "Law."[15] The science that Blavatsky and her followers repeatedly referenced was the "law of evolution," refashioned as "the laws governing spiritual progress" (Sinnett, *Early Days* 31). "Is it too much to believe that man should be developing new sensibilities and a closer relation with nature? The logic of evolution must teach as much, if carried to its legitimate conclusions" (Blavatsky, *Isis Unveiled* 1:v). Blavatsky went on to develop a cosmology and creation myth drawn "from the esoteric Brahmanical, Buddhistic, and Chaldean standpoints, which agree in every respect with the evolutionary theory of modern science" (2:266). Karma provided a nonrandom and utterly just moral system immanent in the naturally divine universe, which she contrasted to what she characterized as the capriciousness and prejudiced judgments of Jehovah. Reincarnation provided the possibility of spiritual progression, "self-help" on a cosmotheistic scale. In one motion, she attempted to immunize her esoteric science using the most virulent strain of natural scientific materialism and to claim some of Darwinism's truth-telling authority for Theosophy. Enlisting both science and Asian religions became common strategies for hybrid religions.

I certainly do not intend to conflate Trollope with Blavatsky—a combination that must end with categorical if not explosive differences—but I do mean to argue that they were at opposite ends of a shared scale. Some of the constituting elements of the most liberal Broad Church Anglicanism reappeared later in the century as essential ingredients of Theosophy and other hybrid religions. Mark Bevir goes so far as to observe that, by the end of the century, "Even Broad Church Anglicans were immanentists who simply combined it with privileging of Jesus Christ as the embodiment of that immanentism and eschewing of Atonement theology for Incarnation theology, appealing to the evolutionary implication that humankind was moving ever toward atonement in the natural divine, building 'God's Kingdom on earth'" ("Welfarism" 651). Theosophy, of course, was considerably further along that trajectory.

## Orientalism, Woman-Centeredness, Spiritual-Social Reformism

The chapters in *Spirit Matters* on Knighton and Leonowens, set in Ceylon (Sri Lanka) and Siam (Thailand) respectively, trace the counterinvasion of Great Britain by Buddhism back to the sites of its origin in the colonial invasion of Buddhist countries. The works by both authors indirectly explore the struggle between, on the one hand, the Anglicist and missionary imperative to justify and spread British, Christian, Anglo-Saxon supremacy and, on the other hand, the Orientalist ideology of respect for indigenous peoples and religions (coupled with co-option of them for purposes that simultaneously served and undermined both British imperialism and those indigenous peoples and religions). Knighton and Leonowens each exemplify the bidirectional interpenetration of Christianity and Buddhism and point toward the subsequent syncretism of "Protestant Buddhism" in Asia and of Buddhism-influenced heterodox religion in Great Britain.

Theosophy completed this trajectory. The name that Blavatsky chose for the ur-religion underlying all world religions from which Theosophy was derived was "prehistoric Buddhism," and her Mahatmas transmitted their teachings from Tibet (*Isis Unveiled* 2:123). Through them she claimed privileged access to "pure" Buddhism, though she also followed the example of comparative religious studies in claiming greater knowledge of Buddhism than its indigenous practitioners: "When we use the term *Buddhists*, we do not mean to imply by it either the exoteric Buddhism instituted by the followers of Gautama-Buddha, nor the modern Buddhistic religion, but the secret philosophy of Sakyamuni, which in its essence is certainly identical with the ancient wisdom-religion of the sanctuary, the pre-Vedic Brahmanism" (2:142). Some thus came to refer to Theosophy by the title chosen by A. P. Sinnett for his popular book, *Esoteric Buddhism* (1883), though, as critics noted even at that time, it is a great deal more esoteric than Buddhist.[16] Karma and reincarnation became central doctrines of Theosophy, as well as of subsequent hybrid religions, though modified away from the Buddhist doctrines through integration with evolutionary science (Lamarckian rather than Darwinian) and Victorian progressivism, since "progress for Blavatsky is simply another term for evolution" in the spiritual realm (Neufeldt 248).

Blavatsky followed through on her commitment to a dharmic origin by taking Buddhist lay vows and moving the Theosophical Society's headquarters to the source of Hinduism and Buddhism, India (though Buddhism had died out in India by the fourteenth century or earlier). During her visit to Ceylon in 1880, she and Olcott became "the first European-Americans to formally embrace Buddhism," in part as a show of solidarity with Buddhist monks resisting Protestant missionaries (Prothero, *White Buddhist* 95). Olcott would go on to become the only Westerner to play a major role in the "southern Buddhist revival" of the nineteenth century and famously to author the "Buddhist Catechism," the "essentialized and intellectualized Buddhism" that "became the Buddhism preferred by Ceylon's emerging elites and [still] . . . dominant among them today" (Young and Somaratna 209). In India, Blavatsky and then Besant similarly built a partnership with the politically engaged and doctrinally purist Hinduism movement, the Arya Samaj, and in 1882 built a new headquarters at Adyar (Chennai).[17] Theosophy thereafter moved more toward Hinduism than Buddhism, though never truly either. Besant went further, courting Hindus in India as a primary audience for Theosophy and becoming a prominent spokesperson for Indian self-rule against the British Raj.[18] In sum, Theosophy brought full circle the bidirectional hybridization of Christianity and Asian religions initiated in the colonial Ceylon and Siam of Knighton and Leonowens and turned the face of heterodox and hybrid religions in the West toward the East ever after.

Blavatsky and Besant shared another defining motivation with Leonowens: social and religious equality for women. As Leonowens felt compelled to battle what she saw as the injustice of the Siamese *Nang Harm*, figuring herself as the protector of women against the specter of patriarchal tyranny, so Blavatsky read the history of Christianity as one of patriarchal suppression of the divine feminine principle within esoteric religions and physical persecution by men especially of women and children in the Inquisition and in witch hunts throughout European and

American history. She took upon herself the role of redressing that history. In designing Theosophy, she reclaimed for the divine feminine coequal status in the Godhead, providing "a theoretical legitimation at the highest cosmological level for mundane notions of equality between the sexes" (Burfield 36). Besant was among the prominent women's rights activists of her day even before she came to Theosophy; "by 1889, when she arrived at Blavatsky's door, Besant was in her early forties, one of the best-known women in England, and the most prestigious and powerful female orator of the time" (Owen, *Place* 24). Like Leonowens, she worked for women on practical issues such as birth control and school-board policy. She never ceased advocating for women's rights, if later more in the way of Blavatsky, for instance in launching the "World Mother" movement in India in 1928 (not to be confused with more recent conservative movements) (Dixon, *Divine Feminine* 207).

Theosophy therefore may be unique among religions in the extent of its egalitarianism. Its founding tenets, given above, explicitly decree against discrimination on the basis of gender, as well as race or creed. In its doctrine as in its leadership, it appealed for and to women. In this, it participated in what Joy Dixon has analyzed as a broader "feminization of religion" from the nineteenth century forward, but it also set a specific pattern of women-centeredness that has persisted in hybrid religions (*Divine Feminine* 67). A number of hybrid religions have been founded or led by women, including Mary Baker Eddy for Christian Science and Katherine Tingley in the American branch of Theosophy. Hybrid religions attracted and continue to attract a majority of women followers to the "unmediated access to spiritual truth and power, outside the male-written scriptures or man-powered churches" (Ellwood and Wessinger 76). In the twentieth and twenty-first centuries, "women continue to be disproportionately represented in the New Age movement for many of the same reasons that drew their great-grandmothers to spiritualism a century ago" (M. Brown 457).

More broadly, the "new occultism" not infrequently was associated with social and political reformism of multiple types. Many at the fin de siècle who sampled Spiritualism, Theosophy, or the Golden Dawn or dabbled in Asian religions also participated in socialism, welfarism, antivivisectionism, women's suffrage, Irish nationalism, Indian nationalism, etc. The "Victorian and Edwardian immanentism" of the "new occultism . . . underlies a definite, historical relationship between religion and social reformism" especially at the end of the century, when "it was considered perfectly feasible . . . to adhere to a communitarian vision and socialist principles while espousing a belief in an unseen spirit world, a cosmic mind, and Eastern religion, and many did" (Bevir, "Welfarism" 651; Owen, *Place* 25). The prerequisite for the syncretism of hybrid religions was an openness to beliefs and views not one's own, an interest in and tolerance of difference, the beginnings of the globalism of the "new occultism" and, what is more, of modernism as a whole. Occultism's immanentism, of a piece with its dissolution of the spirit/matter dichotomy, helped shape a pervasive subculture in which spiritual progress and social progress were considered part of a one-in-the-same divine unity, evolution in one domain causally linked to evolution in the other. For example, ethically motivated socialists at the end of the century, of which Annie Besant was one, "typically regarded the socialist movement, not as a political movement seeking power to construct a new society, but rather as a religious movement based on a spiritual ideal," the "moral idealism" of a less materialistic and thus more equitable and just society in the future (Bevir, "Welfarism" 639, 658). It is not difficult to discern the path by which this cultural formation at the fin de siècle later would become foundational within New Age religions, indeed as one vision of what the New Age itself would be: a more egalitarian, peaceful, and prosperous future for all beings and the entire planet. That view in part had started with Theosophy: "In 1911 members of the Theosophical Society believed that they were about to lead the world into a New Age, spiritually and politically" (Dixon, *Divine Feminine* 8). Thus, the "new occultism" contributed to the cultural construction of what would become a widely diffuse opposition position against the dominant ideologies of laissez-faire capitalism, classical liberal individualism, and the social Darwinism according to which might has the right to subjugate and profit from the "weaker" nation, race, ethnicity, gender, etc. Glancing back to William Knighton and Anna Leonowens earlier in the century, they well understood the potential oppression of dogmatic faith and imperial rule, and in their own complexly conflicted ways they were progressive activists for the religious and racial tolerance upon which the "new occultism" and Theosophy would contribute to building a more modern holistic worldview.

## The Goddess, Trinitarian Resurrectionism, and Spiritual Materialism

H. Rider Haggard's *Cleopatra* participated in the same discourses and social events from which Blavatsky already had drawn key components of Theosophy (or she had preceded them in her own scholarship): Egypt as the origin of the ancient "wisdom literature," as in Blavatsky's "wisdom-doctrine"; the figure of the Goddess, as in Isis, unveiled; pre-Abrahamic monotheism combined with more ancient polytheism and cosmotheism, Blavatsky's "ancient wisdom-doctrine"; and the trinitarian resurrectionism of Osiris-Isis-Horus, a source of the Christian Trinity, though crucially different in retaining the feminine divine. As Blavatsky worked to reinstate the figure of the Goddess, so Haggard's unconvincing recuperation of God the Father at the end of his novel makes his preference for the same clear enough.[19] As *Cleopatra* celebrates the Egyptian trinity, its promised resurrection through reincarnation, so Theosophy, even in its anti-Christianity, retained the Christ figure, the concept of Trinity, and the promise of rebirth, if through multiple lifetimes, as did most subsequent hybrid religions.[20] As the discovery of the pre-Judaic monotheism of Akhenaten threatened to undermine the Mosaic distinction, so Blavatsky intentionally worked in *Isis Unveiled* to do that very thing, as I have shown. Perhaps unique in the history of religions, Ancient Egyptian Atenism was both monotheistic and immanentist, collapsing the dichotomies of divine/natural and spirit/matter. As we have seen, late Victorian hybrid religions, starting with Theosophy, set about deconstructing those same traditional dualisms.

Both Haggard's *Cleopatra* and Stoker's *Dracula* are ultimately about the impossibility of dismantling those dualisms within the enclosure of traditional Western thought and Christian orthodoxy. The most magnetic characters are the unholy demi-immortal figures, with which Blavatsky's Mahatmas share characteristics. Each of these texts demonstrates, however ambivalently, their vitalistic attraction. Dracula's embodiment of the numinous and Isis's fusion of body and soul speak to a deep longing for what had been largely unattainable if ubiquitous within Western discourse: natural supernaturalism and spiritual materialism. Both point to an immanentist cosmotheism that is more directly in contact with spiritual truth than is the prescribed monotheism, perhaps even necessary as an antidote to that patriarchal order. At the end of the century, these texts also express exhaustion at the effort of maintaining the traditional oppositions of soul/body and spiritual/material, which they suggest may have reached, after nineteen centuries, a final collapse that not even orthodox Christianity can redeem. They each are haunted by an ambivalence about the current supremacy of materialism, both scientific and economic, and even about the shining future of the material progress that accompanied the financial, technological, and military supremacy of the British Empire (only a few decades away from its decline). These texts express a deep hunger for forbidden spiritual progressivism, for Spirit. Haggard and Stoker summarize the limitations of the spiritualism/materialism dialectic that I have shown worried the Victorian era from beginning to end. They represent the culmination of the nineteenth-century preoccupations that *Spirit Matters* has excavated. They diagnose the social and cultural conditions in response to which the "new occultism" arose, and they prescribe the treatment that hybrid religions, especially Theosophy, administered.

## From Hybrid Religions to the New Age

Having delineated the causal linkages between the diverse elements of Victorian heterodox religion and spirituality treated in this book and the emergence at the end of the century of the "new occultism," I now will outline the next step in that chain: the historical trajectory that links hybrid religions, especially Theosophy, and the formation of New Age spiritualities in the twentieth century. I then will close *Spirit Matters* by allowing myself several speculations about the ways in which specific themes of the "new occultism" not only shaped New Ageism but diffused throughout Western culture to become defining obsessions and contradictions of the modern era since the nineteenth century.

Historians of the New Age concur not only that its primary point of origin was the "new occultism" of the Victorian fin de siècle but that Theosophy in particular "stands behind much of what we now consider to be the New Age movement" (Bevir, "Annie" 63). The word "occultism" was coined in its current usage as late as 1876—the year before the publication of *Isis Unveiled*—and although there had been a rich variety of esotericisms in Europe for over two millennia, the "new occultism" was a product specifically of the Victorian fin de siècle (Martin 15; Laqueur 111). The *New Age Encyclopedia* starts its "Chronology of the New Age Movement" at 1875, when Blavatsky and Olcott began designing Theosophy, and Gordon Melton, one of the encyclopedia's editors, elsewhere states that "Theosophy became the seedbed that nurtured the important new movements that would emerge so forcefully in the twentieth century," ultimately spawning "several hundred new occult organizations" (Melton 40).[21] Most historians of the New Age also concur that it emerged only fully as late as the 1970s, although, as Steven Sutcliffe and others have analyzed, the American New Thought movement and especially Alice Bailey, a student of Blavatsky, and her Arcane School of the 1920s to 1950s first popularized the idea of a coming New Age. Wouter Hanegraaff distinguishes between the "New Age *sensu lato*" of the 1970s and after, the primary location for which is North America, and the original "New Age *sensu stricto*," which had "its roots primarily in England, a country where Theosophy and Anthroposophy have traditionally been strongly represented" (97). Significantly shaped by the culture of the United States, the New Age *sensu lato* thus varies in fundamental ways from the New Age *sensu stricto*, but "as far as the conditions for the emergence of New Age religion are concerned, this process was completed during the decades around 1900," and the full culmination in the 1970s brought little "*essentially* new" to New Age religion that had not existed in Theosophy (518, 521).

There is a significant body of recent scholarship on the New Age from which I will summarize freely here in extracting a consensus about its constitutive concerns and features.[22] Melton observes that "the prime word used to describe the New Age is holistic" (Melton et al. xx). Holism, the New Age expression of immanentism, is by definition monistic and therefore antidualistic. Thus it is "*against* the idea that human beings are alienated from nature and strangers in the cosmos; *against* human attitudes of domination and exploitation of this alienated nature; *against* the idea that spirit and matter are separate realities, so that spirituality implies an other-worldly transcendence of matter, nature, and the cosmos . . . *against* the overly rationalistic 'parts' mentality of traditional science, which 'murders to dissect'" (Hanegraaff 516). At the same time that it opposes scientific materialism, it insistently makes "use of science as a major vehicle for expressing its perspective" (Melton 36). The New Age inherited this paradox from the "spiritual science" of Theosophy and the "secularization of esotericism" that occurred when the "new occultism" syncretized science and spirituality (Hanegraaff 407). A second defining paradox, or contradiction, is that New Age belief is predominantly immanentist, yet New Agers have not entirely relinquished the hope that there is also a transcendent divinity or force that may intercede on behalf of humanity or the planet. This points to the most obvious feature of all—belief in a coming New Age, whether apocalyptic or millenarian—but also perhaps to a less expected feature: the predominant conception of the universal divine principle as "the Christ." Most New Age religions privilege the West and the Christian heritage, despite Theosophy's rebellion against it. Perhaps in contrast, another constitutive feature of New Age religions is syncretism, the same as that which generated hybrid religions, and, as a result, the integration of elements of Asian religions especially. Thus, it is very common that "New Agers answer the question of survival after death in terms of *reincarnation*," but—swinging back toward the West—they are less true to the Buddhist doctrine than to a combination of two dominant Victorian discourses, evolutionary science and social progressivism, such that New Age "reincarnation" signifies "progressive spiritual evolution" (Hanegraaff 262, 471). The centrality of the spiritually evolving being is a crucial constitutive feature. New Age "Self-spirituality" has been discussed variously as "the monistic assumption that the Self itself is sacred," the "new language of consciousness, creativity, and personal transformation," the "idea of '*creating my own reality*,'" and a culture that "has become obsessed with what the person has come to offer . . . the *value*, the *depth*, the *potential*" of the individual (Heelas 2, 21; Melton et al. xxvii; Hanegraaff 124; Heelas 160). Finally, the last constitutive feature of the New Age that I will mention follows from the previous one: the individualized, diverse, and diffuse nature of New Age practitioners and practices. This is a natural outcome of its alternativeness, its history of opposition to orthodoxy, and its resulting penchant for detraditionalization and deinstitutionalization. In contrast to "organized religion," New Age religion is intentionally de-organized.

It would be quite feasible to start from these constitutive features of the New Age, trace them back to the "new occultism" and hybrid religions of the Victorian fin de siècle, and then extend the historical lineage back to the heterodox religious and spiritual discourses analyzed in *Spirit Matters*, laying out a genealogy that spans two centuries. I leave this to future work or to other scholars. Instead, I will close by touching on three primary themes of the "new occultism" that not only have persisted in New Age spiritualities but still are contributing to pervasive discourses that characterize modern and postmodern culture and society.

*Syncretism*: The syncretism that generated and still is generating new hybrid religions "is the pluralistic and accommodatory opposite of fundamentalism" that, as such, "desacralizes the transparent assumptions of cultural supremacy" (Bramble 1; Bhabha 228). Syncretism makes it problematic to maintain a "one true God" who had chosen one's own people as more special than all other people. Syncretism occurs when two religious cultures interface, then interpenetrate. It happens historically without design. All religions that institutionalize do so through a historical process of syncretism, though the monotheistic world religions disclaim their syncretic roots by claiming origin in an extrahistorical event of divine revelation, as in the "Mosaic distinction."[23] Empire and colonization were in the nineteenth century the leading vehicles of religious syncretism. Comparative religious studies accelerated this process. Then, something new happened: H. P. Blavatsky and other leaders of Theosophy chose to design and implement an *"intentional programme for syncretism"* (Kraft 156). They chose to syncretize, and they chose diverse elements not only of religions and esoteric spiritualities but also of popular culture and ideology, such as evolutionary science, self-help, and progressivism. They demonstrated that syncretism "may occur between currents of one religion, between a religion and an ideology, between religion and science, and between religion and culture" (Droogers 13). Then (for many complex reasons that I am not taking time here to unpack), this program of intentional syncretism spread throughout Western culture. It became a defining principle of modernism, proliferating in psychology, anthropology, philosophy, and art, with growing implications for international business and politics. Thus, "the occult/syncretic . . . is as crucial to modernism as Platonism and high magic were to the Renaissance" (Bramble 134). T. S. Eliot wrote the most famous poem of the twentieth century effectively about that event, *The Waste Land*, which enacts that syncretism by combining bits and pieces from across the history of European culture with bits of Buddhism and Hinduism. Pablo Picasso integrated the facial planes of carved African masks, among other things, to create Cubism.

Carl Jung drew psychoanalytic research together with "esoteric traditions, Romantic *Naturphilosophie*, evolutionist vitalism, 'neopagan' solar worship, *völkisch* mythology and considerable doses of occultism" to produce his model of the modern human psyche, presumed to be applicable to all human beings (Hanegraaff 507; Bramble 33). "Humanity" and "planet" became more conceivable as wholes, with the potential for ecological holism. Then something even bigger happened: syncretism went viral when the bits became bites on the World Wide Web and accelerated toward infinite combinatorics and exponential growth. It became possible to draw together and juxtapose images and ideas of art, language, race, nationality, etc. from any and all places, cultures, and peoples on the planet. Syncretism that had begun between religions in the nineteenth century culminated in a defining process of postmodernism. Religious hybridity was the original type of global hybridization (in the sense described by Homi Bhabha). Syncretism was the product of, and has the potential to generate, globalization and tolerance of difference. The stakes of this inevitable cultural and social process are very real and profound, given that the alternatives are isolationism, racism, fundamentalism, and terrorism/war.

*Immanence*: Annie Besant, one of the authors of modern syncretism, well understood these stakes, speaking and writing as she did from an India torn by colonial violence involving multiple religions. She published *Evolution of Life and Form* (1898) to delineate the difference and the ultimate unity between "Life," the immanent "Force" of the "One existence," and "Form," the materialism to which some modern scientists mistakenly reduce Life and, therefore, fail to understand that the evolution of the human species is inseparable from its progressive spiritual evolution (24). Humankind (expressed in what follows as "he") could not reach this complete understanding "until he had learned that life was everything and form nothing—and that is the lesson which war teaches when it is rightly understood—until that lesson was learned, he was not prepared for the far harder evolution of the life, which is to master the lesson of unity beneath diversity, of love beneath antagonism, of being the friend of every creature and the foe of none" (118). This was felt and expressed similarly by Christian socialists in England at that same time, for whom, as William Jupp summarized in 1906, religion came to signify "an impassioned sense of the Unity and Order of the world and of our own personal relation thereto; an emotional apprehension of the Universal Life in which all individual lives are included and by which they are sustained; the communion of the human spirit with the Unseen and Eternal; faith in God as the Principle of Unity'" (Jupp in Bevir, "Welfarism" 646). This was immanentism at the end of the nineteenth century.

That immanetism became the "holism" of the New Age, and its primary sociopolitical vehicle became not socialism, which was and is too antithetical to dominant American ideology, but rather environmentalism, the green movement, sometimes infused with elements of Asian religions. Besant's "unity beneath diversity" became "the emphasis on unity-which-includes-diversity [that] is highly characteristic of New Age culture criticism" (Hanegraaff 34). That unity has come to include all difference, whether of nationality, race/ethnicity, gender or gender-identity, sexual preference, etc., and, beyond that, all sentient beings and the planet as a living biosphere. The opposition to that unity remains the same in the twenty-first century as it was in the nineteenth century: the traditional Christian dualisms that separate rather than unify God, the human, and nature. God made the earth for man to "subdue it" and "have dominion over" it, which the masters of industry and empire interpreted conveniently as a God-given right to the "power to control nature achieved by a civilization that had inherited the license to exploit it" (Genesis 1:28; Garreau 63). Even so, as strands of the New Age have diffused throughout Western culture and environmentalism has "gained much mainstream acceptance," orthodox Christians from diverse denominations increasingly have embraced "stewardship" of God's earth as appropriate "Creation Care," although at the same time they may remain highly critical of environmentalism when it takes on the evangelical qualities of a "secular religion" (Kemp 31; Garreau 65, 66).

One source of the evangelical impetus behind New Age holism is the perceived underwriting of environmentalism by certain doctrines of Asian religions that were more thoroughly absorbed in the twentieth century than could yet have occurred by the end of the nineteenth century. For example, the fundamental Buddhist doctrine of *pratītya-samutpāda* in Sanskrit or *Paticca-samuppāda* in Pali, translated as "dependent origination" or "interdependent arising," states, in sum, the ultimate inseparability of any person or thing from every other person and thing in the universe: fundamental and inescapable oneness.[24] One cannot do violence to others or to the earth without doing violence to oneself. This thinking disseminated across Western culture in the twentieth century, for instance through Thich Nhat Hanh's popularization of his Westernized conception of "interbeing." This is ecological thinking. One finds it in New Age theories such as the "Gaia hypothesis": that the planet, all of its processes biological and inorganic, including humans as one natural and potentially disruptive component, is an integrated and self-regulating ecosystem. That this concept was formulated by a scientist, James Lovelock, points to one significant change between the immanentism of the "new occultism" and the holism of the New Age. The latter is more supported by, if not integrated with, science. Thus the New Age has partly fulfilled the historical trajectory initiated by Blavatsky and Besant—or by the entire history of Western physicotheologies (summarized in chapter 1)—by continuing to close the gap between science and spirituality. The large majority of geoscientists and climate scientists support the theory of global climate change; whether they also entertain New Age spirituality or not, they add legitimacy to the arguments of those who believe that the "Unity of Self and world" is a manifestation of the blessing of natural divinity (Besant, *Evolution of Life* 20). The immanentism articulated in the Victorian fin de siècle has contributed not only to New Age holism but to the postmodern mainstream discourse of "sustainability," upon which hangs nothing less than the long-term survival of the human species, among others.

*Modern Subjectivity*: The architects of Theosophy wanted to unseat the dominant and historically intertwined ideologies of the traditional Christian soul and classical liberal individualism. Both appeared as oversimplified and reductive. Neither sufficiently explained the multifaceted complexity of the relationship between the self and the divine, on one hand, or the self and the social collective, on the other hand. The singularity of the soul segregated it from the communal Spirit and reduced the potential for shared "spiritual work" and progressive spiritual evolution to "higher" selfhood. Liberal individualism seemed, by the end of the century, increasingly atomized and autonomous, untethered from any reference either to the divine or to social responsibility, on its way to the self-determining freedom-in-isolation of modern existentialism and the un-self-reflective "individual freedom" of twentieth-century American ideology. In contrast, Theosophy strove to give depth and dimensionality to occult subjectivity in its seven-level model of the split-and-multiplied self, which also facilitated a distinction between the mundane "self" of the lower levels and the "Higher Self" of the upper levels. On the one hand, this system may appear to cast the individual as divine, the self-as-the-divine, as when Besant writes, "for the SELF of the universe and the SELF of man are one, and in knowing the SELF we know That which is at the root of the universe and of man alike" (Besant, *The Self* 5). This can and has been read, or misread, as making the Self the monomaniacal center of the universe, and there are strands of this in New Ageism.

New Age subjectivity, in its manifold expressions in the twenty-first century, is conflicted between self-as-the-divine and self-in-the-divine, Self and Unity. The "new occultism" had included both possibilities. "In proposing the immanence of the self-referential subject," the unity of self with both the divine and the natural, "the occult articulated a unique expression of both the modern drive for 'self-realization' and a contemporary impulse towards spirituality," a drive toward both Self and Spirit (Owen, *Place* 147). This pattern was augmented by the contemporaneous rise of the discipline of psychology, which made the interior seat of the soul the object of scientific investigation and lifted selfhood to a primary object of analysis and cultivation. This in part has defined the "Self-spirituality" of the New Age. Thus, Hanegraaff analyzes "*the psychologization of religion and sacralization of psychology*" as a constitutive feature of New Age religion (366), and Heelas's *The New Age Movement: The Celebration of the Self and the Sacralization of Modernity* argues that the New Age "is, above *all* else, about the self and its sacralization" (160). Heelas's subtitle reminds us that the sacralization of the self was a defining characteristic of modernism before the New Age "movement" existed ("the right to individual belief is the surviving—indeed, permissible—form of religion in modernity") and that to a significant extent the "movement" was a construction of twentieth-century American culture and its fixation on particular forms of individualism (Viswanathan xvi). New Age "utilitarian individualism," which believes "that something powerful lies within the person; that this can be tapped and improved; and that it can then be utilized to enable the person to operate more successfully in obtaining what the materialistic world has to offer," is more a product of Dale Carnegie, "prosperity theology," and corporate leadership trainings than it is of Blavatsky, Besant, and the "new occultism" (Heelas 166). But it is true that the "New Age movement is now a multimillion-dollar industry" and that not a few New Agers are justifying financial enrichment as self-realization, cultivating "spiritual" self-discipline for power over others, or just selling easy enlightenment to the growing hoard of seekers (Dixon, *Divine Feminine* 230). This is the self-as-the-divine side of the New Age, which for some obscures what I believe is the more historically predicated and authentic self-in-the-divine side.

Victorian Theosophists, in their social and political engagements, cast the individual as always part of Unity, social as spiritual. In the parallel example of ethical socialism in England at the same time period, "this belief in the universe as a single, spiritual whole encouraged the immanentists to call for a higher individualism proclaiming both that individuals must follow their own instincts in their progress toward God, and yet that individuals are intrinsically a part of a wider community" (Bevir, "Welfarism" 647). Likewise in the old New Age religions such as Theosophy and Anthroposophy, self always is a component of the Higher Self, and one's evolution toward oneness with it enables and is enabled by the evolution of all other sentient beings toward the same, similar to the Bodhisattva ideal of Mahayana Buddhism. Thus in some New Age religions, Engaged Buddhism, and New-Age-influenced strains of Quakerism and other liberal forms of Christianity, transforming one's self is but the first necessary step in transforming the world, inescapably so, since self and world are holistically part of a unified continuum. One's individual progress toward the divine—or toward Spirit, as some Victorians expressed it—only can occur if in unity with the progression of the community, the common good, toward a more compassionate, egalitarian, and peaceful world in a better future, a New Age.

# Notes

**1. Orthodox Christianity, Scientific Materialism, and Alternative Religions**

1. "Age of doubt" is a stereotype of the Victorian period; see for example Lane, *Age of Doubt*. For "age of agnosticism," see Schlossbert (275) or, in general, Lightman, *Origins*. For "age of materialism," see Foote (152) and, more generally, Fuller, B. Morgan, Vitzthum, and many sources in the nineteenth century that I cite subsequently. "Age of scientific naturalism" comes especially from Turner, *Between*; Dawson and Lightman, *Victorian Scientific Naturalism*; and Lightman and Reidy, *Age of Scientific Naturalism*.

2. I capitalize "Spiritualism" when using it to refer to the historically specific movement that began in 1848 in Hydesville, New York, and continued as an identifiable movement at least into the 1920s–1930s. Lowercase "spiritualism" signifies a much older and broader meaning. By the eighteenth and nineteenth centuries, it often was defined in opposition to "materialism." Long before the connotations of "materialism" as desire for material possessions or as "historical materialism" in the Marxist sense, "materialist" meant "one who denies spiritual substances," according to Samuel Johnson's 1755 *Dictionary of the English Language* (n.p.). In this sense, "spiritualism" was used most broadly to mean any belief in the existence of spiritual beings and states that transcend material existence.

3. This is the thesis of Franklin, "The Merging of Spiritualities."

4. Stanley defines "naturalism" most simply as "the exclusion of supernatural or religious matters" and situates it historically as "a distinctively British creation" of the nineteenth century (*Huxley's Church* 1, 2).

5. On Clerk Maxwell and the North England physicists, see Dawson and Lightman; Fichman; Heimann; Lightman, "Victorian Sciences"; Turner, *Between*; and, most recently, Stanley, *Huxley's Church*.

6. There are many fuller and more nuanced treatments of Enlightenment Deism; see, for a start, Byrne, as well as Lightman, "Unbelief."

7. As Turner observes in this regard, "natural theologians contended that the manner in which Europeans and more particularly the British could exploit the earth for its own benefit provided evidence of God's providential care for human beings and his approval of a competitive, commercial society tempered by benevolence"; they "plac[ed] Anglican theology as well as science on the side of material and economic progress and social stability," especially for the British (*Contesting* 104, 106).

8. Carlyle's *Sartor Resartus*, book 3, chap. 8, titled "Natural Supernaturalism," defines that concept as "this tendency to reformulate theological ideas (the Fall, redemption) within the realm of mind and nature alone—the human imagination becoming our means of salvation" (A. Williams 105). As Turner notes, "natural supernaturalism represented a new mode of natural theology" (*Contesting* 141).

9. One area that has received significant scholarly attention that I have chosen not to investigate is the relationship between aesthetics, the late Victorian Aestheticism movement, and spiritualism or the occult. See especially Levine, "Ruskin," or B. Morgan; also, for instance, DeWitt; Higgins; and Knight.

10. For a thorough reading of the relationship between Wallace's science and his spiritualism, see Prasch.

11. On the "secularization thesis," see Turner, *Contesting* 1–17; Chadwick, *Secularization*; and Lightman, "Victorian Sciences," which observes that "scholars studying Victorian science and religion in Britain began to question the conflict thesis back in the 1970s" (344).

12. Among many other possible sources, see Beer's groundbreaking work, *Darwin's Plots*; Lightman, *Evolutionary Naturalism*; and Helmstadter and Lightman.

13. I use "liberal intellectual" in the sense developed throughout Cottom, *Social Figures*.

14. I use the language of the "bride of religion" and the "groom of science" realizing that I am reproducing gender assumptions of the period that I am analyzing, but for that very reason: this is how many Victorians would have gendered religion and science. As Callum Brown argues, the nineteenth century witnessed a "feminization of piety" (and when, in the 1960s, women cast off the role of maintaining piety, Christianity in Britain died). If I am falling short of Dixon's charge to "find ways to write the history of religion and gender without allowing our analyses to collapse back in the Victorian binary of the 'secular man' and the 'spiritual woman'" ("Modernity" 212), I do so intentionally and with awareness that "woman" was not a monolithic category.

15. I place "discovered" in scare quotes for reasons amply explained by Almond.

16. The use of "law" to designate the dharma can be seen, for instance, in the title of Alabaster's influential 1871 work, *The Wheel of the Law*, and throughout Edwin Arnold's 1879 best-selling verse narrative of the life of the Buddha, *The Light of Asia*, which uses terms like "the great Law" (VIII.212). For works that equate the law of the dharma to the law of evolution, either criticizing or celebrating the "scientific" qualities of Buddhism, see Eitel 62, 66; Lilly, "Message of Buddhism" 209; and *Literary Digest* 162. For an analysis of the Victorian conflation of Buddhism and Darwinism, especially within Theosophy, see Clausen 7, and Bevir, "The West" 764. I generally have chosen to standardize on the Sanskrit rather than the Pali terminology for Buddhist doctrines. This does not reflect a preference but rather a practical recognition that a larger number of Westerners are more familiar with "dharma" than "dhamma," "karma" than "kamma," and "nirvana" than "nibbana," for instance. However,

and at the risk of confusion, in my treatments of Knighton and Leonowens I use the Pali terms because those authors' texts are set in countries where Theravada Buddhism is predominant.

17. Here I draw upon Bakhtin's concepts of the "monological" and the "dialogical."

## 2. The Evolution of Occult Spirituality in Victorian England and the Representative Case of Edward Bulwer-Lytton

1. I open with the now infamous opening clause of Edward Bulwer-Lytton's novel *Paul Clifford*. In this paragraph, I take the liberty of imaginatively condensing into a short period historical facts from Bulwer-Lytton's biography that occurred over a longer time frame. On the fair-haired boy's ghost, see Mitchell 147.

2. On Bulwer-Lytton's twenty-three-year political career, see Mitchell 88, 133, 188–90, and 211. In short, Bulwer-Lytton's politics, aesthetics, and views on the occult coincided: in all three arenas he professed himself a traditionalist or conservative and an elitist, believing always in aristocratic order, refined sensibility, and adept knowledge. He opposed the materialism and progressivism of his age.

3. Bulwer-Lytton's novel *Zanoni* opens with just such a scene in a rare-book shop in London where the narrator encounters an aged adept of Rosicrucianism.

4. This fact comes from Woolf 237. Other sources on Elliotson or his connections with Dickens or Bulwer-Lytton include Kaplan; Willis 96; and Winter 59.

5. On Martineau's connection with Bulwer-Lytton, see Winter 221 and Wolff 235. Martineau had been so impressed with *Zanoni* that she wrote a celebratory summary of it that came to be published as an appendix to the novel.

6. All references to Theosophy are to the Theosophical Society International, which should not be confused with the Theosophical Society Pasadena. My primary sources on Theosophy and Blavatsky are those by Blavatsky; Olcott; and Sinnett, *The Early Days of Theosophy in Europe*. Useful secondary sources include Bevir, "The West Turns Eastward"; Dixon, *Divine Feminine*; Godwin; Mead; Prothero, *The White Buddhist*; and Washington. On Bulwer-Lytton's influence on Blavatsky, see Christensen 234; Mitchell 149; and Wolff 186.

7. "Mesmeric mania" is from the title of Bennett's *Mesmeric Mania of 1851* (1851), from which Kaplan derived his essay's title, "'The Mesmeric Mania,'" and Winter uses the phrase "Mesmerism Mania" throughout her book.

8. Among the most significant of these for the popularization of Mesmerism were Elliotson, *An Introduction to the Study of Animal Magnetism* (1840); Townshend, *Facts in Mesmerism* (1840); and Martineau, *Letters on Mesmerism* (1845). Other influential sources include Jung-Stilling; Colquhoun; Dupotet [De Sennevoy]; Braid; and Esdaile.

9. The histories to which I allude are Darnton; Tartar; Willis; and Winter.

10. Spiritualist practice was highly diverse and only ever partially codified or institutionalized, which permitted a critic of the movement such as Davis in 1875 to summarize it reductively: "It is simply a belief, first, that man has a Spirit; second, that this Spirit lives after death; third, that it can hold intercourse with human beings on earth" (5).

11. The studies of Spiritualism to which I allude are those by Brandon; Goldfarb and Goldfarb; Noakes; Oppenheim; Owen, *The Darkened Room*; Tromp; and Wilburn. Nineteenth-century histories and studies include W. Carpenter; Doyle; Podmore; Robertson; Sargent; and Tuttle.

12. My sources on women and nineteenth-century spiritualisms include those by Braude; Burfield; Dixon, especially *Divine Feminine*; Ellwood and Wessinger; Oppenheim; and Tromp.

13. As Podmore argued in 1902, "historically, moreover, Spiritualism is the direct outgrowth of Animal Magnetism" (xiv). Oppenheim notes that "Mesmerism expanded effortlessly into spiritualism for a rich variety of reasons, not the least important of which was

the combination of scientific, religious, and occult sources on which both movements drew" (222).

14. Christensen quotes from Bulwer-Lytton's "Art of Fiction." Bulwer-Lytton was well aware that the Gothic romance, like romance in general, was in direct competition with realism and that it was criticized as morally irresponsible in its failure to portray social and emotional life realistically. He one-upped such criticisms by claiming for his fiction a more noble and necessary mission to represent spiritual, not material, reality.

15. The "demi-immortal oriental," theorized in Franklin, *Lotus*, is a nineteenth-century character type that possesses indefinite bodily or material longevity, derived from an "Eastern" source, but whose spiritual immortality is thereby placed in jeopardy. As an alternate form of immortality, it poses a threat to the traditional Judeo-Christian soul and afterlife. Vampires are a prime example.

16. On Natural Supernaturalism, see Carlyle's *Sartor Resartus*. Carlyle in fact wrote to Bulwer-Lytton that *Zanoni* "will be a liberating voice for much that lay dumb imprisoned in many human souls" (in Christensen 80).

17. See Braid's *Neurypnology* (1843) for his theorization of hypnotism.

18. The landmark "argument from design" within Natural Theology is most famously articulated by Paley.

19. My primary source on the 1851 census is McLeod.

20. Wilburn, *Possessed Victorians*, provides a counterpoint to my argument here. She develops the concept of "possessed individualism" to describe an alternative among practitioners of spiritualism and in the novels of certain authors to the liberal "possessive individualism" that is more akin to the endpoint of Protestant individualism that I find to have been more pervasive in Victorian culture.

21. On Rosicrucianism in Bulwer-Lytton, see J. Coates as well as Findlay. In arguing against the centrality of Rosicrucianism to *Zanoni*, I am siding against J. Coates and Findlay with Wolff 163–65, 183–85, and 233.

22. "Theurgy," according to the *Encyclopedia of Religion*, "refers to actions that induce or bring about the presence of a divine or supernatural being"; "it is distinguished from ordinary magical practice less by its techniques than by its aim, which was religious (union with the divine) rather than secular," in other words, spiritual rather than material (Norris 9156).

23. For consideration of the relationship between Bulwer-Lytton's aesthetics and spiritualism, see G. Budge, "Mesmerism" 47, and Fradin 15. Cottom develops the point that "art came to be the legitimate supernatural in that it was understood to be the proper medium for the exercise of the powers traditionally attributed to the supernatural" (*Abyss of Reason* 94).

24. The figure of the "demi-immortal oriental" multiples in the twentieth century in early horror cinema, followed by superhero cinema and films in the subgenre I call martial-arts-Buddhism, which include *Star Wars* (1977), *The Matrix* (1999), *Crouching Tiger, Hidden Dragon* (2000), *The Last Samurai* (2003), and *Bullet-Proof Monk* (2003), among many others.

### 3. Anthony Trollope's Religion

1. apRoberts makes a similar observation: "It seems surprising at first, for an author who writes so much about the clergy and politicians and lawyers, about what seem to be actual affairs, that one is puzzled to define his position" ("Introduction" 13).

2. For an introduction to the religious context of nineteenth-century England and the delineation of High Church, Low Church, and Broad Church positions within the Church of England (Anglicanism), see Jay; McLeod; and Parsons.

3. Mullen and Munson observe in this regard: "Trollope's novels do not discuss an individual's private religious life or, normally, religious belief and hence some have concluded that Trollope lacked firm religious belief. What he lacked was the ability glibly to discuss such things in fiction" (433).

4. The Ecclesiastical Commission had been launched in 1836 to regulate the distribution of the "11,600 total benefices in England and Wales" and to correct the excesses and inequalities of the patronage system by which they were distributed to clergy (Melnyk 7). The most common "abuses" were nepotism (favoritism in distributing incumbencies), pluralities (clergy holding multiple incumbencies), and absenteeism (clergy not in residence at one of their held parishes), all of which Trollope's novels incorporate into their plots.

5. This is not to mention a broader array of challenges to Christianity in general, including the emergence for the first time of public atheism, for instance in the 1844 founding of the British Anti-State-Church Association or "Liberation Society," and the 1851 Census of Religious Worship, which found that only 51 percent of those who attended services reported themselves to be Anglicans, establishing "the impossibility of treating the establishment as privileged on the ground that it was the church of the immense majority of the country" (Chadwick, *Victorian Church* 151, 369).

6. Early to mid-Victorian evangelicals "placed a stress on personal religion, the state of an individual's soul, and the relation of the individual to the atoning death of Christ," as well as on the literalness of the Bible and an evangelical mission (Shea and Whitla 7). Not all of Trollope's evangelical characters are represented unfavorably. Mr. Saul in *The Claverings* (1867) is one among several examples of a sympathetic evangelical (apRoberts, "Introduction" 30). Trollope later even defended Mrs. Proudie as "conscientious, by no means a hypocrite, really believing in the brimstone which she threatened, and anxious to save the souls around her from its horrors" (*Autobiography* 276).

7. The High Church "stressed the historic institution of the church, its hierarchy and sacraments, and was bound to the Tories" (Shea and Whitla 7). Critics who argue that Trollope was a High Churchman include Bankert (153) and Mullen and Munson (78). Trollope's mother, Fanny, "belonged to the same church as Mrs Grantly in *Barchester Towers*: 'the high and dry church, the High Church as it was some fifty years since, before tracts were written and young clergymen took upon themselves the highly meritorious duty of cleaning churches'" (Neville-Sington 254). His sister, Cecilia, was a Puseyite—a follower of Oxford movement leader Edward Pusey—and Anthony had personal connections with Pusey and other Anglo-Catholics, which contextualizes his sympathetic portrayal of Mr. Arabin's struggle in *Barchester Towers*.

8. Letwin's observation in this regard, if a bit overstated, is relevant: "Indeed all of the controversies, whether between the high and the high and dry Church, or between high and low churchman, whether about chanted services and intoned prayers, genuflection and the length of sermons, lecterns and credence tables, candles and embroidered alter cloths, are treated as something of a joke" (232).

9. Markwick is guided by Vance, who writes, for example, that Victorians in this tradition loathed "the 'Manichee' contempt of the world characteristic both of the older generation of Evangelicals and of Newman and the Tractarians [that] tended to involve a rejection of ordinary human nature 'in the flesh,' a rejection of everyday human society as the proper sphere of Christian activity, and a rejection of the physical world as of no consequence in comparison with the heavenly world which forms the goal of Christian aspiration" (Vance 31–32).

10. Thus Mayne, writing in 1998 as the former dean of Westminster Abbey, described Trollope as possessing "what one might call the defining marks of Anglicanism: tolerance

within a broad spectrum of belief and interpretation; a high regard for the individual conscience; moderation in face of extremism; a recognition that truth may sometimes lie in both extremes rather than somewhere in between" (xii). It also may be that Mayne is projecting his late twentieth-century, Broad Church–derived assumptions back upon Trollope.

11. As Kimball observes in this regard: "Many modern commentators, reading themselves back into Trollope, have depicted him as a kind of closet atheist. But . . . this is to misunderstand the complexity of Trollope's situation and the religious milieu of his time. Whatever religious doubts Trollope entertained, they did not capsize his spiritual equanimity. And why should they have? We may be reasonably certain he would have regarded the deliberate *cultivation* of doubt—something we take more or less for granted—as a culpable self-indulgence" (n.p.).

12. I speculate that the Broad Church gentleman's avoidance of public displays of "strong religious emotions" parallels the Oxford movement's "'doctrine of reserve,' best described in Tract 80, which held that some spiritual truths should not be communicated promiscuously to the uninitiated" (Melnyk 24), and may be a historical residue of the lesson from the centuries of religious violence of the Reformation and the Jacobite rebellions that it may be best for civility and order to hold one's peace on issues of faith.

13. A relevant counterpoint, observed by Cockshut, is that the majority of Protestants in England did not agree that traditional Christian doctrine might be reduced to "a matter of common sense and the gentlemanly virtues" and "agreed in rejecting the [*Essays and Reviews*] essayists' implicit claim that Christianity was largely to be understood as a great civilizing force, akin to benevolence, scholarship, and higher education" (84, 85).

14. Another insightful treatment of the figure of the gentleman in Trollope is Gilmour, especially in reference to *The Vicar of Bullhampton* on 152–56.

15. Kincaid observes in the same vein that "the Vicar is certainly Trollope's most explicitly religious figure and this novel his most radical statement on the uses of Christianity" (155).

16. On Trollope's treatment of fallen women, see Morse, *Women*.

17. As Trollope similarly wrote elsewhere, "In regard to a sin common to the two sexes, almost all the punishment and all the disgrace is heaped upon the one who in nine cases out of ten has been the least sinful" (*Autobiography* 333).

18. Trollope acknowledged that he "worked always on Sundays,—as to which no scruple of religion made me unhappy" (*Autobiography* 277). Also see the article he published in *The Fortnightly Review* titled "The Fourth Commandment."

19. The Broad Church compromise may have echoed the Tudor settlement between church and state at the founding of the Church of England, a "complicated compromise in which the Crown assumed responsibilities for the appointment of archbishops and bishops under specified conditions, and they in turn have places in the civil government in the House of Lords" (Shea and Whitla 76). The working out of the resulting conflicts between church and state is present behind all of Trollope's writings about clergymen, from Mr. Harding's wardenship to Rev. Crawley's curacy to Fenwick's right to the land that the marquis has given to the Methodists.

20. There is a more specific parallel between Carry and Mary (as their names imply), and Trollope's complex and subtle point is this: the fact that Carry has committed a sin of passion and perhaps love (and that Fenwick's motivations in relation to her are mixed for those reasons), does not mean that Mary should not marry with consideration for passion and love but rather that she should do just that. This is the Trollopian dialectic.

21. For some nineteenth-century conceptions of fully "modern Christianity," see Patterson; Sabatier; and Walker.

## 4. The Influences of Buddhism and Comparative Religion on Matthew Arnold's Theology

1. For an introduction to the religious context of nineteenth-century England and the delineation of High Church, Low Church, and Broad Church positions within the Church of England (Anglicanism), see Jay; McLeod; and Parsons.

2. As Müller observed in 1867, "the real beginning of an historical and critical study of the doctrines of Buddha dates from the year 1824" when Brian Houghton Hodgson published "the fact that the original documents of the Buddhist canon had been preserved in Sanskrit in the monasteries of Nepal" (*Chips* 189). Among the best secondary background studies for the subject area of this essay are Almond; Lopez, *Curators*; and Schwab.

3. A search of the Periodicals Content Index database for articles published with "Buddha" or "Buddhism" in the title reveals this pattern: 3 in the period 1841–50; 0 in 1851–60; 13 in 1861–70; 74 in 1871–80; 148 in 1881–90; 367 in 1891–1900; 287 in 1901–10; and 243 in 1911–20.

4. I derive this point from Almond, whose premise is summed up as follows: "Originally existing 'out there' in the Oriental *present*, Buddhism came to be determined as an object the primary location of which was the West, through the progressive collection, translation, and publication of its textual *past*" (13).

5. On the Victorian "Aryan question," see, among nineteenth-century sources, Huxley, *Aryan Question*; Müller, *Lectures* 31; Oldenberg 5; T. W. Rhys Davids, *Buddhism: Being* 22, and *Lectures* 23; and, among more recent sources, Bishop 120, 290–95; Davies; and van der Veer 50, 134–41.

6. For representative examples, see Müller, *Chips* 220, and T. W. Rhys Davids, *Buddhism: Being* 80.

7. As T. W. Rhys Davids summarized this point: "such questions as—What shall I be during the ages of the future? . . . [or] This is being: Whence did it come? And wither will it go?—are regarded as worse than unprofitable, and the Buddha not only refused to discuss them, but held that the tendency, the desire to discuss them as a weakness, and that the answers usually given were delusion" (*Buddhism, Its* 210).

8. For Arnold's uses and citations of Burnouf, see Arnold, *Literature and Dogma* 239, 272, 333; Arnold, *Letters*, Lang, vol. 1, 365, 375; and Arnold, *Note-books* 486, 495. On Arnold and Barthélemy-Saint-Hilaire, see Arnold, *Unpublished Letters* 43, or *Complete Prose Works* 518–19. Secondary sources on this include apRoberts, *Arnold and God* 85, 203; Jarrett-Kerr, "Arnold" 135–36, 142; and Whitlark 9.

9. On Buddhism in relationship to Arnold's poems, see Honan; Jarrett-Kerr, "Arnold versus the Orient"; McGhee; and Whitlark.

10. Arnold's attraction to Buddhist morality is further evidenced by the fact that in his *Note-books* he recorded the following passage from Burnouf's translation of the Lotus Sūtra (translated here from the French by my wife, Judith C. Lucas): "The perfection of courage or energy 'conducts through the perfect maturity of the indolent being' and revives in him all of the languishing (or pining) seeds (or semen) of virtue. The perfection causes him to travel through 'these desert regions and these sterile lands empty (or void) of all merit (or worth)'; this perfection causes him to cultivate the fecund (or fertile) seeds that the practice of duty deposits always in the heart of being gifted in morality (or morally gifted)" (486). The focus of this passage is virtue, duty, and morality, in short, righteousness.

11. On the nineteenth-century nirvana debate, see Droit; Franklin, *Lotus*; and Welbon.

12. For one representative example of contemporary criticisms of *Literature and Dogma*, in part for reducing religion to morality, see Traill.

13. Thus Arnold writes dismissively: "now comes M. Émile Burnouf, the accomplished kinsman of the gifted orientalist Eugène Burnouf, and will prove to us in a thick volume that the oracles of God were not committed to a Semitic race at all, but to the Aryan" (*Literature and Dogma* 239). He sees a link between the undesirably metaphysical elements he finds in the Gospels and Eastern influence: "And undoubtedly the writer of the Fourth Gospel seems to have come into contact, in Asia or Egypt, with Aryan metaphysics whether from India or Greece" (272). But his ultimate judgment is here: "but with this natural bent in the authorities of the University of Cambridge, and in the Indo-European race to which they belong, where would they be now if it had not been for Israel, and for the stern check which Israel put upon the glorification and divinization of this natural bent of mankind" toward metaphysics, miracles, and dogma (187).

14. For representative Victorian descriptions of Buddhist self-renunciation as too extreme, see Eitel 78–84, and Monier-Williams 558. Many other examples exist.

15. The circle of influence began to close earlier in 1870 when an anonymous author of a review of Alabaster's *Wheel of the Law* published in *Littell*'s *Living Age* titled the piece "A Buddhist 'Matthew Arnold,'" comparing a Siamese Buddhist, Chao Phya Thipakon, to Arnold.

## 5. Interpenetration of Religion and National Politics in Great Britain and Sri Lanka

1. I place "discovered" in scare quotes for reasons amply explained by Almond. I analyze the appropriation of Buddhism in colonial contexts in Franklin, *Lotus* 4–9.

2. My sources on the Sinhalese Buddhist revival of the nineteenth century include De Silva; Harris; Prothero, *The White Buddhist*; and Young and Somaratna. Malalgoda is one of the most authoritative sources.

3. According to Harris, "Protestant Buddhism" first was theorized in 1970 by Obeyesekere as "the form of Buddhism that arose in Sri Lanka in the latter part of the nineteenth century as a response to Christian missionary activity" (6–7). The more recent, partially synonymous term is "Buddhist modernism," as in McMahan's *The Making of Buddhist Modernism*. See Harris 168 for a fuller definition of the features of Protestant Buddhism.

4. For a contrasting perspective on Orientalism to van der Veer's, see Suleri.

5. For examples of what I am calling the "colonialist's owner's manual" genre, see the works by E. Carpenter; Percival; Sirr; and Tennent, *Ceylon*.

6. The more usual definition of "Mudaliar" or "Mudliyar" is as minister or chief. Gooneratne defines "Mudaliyars" as "leaders of the low-country Sinhalese society" (*English Literature* xiv). I focus here on Marandhan, recognizing that the figure of Hormanjee, the Parsee, equally deserves analysis, which will have to wait for another occasion.

7. *Forest Life* was preceded most importantly by Robert Knox's *An Historical Relation of the Island of Ceylon* (1681), which was one potential inspiration for Daniel Defoe's *Robinson Crusoe* (1719), as discussed in Allen. It was followed by Langdon's missionary conversion novel, *Punchi Nona* (1884), and L. Woolf's *Village in the Jungle* (1913).

8. The three primary publications representing the Carlyle–Mill debate were Carlyle's infamous essay "Occasional Discourse on the Negro Question" of 1849; Mill's response with "The Negro Question"; and Carlyle's critical commentary in *Shooting Niagara* (1867) on the Jamaica Committee, on which Mill served.

9. I draw throughout on the body of scholarship on masculinity in nineteenth-century Britain represented, for instance, by Dowling and Sussman. I follow Sussman's recognition of multiple "masculinities" in competition.

10. On the formation of missionary societies and influx of them into Ceylon, see Harris 13.

11. Hardy's *A Manual of Buddhism* (1853) was one of the most authoritative early sources published in English, and he was "influential in propagating the view, not only that it was 'the bounden duty of the government of the country, from its possession of the Truth, to discountenance the system [of Buddhism] by every legitimate means,' but also that Christianity and Buddhism were involved in a conflict the only victor in which could be the former" (Almond 134).

12. On the Buddhist Temporalities Question, also see "Buddhism and the British Government," 444–48.

13. On British taxation of the Sinhalese as one bone of contention, see Evers 327, and Sirr 361.

14. For nineteenth-century works that equated the law of the *dhamma* to the law of evolution, either criticizing or celebrating the "scientific" qualities of Buddhism, see Eitel 62 and 66; Lilly, "Message of Buddhism" 209; and *Literary Digest* 162. For an analysis of the Victorian conflation of Buddhism and Darwinism, especially within Theosophy, see Clausen 7, and Bevir, "The West" 764.

15. On the influence of the *Jatakas* on the Western folkloric tradition, start with T. Rhys Davids, *Buddhist Birth Stories*.

16. Knighton cites the "Damma Padan" translated by Daniel J. Gogerly, but that may have been published only in Ceylon or provided personally in unpublished manuscript (2:24). The first translation in Europe was by the Danish scholar Viggo Fausbøll in 1855, upon which Max Müller based the first translation in England in 1881.

17. On the influence of the *Jatakas* on Kipling, see Caracciolo.

18. As J. Warren argues, Mill believed that only the establishment of an equitable rule of law would promote "the dependence of individuals on society and provide them with the potential to realize a type of individualism" that was conducive to building his model of a liberal society and "that was at the heart of a masculinity he associated with mid-nineteenth-century bourgeois men" (48).

19. I allude to the distinction, problematized by postcolonial theorists such as Bhabha, Young, and Viswanathan, between "First Empire" and "Second Empire" colonialism. Similar to my category of bully masculinity, the First Empire model "rested on the application of a mute physical force applied directly to the bodies" of slaves and colonial subjects (Scott 335). Second Empire ideology was "concerned rather to develop techniques of subjectification, surveillance, and discipline" (335). Sharing the inherent ambivalence of Orientalism, it carried a mission of liberating, civilizing, educating, and improving, often exercised through conversion to Christianity, but, however much more humane, was not necessarily less of a vehicle for repression of difference and exploitation of people and resources.

20. The "passive Buddhist" stereotype can be found in Eitel 76, and Monier-Williams 560, among many others.

21. The immensely complex figure of the Victorian gentleman has of course been much analyzed. See, for example, the works by Adams and by Waters.

22. In this Knighton was aligned with the English-educated Sinhalese author James De Alwis, who was convinced that teaching scientific knowledge to the Sinhalese would make them better able "to adopt the religion of the Bible" (in Almond 92).

23. To give one of many possible examples, Eitel, a noted scholar and fierce critic of Buddhism, wrote indignantly that a "Buddhist may adopt all the results of modern science, he may become a follower of Newton, a disciple of Darwin, and yet remain a Buddhist" (63).

24. As Darwin (in)famously wrote in chapter 21, the conclusion, of *Descent of Man*: "For my own part I would as soon be descended from that heroic little monkey . . . as from a savage who delights to torture his enemies, offers up bloody sacrifices" (n.p.).

25. For examples from the many Victorian descriptions of Buddhism as a cold, heartless, metaphysical system, see Eitel 3, 97; Monier-Williams 13, 537, 559; and Tennent, *Christianity in Ceylon* 226.

26. Beal mentions the form of Buddhism to which Marandhan refers here: "It [the doctrine that there is *"no cause,* but all things exist 'of themselves'"] appears to have finally resolved itself into the form of belief maintained by the Svabavika school, which yet exists in Nipal, and is opposed to that known as the Aishvarika, or Theistic School" (lvii).

27. On the Buddhist ethical system as second only to that of Christianity, see for example Amberley 316; Claughton 141; Knighton 2:416; and Monier-Williams 217, 537. Reginald Copleston, the bishop of Colombo, writing from Ceylon, worked to reverse this Western endorsement of Buddhist ethics in multiple highly critical essays, some published anonymously: see [Copleston] and Colombo.

28. It is significant that some pre-nineteenth-century European reports from Ceylon described the Sinhalese as a highly ethical people; see for example Knox, quoted in Sirr 278–79. Then, as missionary interest in Ceylon intensified during the Anglicist-Orientalist debates, descriptions shifted to emphasize their extreme need for ethical instruction and, in particular, their sexual immorality; see for example Claughton and Colombo.

29. I speculate in this paragraph about the reception of *Forest Life* without reference to sources because I found very little in terms of contemporary reviews, which may be significant in itself. The writings by Copleston/Colombo give a sense of what critical responses from Christian apologists looked like.

30. We know from missionary reports that many Sinhalese converts were claimed but that many reverted to Buddhism or simply practiced Christianity in parallel. "Missionaries boast of the multitude of converts made in Ceylon," wrote Henry C. Sirr in 1850, but, "Alas! alas! strangely do they omit to mention the number of these professed converts who attend devil-dances, and make offers to Buddha, his temples, and priests" (53).

## 6. Identity, Genre, and Religion in Anna Leonowens's *The English Governess at the Siamese Court*

1. For examples of the types of charges and evidence against Leonowens's veracity, see Bristowe; Griswold; and W. Warren.

2. King Mongkut's full name was Phra Bat Somdet Phra Poramenthramaha Mongkut Phra Chom Klao Chao Yu Hua. For convenience, but with all respect, I will use his shorter, more familiar name throughout.

3. As one biographer of King Mongkut notes in this regard, "Years later in London, when the Siamese Ambassador reproached her for slandering her former employer, she excused herself by saying that readers wanted sensational revelations about the Orient and she had to provide them in order to satisfy her publisher" (Griswold 49). But I also agree with Lorraine Mercer's assessment that "Leonowens's ability to create such interest and empathy in her readers was born in her social and political beliefs that no people should be enslaved to a master, an owner, or a religious creed, but instead should be free to seek their own happiness" (225).

4. Sir John Bowring wrote that King Mongkut himself compared his reformation of Buddhism to the Protestant Reformation (see Bowring 302). We know that King Mongkut had friendships with French Catholic missionaries in Siam and that Protestant critics of Buddhism frequently compared it to Catholicism, as Leonowens does in *English Governess* 134. For anti-Catholic, anti-French discourse in *English Governess*, see 33, 138, 226, 256, and 264.

5. Leonowens's casting of herself as the hero illustrates what Chu-Chueh Cheng analyzes as "the empowerment of travel" via the author's license to redefine her social positions (125).

As Maria Frawley notes, this applied especially to women writers, whom travel enabled "to create a connection to and establish authority with a part of English culture that hitherto had evaded them because they lacked the education that decreed cultural authority" (in Cheng 125). This deficit of authority and commensurate need for validation applied all the more to "the ex-centricity of Leonowens's position in terms not only of gender but also of class, racial, and national origin," and this "is evident in the degree to which her texts seem to resist the discursive positions [of "feminine" decorum and passivity] frequently adopted by other nineteenth-century women travelers" (S. Brown 602).

6. Burton concludes, for example: "A review of feminist periodical literature reveals that British feminists constructed the image of the helpless Indian womanhood on whom their own emancipation in the imperial nation state ultimately relied. Thus, in both practice and theory, the Indian woman served as a foil against which British feminists could gauge their own progress" (295).

7. On Leonowens's relationship with Reverend Badger, see S. Morgan 4–6 and 52–54.

8. The influence of Burnouf on Leonowens raises an intriguing question, which I cannot pursue here: what, if any, is the causal relationship and direction of influence between Burnouf's principle of giving primacy to the most original textual sources and King Mongkut's "pure Buddhism"? Was Burnouf part of Mongkut's library in the 1840s?

### 7. Ancient Egyptian Religion in Late Victorian England

1. The name chosen by the founders of the Hermetic Order of the Golden Dawn invokes Egypt twice, in the name of Hermes, the Greek counterpart to the Egyptian god Thoth, and in "Golden Dawn," which references the sun god Ra or Amen-Ra (Luckhurst 219).

2. In Joshua 13:2–3, the Lord tells Joshua, "This is the land that yet remains: all the regions of the Philistines, and of those of the Gesh'urites (from the Shihor, which is east of Egypt, northward to the boundary of Ekron, it is counted as Canaanite)," and so on, listing all of the lands he will allot to Israel as an inheritance. The Sihor River apparently marked the western boundary with Egypt.

3. As a range of scholars have observed, "the reanimated figure of the embalmed Egyptian stalks the pages of more than thirty Victorian and Edwardian novels, short stories, poems, and plays," and "by the mid-1890s many more works of fiction set in ancient Egypt were being produced each year than had been written in the whole of the first half of the century put together" (Bridges 137; Gange, "Religion" 1102, n. 75). Loudon's *The Mummy* (1827) was among the earliest in the century and was followed by these, to give only a selection: Théophile Gautier, *The Romance of a Mummy* (1863); Grant Allen, "My New Year's Eve Among the Mummies" (1878); H. Rider Haggard, *She* (1887); Arthur Conan Doyle, "The Ring of Thoth" (1890) and "Lot No. 249" (1892); Florence Farr, *Egyptian Magic* (1896); Marie Corelli, *Ziska: The Problem of a Wicked Soul* (1897); E. and H. Heron, "The Story of Baelbrow" (1898); Guy Boothby, *Pharos the Egyptian* (1899); Richard Marsh, *The Beetle* (1899); Bram Stoker, *The Jewel of the Seven Stars* (1903); Algernon Blackwood, *The Wave: An Egyptian Aftermath* (1916); and Sax Rhomer, *Tales of Secret Egypt* (1918).

4. Other examples contemporary to Nilan include Cook; Hoare; and A. Williams.

5. Egyptian "wisdom literature," such as *The Instructions in Wisdom*, *The Instruction of Any*, or *The Instruction of Amenemope*, emphasizes middle-class ethics and righteousness and is "closer in style and content to Hebrew literature than to any other Egyptian writings," in particular to Proverbs 22 and 23 (David 262, 263).

6. Thomas "Mummy" Pettigrew, author of *History of Egyptian Mummies* (1834) and famed for his scholarly and then public commercial "unwrappings," "was particularly interested in using the skulls of his mummies to 'prove' by craniometric analysis that Ancient

Egyptian had not been African but Caucasian in origin"; "even as late as the public unravelling of a mummy by Wallis Budge in 1889 at University College, the main conclusion of a rather uninteresting exercise was that Egyptian mummies were not 'Negroes'" (Luckhurst 100–101). Petrie also brought a eugenics agenda to his scholarship.

7. Breasted was a primary source for Sigmund Freud in his argument in *Moses and Monotheism* (1939) concerning the debt of Moses to Akhenaten. Freud was a fascinated student of ancient Egypt and also of the novels of H. Rider Haggard. On Freud and Akhenaten, see Assmann 148–69, and Parramore 154–58. On Freud and Haggard, see Mazlish and Young.

8. On the dating of Moses, see Gabriel 191, and David 267.

9. For comparative analysis of the Amarna texts and the Bible illustrating the debt of the latter to the former, see David 228 and 262.

10. As Assmann notes in this regard: "What Akhenaten actually discovered, what he was probably the first to discover, and what he certainly experienced himself as a revelation, was a concept of *nature*. With regard to the Divine, his message is essentially negative: God is *nothing else than* the sun, and he is also nature" (188–89).

11. I have made a similar argument in relationship to the Victorian responses to components of Buddhism; see Franklin, *Lotus* 23.

12. Simon Magus points out that in a number of his novels subsequent to *Cleopatra* "Haggard focuses specifically on the actual historical monotheism of the pharaoh Akhenaten during the Amarna period" (7). His reading of Haggard, to which my analysis is indebted, concludes: "We can summarise, then, the fundamental framing elements of what are in effect the Egyptosophical components of Haggard's oeuvre: an 'original monotheism' conflated with an explicit Atenism, and—again, reprising Budge—an Osiride Christology" (9).

13. On the "curse of the mummy," see Bridges; Deane; Glover, "The Lure of the Mummy"; and Luckhurst.

14. As Pearson puts this point, though Haggard's stories often are driven by the fulfillment of male desire, "the narrative always in the end thwarts this desire and leaves the male protagonist in a state of unsatisfied frustration and prolonged repetition of desire" (228).

15. Haggard figures Cleopatra in part as a Victorian New Woman, one who possesses the confidence to define her own ambitions and desires. On the topic of marriage, she exclaims, "Marriage! I to marry! I to forget freedom and court the worst slavery of our sex" (*Cleopatra* 104).

## 8. The Economics of Immortality

1. I allude to the distinction between "horror" and "terror," one source of which was Ann Radcliffe (1764–1823), one of the originating authors of the Gothic novel. On horror versus terror, see for example Hume.

2. Prior to Halberstam, Moretti made a similar point: "The central characters of this literature—the monster, the vampire—are *metaphors*, rhetorical figures built on the analogy between *different semantic fields*. Wishing to incarnate Fear as such, they must of necessity combine fears *that have different causes*: economic, ideological, psychical, sexual (and others should be added, beginning with religious fear)" (105). The current chapter focuses on that religious fear. For an observation related to Moretti's, see Hurley 197.

3. On the demi-immortal Oriental in Corelli's novels, see Franklin, "Counter-Invasion of Britain."

4. For example, after midcentury, phrases like "the laws governing spiritual progress," "Progressive evolution," and the "Eternal progress open to every soul" became common among spiritualists and Theosophists (Sinnett, *Early Days* 31; Tuttle 14; Doyle 260).

5. On the antiprogressive spirituality of Haggard's Ayesha, see Coates, "'Spiritual,'" as well as Franklin, "Memory."

6. The Victorian concept of spiritual de-evolution, derived in part from various understandings of karma and reincarnation, appears in the principle texts of Theosophy as well as in late Victorian romance novels. Corelli writes, for example, about "Retrogression of the Soul" or "Eternal Retrogression" (*Romance* x, 249). Though few critics have focused on Dracula's spiritual devolution, many have commented upon the related topic of his association either to the Decadent movement or to degeneration theory. See for example Tomaszewsha or Glover, "'Our Enemy.'"

7. "Mesmeric mania" comes from the title of Bennett's 1851 book. My sources on Mesmerism include Kaplan; Tartar; Willis; and Winter.

8. See, for example, Andriopoulos, Banerjee, Bigelow, Coe, and, most importantly, Halberstam as well as Moretti.

9. Concerning the humanistic as opposed to divine understructure of Smith's economics, Packham concludes that "Smith's 'invisible hand' initially seems to suggest a role for a Newtonian divine force sustaining the operation of his economy; yet far from indicating the presence of an external controlling power, the hand expresses the actions of 'natural forces internal to man'" (480).

10. The vampire-novel series to which I refer include P. C. Cast's "House of Night" series, Melissa De La Cruz's "Blue Blood" series, Laurell K. Hamilton's "Anita Blake Vampire Hunter" series, Charlaine Harris's "Sookie Stackhouse" series, Stephanie Meyer's "Twilight" series, and, of course, Anne Rice's "Vampire Chronicles" series.

11. Enns makes an analogous point about Mesmerism: "In other words, rather than conceiving of consciousness and the body in terms of the Cartesian mind/body split, mesmerism introduced a new conception of materiality, which suggested that the body and consciousness were both bound together and material. Mesmerism provides an ideal starting point for understanding the emergence of a strange new kind of embodiment in the electric age" (64).

## Conclusion

1. For a more complete definition of late Victorian hybrid religions, see Franklin, *Lotus* 59. By "Theosophical Society" I mean the Theosophical Society International, originally founded by H. P. Blavatsky and H. S. Olcott, which should not be confused with the subsequent American branch, the Theosophical Society Pasadena, which W. Q. Judge broke from Blavatsky to form in 1895 (and which itself should not be confused with the American branch of the Theosophical Society International in Wheaton, Illinois). The focus here is only on the International.

2. A. P. Sinnett, the primary spokesperson for Theosophy in England at the end of the century, summarized H. P. Blavatsky's sevenfold structure of subjectivity in this way: 1. The Body (Rupa); 2. Vitality (Prana); 3. Astral Body (Linga Sharira); 4. Animal Soul (Kama Rupa); 5. Human Soul (Manas); 6. Spiritual Soul (Buddhi); 7. Spirit (Atma) (Sinnett, *Esoteric Buddhism* 65).

3. Though I focus here only on the two official leaders of the Theosophical Society, Blavatsky and Besant, they collaborated with others who also played major roles. Most important was H. S. Olcott, who cofounded the society with Blavatsky and helped her revise *Isis Unveiled*, followed by W. Q. Judge, A. P. Sinnett, and C. W. Leadbeater, among others. Judge initially served as vice president under Blavatsky, but he then led the American Section to declare autonomy. Sinnett was a primary organizer in England and India; his *Occult World* (1881) was a Theosophical best seller. Olcott, Blavatsky's primary (probably nonromantic) partner and a leading spokesperson, developed the relationship between Theosophy

and Buddhism, while Blavatsky, after moving the society to India, and then especially Besant, led Theosophy toward a relationship with Hinduism (one of the reasons that Rudolf Steiner separated from the society to found Anthroposophy).

4. I place "New Age movement" in scare quotes because there is no clear consensus among scholars who specialize in it about whether it is accurate or not to refer to it as a "movement," given that it is diffused throughout modern Western culture and largely not institutionally structured. While Hanegraaff states that "the *New Age is synonymous with the cultic milieu having become conscious of itself as constituting a more or less unified 'movement'*" in the 1970s (17), Sutcliffe argues that it originally was an "apocalyptic emblem" signaling the dawning of a New Age and is better understood after that connotation has partly waned as a "sensual and somatic idiom of contemporary popular religion" or "a diverse collectivity of questing individuals" (30, 223). Given that it is quite possible to characterize the New Age in terms that apply across a large number of its practitioners, categorize prevalent types of beliefs and practices and trace the histories of them, and so study it systematically as a scholarly object, I see no difficulty in using "movement," but given this debate I have chosen in this book to refer to "New Age religions" or "New Age spiritualities."

5. Biographical treatments of Blavatsky include Gomes, *Dawning*; Mead; Washington; and Wessinger et al.

6. In the nineteenth century, sympathetic histories and summaries of Theosophy were written by Olcott and by Sinnett, and critical commentaries were published by Max Müller and MacDonald, among others. Subsequent histories include those by Campbell; Dixon, *Divine*; Goodrick-Clarke; Goldfarb and Goldfarb; Gomes, *Dawning*; Godwin; Oppenheim; Ransom; and Washington. Bevir and Burfield have published useful essay analyses. Perhaps the best sources are Gomes's *Dawning* and Dixon's *Divine Feminine*.

7. In 1884, the Society for Psychical Research sent Richard Hodgson to Adyar, India, to investigate the authenticity of the Mahatma letters; in his 1885 report published in the society's proceedings, he denounced Blavatsky as "one of the most accomplished, ingenious and interesting impostors in history" (in Sinnett, *Early Days* 66). On the Mahatma letters and related scandal, see Gomes, *Theosophy* chap. 6. The letters themselves are preserved in the British Library.

8. Many twentieth- and twenty-first-century Theosophists would defend the authenticity of the Mahatma letters, as does the scholar and Theosophist Christmas Humphreys in 1940 when he writes, "Our knowledge of Theosophy, then, comes from the two Masters [the Mahatmas of the letters] who trained H. P. Blavatsky for her mission in the world, and taught her by divers means the wisdom outlined in her writings" (165).

9. This estimation of the number of Besant's publications comes from Open Library, openlibrary.org/authors/OL16933A/Annie_Wood_Besant, accessed October 10, 2016.

10. According to data provided via personal correspondence with Mr. Conrad Jameson, the public relations officer for the Theosophical Society International in Adyar, India, in 2001 there were 1,081 lodges across fifty-one different nations with a total of 31,996 memberships.

11. On Bulwer-Lytton's influence on Blavatsky, see Christensen 234; Mitchell 149; and Wolff 186.

12. These rough statistics come from Gomes, *Theosophy* 145 and *Dawning* 153. Another scandal surrounding Blavatsky's work concerned whether or not she had plagiarized portions of *Isis Unveiled*. Certainly she borrowed from a dizzying array of sources and did not quote or footnote according to MLA standards. Some critics repeatedly attacked her in print for plagiarism, while some others defended her citation practices. On this, see Gomes, *Theosophy* 143–53.

13. The term "Aryan," which since its adoption by the Nazis bears a tragically racist connotation, referred in the nineteenth century to the ancient people and area of what is now northern India or Pakistan, from which Siddhartha Gautama (ca. 563–ca. 483 BC), and therefore Buddhism, issued. The "Aryan question" that interested Victorians, which was stimulated by the earlier discovery of the membership of English in the Indo-European language group, concerned the extent to which northern European peoples were linguistically and genetically related to the people of northern India, a question with implications for British occupation of India. See Batchelor 266, and van der Veer, the chapter "Aryan Origins" 134.

14. Comparative analogy is a primary rhetorical strategy in *Isis Unveiled*, and though it is a logically and historically weak strategy, Blavatsky uses it to convincing effect, especially in the two- and three-column tables that appear throughout. She sets a column of Pythagorean verses next to one of similar New Testament verses, for instance, or a column of Hindu scripture beside analogous Old and New Testament passages. By juxtaposing the mythical/biographical events in the lives of Krishna, Buddha, and Jesus, she persuasively suggests a precedent for the latter in the former two. The purpose is to demonstrate that every symbol and idea that Christianity has claimed as its own in fact derived directly from previous "pagan" mythologies and systems of belief.

15. The use of "law" to designate the dharma can be seen, for instance, in the title of Alabaster's influential 1871 work, *The Wheel of the Law*, and throughout Edwin Arnold's 1879 best-selling verse narrative of the life of the Buddha, *The Light of Asia*, which throughout uses terms like "the great Law" (VIII.212).

16. For contemporary rebuttals of Theosophy's claim to be "esoteric Buddhism," see Snell and MacDonald, the latter of which argues, "We are able to prove *all* of the statements concerning the inner meaning and purpose of Gotama Buddha's teaching made through Mr. Sinnett by the Theosophical Society, or (if it be preferred) by the Tibetan Brotherhood, to be one by one baseless and false" (713).

17. On the association between the Theosophical Society and the Hindu Arya Samaj in India, see Gomes, *Dawning* 13 and the section "Pilgrimage to India," as well as Godwin 320.

18. On Besant's role in socially engaged religious and political movements both in England and in India, see Beckerlegge 235; Bevir, "A Theosophist in India"; Burfield; Dixon, *Divine Feminine*, 206; Ellwood and Wessinger; van der Veer 77; and Viswanathan 177–207. There is critical disagreement concerning the extent to which Besant served or subverted both Indian nationalism and British imperialism.

19. For a summary of Blavatsky's argument in *Isis Unveiled* about the historical basis for and suppression of the figure of the Goddess, see Franklin, *Lotus* 73–74.

20. I have not elaborated here the nature of the concept of trinity within Theosophy, but it is a recurring tenet taking multiple forms that are not identical either to the ancient Egyptian trinity or to the Christian Trinity. Blavatsky writes as if there is a divine triune principle governing the natural-spiritual universe, as when she writes, "*The trinity of nature is the lock of magic, the trinity of man the key that fits it*" (*Isis Unveiled* 2:635). See Besant, *Evolution of Life* 19 for one example of her variation of this concept.

21. Some historians also note the popular journal *The New Age*, founded in London in 1894, but it was more a vehicle first for Christian socialism and then modernist literature and criticism than for occult spirituality (though its editor from 1907 to 1922, A. R. Orage, was interested in occultism, and there were complex interconnections between Christian socialism, modernist aesthetics, and occultism). One avenue that I have chosen not to pursue in *Spirit Matters* is the linkages between heterodox religion or occult spirituality and the Aestheticism or Decadent movement of the fin de siècle, on which there is a substantial body of scholarship, including works by DeWitt; Higgins; and Knight, *Victorian Christianity*.

22. My primary sources on the New Age are Goodrick-Clarke; Hanegraaff; Heelas; Kemp; Melton; and Sutcliffe.

23. On the syncretic origin of all religions, see Byrne 99; Kraft 143–44; and Shaw and Stewart 7.

24. Nineteenth-century sources on "dependent origination" include Monier-Williams 102–4, and T. Rhys Davids, *History and Literature* 101–8. More recent sources include Nhat Hahn 221–49, and Rahula 53–54.

# Bibliography

**Primary Sources**

Alabaster, Henry. *The Wheel of the Law: Buddhism Illustrated from Siamese Sources by the Modern Buddhist, a Life of Buddha, and an Account of the Phrabat*. Trübner & Co., 1871.

Alford, Henry. "Mr. Anthony Trollope and the English Clergy." Review of *Clergymen of the Church of England*, by Anthony Trollope. *The Contemporary Review*, vol. 2, May–Aug. 1866, pp. 240–62.

Amberley, John R. "Recent Publications on Buddhism." *The Theological Review*, vol. 9, 1872, pp. 293–317.

Arnold, Edwin. *The Light of Asia, or The Great Renunciation (Mahābhinishkramana), Being the Life and Teaching of Gautama, Prince of India and Founder of Buddhism (as Told in Verse by an Indian Buddhist)*. 1879. Theosophical Press, 1997.

Arnold, Matthew. *The Complete Prose Works of Matthew Arnold*. Vol. 11, *The Last Word*. Edited by R. H. Super. UP Michigan, 1977.

———. *Culture and Anarchy*. 1869. Edited by Samuel Lipman, Yale UP, 1994.

———. *Essays, Letters, and Reviews by Matthew Arnold*. Edited by Fraser Neiman, Harvard UP, 1960.

———. *The Letters of Matthew Arnold*. Vol. 1, *1829–1859*. Edited by Cecil Y. Lang, UP Virginia, 1996.

———. *The Letters of Matthew Arnold to Arthur Hugh Clough*. Edited by Howard Foster Lowry, Clarendon Press, 1932.

———. *Literature and Dogma: An Essay Towards a Better Apprehension of the Bible*. 1873. *The Complete Prose Works of Matthew Arnold*, vol. 6, *Dissent and Dogma*, edited by R. H. Super, UP Michigan, 1968, pp. 139–411.

———. *The Note-Books of Matthew Arnold*. Edited by Howard Foster Lowry, Karl Young, and Waldo Hilary Dunn, Oxford UP, 1952.

———. *Unpublished Letters of Matthew Arnold*. Edited by Arnold Whitridge, Yale UP, 1923.

Baildon, Henry Bellyse. *The Spirit of Nature, Being a Series of Interpretive Essays on the History of Matter from the Atom to the Flower*. J. & A. Churchill, 1880.

Baker, Samuel White. *Eight Years Wanderings in Ceylon*. 1855. J. B. Lippincott & Co., 1877.

Barthélemy-Saint-Hilaire, J. *La Bouddha et sa Religion*. Librairie Académique, 1860.

———. *The Buddha and His Religion*. Bracken, 1996.

Beal, Samuel, translator. *Travels of Fah-Hian Sung-Yun, Buddhist Pilgrims, from China to India (400 A.D. to 518 A.D.)*. Trübner, 1869.

Bennett, John Hughes. *The Mesmeric Mania of 1851, with a Physiological Explanation of the Phenomena Produced*. Sutherland and Know, 1851.

Besant, Annie. *The Evolution of Life and Form: Four Lectures Delivered at the Twenty-Third Anniversary Meeting of the Theosophical Society at Adyar, Madras, 1898*. Theosophical Publishing Society, 1905. Project Gutenberg, www.gutenberg.org/files/40224/40224-h/40224-h.htm. Accessed 24 Dec. 2016.

———. *Materialism Undermined by Science: A Lecture by Annie Besant*. Pamphlet Series 17. Theosophical Publishing Society, 1895.

———. *The Self and Its Sheaths: Four Lectures*. Theosophical Publishing Society. 1895. *Theosophy, Christianity*. www.anandgholap.net/Self_And_It's_Sheaths-AB.html. Accessed 24 Dec. 2016.

Bigandet, The Right Rev. P. [Paul Ambrose]. *The Life or Legend of Gaudama, the Budha of the Burmese, with annotations. Notice on the Phongies, or Budhist Religious, and the Ways to Niban*. Pegu Press, 1858.

Blavatsky, H. P. *Isis Unveiled: A Master-Key to the Mysteries of Ancient and Modern Science and Theology*. Vol. 1, *Science*. 1877. Theosophical UP, 1972.

———. *Isis Unveiled: A Master-Key to the Mysteries of Ancient and Modern Science and Theology*. Vol. 2, *Theology*. Theosophical Publishing, 1910.

———. *The Key to Theosophy: Being a Clear Exposition, in the form of Question and Answer, of the Ethics, Science, and Philosophy for the Study of which the Theosophical Society Has Been Founded*. Theosophical Publishing Company, 1889.

———. *The Secret Doctrine: The Synthesis of Science, Religion, and Philosophy*. Theosophical Publishing Company, 1888.

Boothby, Guy. *Dr. Nikola*. D. Appleton and Company, 1896.

Bowring, Sir John. *The Kingdom and People of Siam*. 1857. 2 vols., Oxford UP, 1969.

Braid, James. *Neurypnology, or, The rationale of nervous sleep, considered in relation with animal magnetism: illustrated by numerous cases of its successful application in the relief and cure of disease*. John Churchill, 1843.

"Buddhism, and the British Government" ["The British Government and Buddhism"]. *London Quarterly Review*, vol. 3, 1854, pp. 436–57.

Brontë, Charlotte. *Jane Eyre*. 1847. Edited by Richard J. Dunn, 2nd ed. W. W. Norton, 1987.

Budge, Wallis, Sir. *Egyptian Religion: Egyptian Ideas of the Future Life*. 1900. University Books, 1959.

"A Buddhist 'Matthew Arnold.'" *Littell's Living Age*, no. 1351, 23 Apr. 1870, pp. 235–38.

Bulwer-Lytton, Edward. *The Coming Race*. 1871. Book Jungle, 2007.

———. *Paul Clifford*. 1830. Project Gutenberg. www.gutenberg.org/files/7735/7735-h/7735-h.htm. Accessed 24 Dec. 2016.

———. *A Strange Story*. 1862. *The Worlds of Edward Bulwer Lytton*, vol. 10., P. F. Collier and Son, 1901.

———. *Zanoni*. 1842. Wildeside Press, 2009.

Burnouf, Eugène. *Introduction to the History of Indian Buddhism*. 1844. Translated by Katia Buffetrille and Donald S. Lopez, Jr., UP Chicago, 2010.

Carlyle, Thomas. "Occasional Discourse on the Negro Question." *Fraser's Magazine*, vol. 40, Dec. 1849, pp. 670–79.

———. *Past and Present*. 1843. Oxford UP, 1960.

———. *Sartor Resartus: On Heroes and Hero Worship*. 1832. J. M. Dent & Co., 1959.

———. *Shooting Niagara: And After?* Chapman and Hall, 1867.

Carpenter, Edward. *From Adam's Peak to Elephanta: Sketches in Ceylon and India*. Swan Sonnenshein & Co., 1892.

Carpenter, William B. *Mesmerism, Spiritualism: Historically & scientifically considered, being two lectures delivered at the London Institution, with preface and appendix*. Longmans, Green and Co., 1877.

Claughton, Peter C. "Buddhism." *Journal of the Transactions of the Victoria Institute*, vol. 8, 1874, pp. 138–66.

Colebrooke, Henry Thomas. *Essays on the Religion and Philosophy of the Hindus*. Trübner, 1837.

Colombo, Reginald Stephen [Copleston, Reginald]. "Buddhism." *The Nineteenth Century*, July 1888, pp. 119–35.

Colquhoun, James Campbell. *Isis revelata: An inquiry into the origins, progress, and present state of animal magnetism*. Maclachlan & Stewart, 1836.

Cook, Keningale. "The Ancient Faith of Egypt." *Dublin University Magazine*, vol. 90, 1877, pp. 27–51.

[Copleston, Reginald]. Review of Monier-Williams, *Buddhism*, and Oldenberg, *Buddha*. *The Quarterly Review*, vol. 170, no. 340, Apr. 1890, pp. 318–46.

Corelli, Marie. *The Life Everlasting: A Romance of Reality*. 1911. Borden Publishing Co., 1966.

———. *A Romance of Two Worlds*. 1886. Borden Publishing Co., 1947.

Darwin, Charles. *The Descent of Man, and Selection in Relation to Sex*. 1871. Project Gutenberg. www.gutenberg.org/cache/epub/2300/pg2300.html. Accessed 13 Aug. 2000.

Davis, Mary F. *Danger Signals: An Address of the Uses and Abuses of Modern Spiritualism*. A. J. Davis & Co, 1875.

"Death of Mr. W. S. Lilly. Essayist and Catholic Champion." *The Times*, no. 42193, 1 Sept. 1919, p. 13.

de Harlez, C. "Buddhist Propaganda in Christian Countries." *Dublin Review*, vol. 107, no. 3S24, 1890, pp. 54–73.

De Quincey, Thomas. "Ceylon." *Blackwood's Edinburgh Magazine*, vol. 54, Nov. 1843, pp. 623–36.

Doyle, Arthur Conan. *The History of Spiritualism*. Vols. 1 and 2. 1926. Arno Press, 1975.

Driesch, Hans. *The History and Theory of Vitalism*. Translated by C. K. Ogden, London: MacMillan and Co., Limited, 1914.

Dupotet [De Sennevoy], Jean. *An Introduction to the Study of Animal Magnetism. With an appendix, containing reports of British practitioners in favour of the science.* Saunders & Otley, 1838.

Edwards, Amelia. "Was Ramses II the Pharaoh of the Exodus?" *Knowledge*, vol. 2, 1882, pp. 108–9, 141–42, 192–93, 228–29, 244, 226–61, 291–93, 324–26, 387, 450.

Eitel, Ernest J. *Buddhism: Its Historical, Theoretical and Popular Aspects*. 3rd ed., Land, Crawford & Co., 1884.

Ellinwood, F. F. "Buddhism and Christianity—A Crusade which Must Be Met." *The Missionary Review of the World*, vol. 4, 1891, pp. 108–17.

Elliotson, John. *An Introduction to the Study of Animal Magnetism*. Longman, Orme, Brown, Green, and Longmans, 1840.

"The English Governess at the Siamese Court by A. H. Leonowens." *North American Review*, vol. 112, no. 23, Apr. 1871, pp. 422–24.

Esdaile, James. *Mesmerism in India, and Its Practical Application in Surgery and Medicine*. London, Longman, Brown, Green, and Longmans, 1846.

Everett, Charles C. "Recent Studies in Buddhism." *The Unitarian Review and Religious Magazine*, vol. 18, 1882, pp. 421–36.

Feuerbach, Ludwig. *The Essence of Christianity*. Translated by Marian Evans, John Chapman, 1854.

Gardner, Percy. "Modernism and Philosophy." *Modernism in the English Church*, Methuen, 1926, pp. 26–41.

Gogerly, Daniel J. *Ceylon Buddhism*. 2 vols. Edited by Arthur Stanley Bishop, Wesleyan Methodist Book Room, 1908.

Haggard, H. Rider. *Ayesha: The Return of "She."* 1905. *The Classic Adventures: "Ayesha: The Return of She," "Benita: An African Romance,"* New Orchard Editions, 1986.

———. *Cleopatra, Being an Account of the Fall and Vengeance of Harmachis, The Royal Egyptian, as Set Forth by his Own Hand*. 1889. *The Works of H. Rider Haggard*, Black's Readers Service Company, 1928.

———. *The Days of My Life, An Autobiography*. 2 volumes, edited by C. J. Longman, Longmans, Green and Co., 1926.

———. *She*. 1887. Oxford UP, 1998.

Hardy, R. Spence. *A Manual of Buddhism, in its Modern Development; Translated from Sinhalese Mss.* 1853. Williams and Norgate, 1860.

Hoare, John Newenham. "The Religion of the Ancient Egyptians." *The Living Age*, vol. 140, no. 1803, 4 Jan. 1879, pp. 33–41.

Huxley, Thomas Henry. *The Advance of Science in the Last Half-Century*. D. Appleton and Company, 1889. Project Gutenberg. www.gutenberg.org/files/15253/15253-h/15253-h.htm. Accessed 6 June 2015.

———. "Agnosticism: A Rejoinder." 1889. *Collected Essays*, Vol. 5, *Science and Christian Tradition*. D. Appleton and Company, 1902. Project Gutenberg. www.gutenberg.org/files/15905/15905-h/15905-h.htm. Accessed 6 June 2015.

———. *The Aryan Question and Pre-historic Man*. Kegan Paul, Trench, 1890.

Johnson, Samuel. *A Dictionary of the English Language*. W. Strahan, 1755.

Jung-Stilling, Johann Heinrich. *Theory of pneumatology: In reply to the question, what ought to be believed or disbelieved concerning presentiments, visions, and apparitions, according to nature, reason and scripture*. Longman, Rees, Orme, Brown, Green, and Longman, 1834.

Knighton, William. *Forest Life in Ceylon*. 2 vols. Hurst and Blackett Publishers, 1854.

Knox, Robert. *An Historical Relation of the Island Ceylon, in the East-Indies: Together, with an account of the detaining in captivity the author and divers other Englishmen now living there, and of the authors miraculous escape: illustrated with figures, and a map of the island*. Richard Chiswell, 1681.

Langdon, Samuel. *Punchi Nona: A Story of Female Education and Village Life in Ceylon*. T. Woolmer, 1884.

"Lecture by Mrs. Leonowens on 'Buddha' in the Free Religious Course." *Boston Daily Globe*, 9 Feb. 1874, p. 2.

Legge, F. "The Origin of Modern Occultism." *The National Review*, vol. 14, Sept. 1889, pp. 10–22.

Leonowens, A. H. [Mrs. A. H.] "The City of Forbidden Women." *The Youth's Companion*, vol. 50, 1 Feb. 1877, p. 35.

———. *The English Governess at the Siamese Court; Being Recollections of Six Years in the Royal Palace at Bangkok*. 1870. UP Michigan, 2005.

——— [Mrs. Anna Harriette]. "The Religion of Siam." *The Open Court*, vol. 16, May 1902, pp. 149–51.

———. "The Siamese Christmas." *The Aldine*, vol. 6, no. 12, Dec. 1873, pp. 230–31.

——— [Mrs. A. H.]. "Tree Consecration: (A Buddhist Ceremony)." *Christian Union*, vol. 10, no. 4, 29 July 1874.

——— [Anna Harriette]. "A Visit from a Siamese Princess." *The Aldine*, vol. 7, no. 10, Oct. 1874, pp. 202, 205.

Lilly, William Samuel. *Ancient Religion and Modern Thought*. 2nd ed., London: Chapman and Hall, 1885.

——— [W. S.]. "The Message of Buddhism to the Western World." *The Fortnightly Review*, vol. 78, July–Dec. 1905, pp. 197–214.

*Literary Digest*. Vol. 1, no. 6, May 31, 1890, p. 162.

Lodge, Oliver. "Matter and Spirit: Connexion between Material and Spiritual." Privately printed, Spottiswoode and Co., 1905.

MacDonald, Frederika. "Buddhism and Mock Buddhism." *The Fortnightly Review*, vol. 37, Jan.–June 1885, pp. 703–16.

Martin, Alfred W. *Psychic Tendencies of To-Day: An Exposition and Critique of New Thought, Christian Science, Spiritualism, Psychical Research (Sir Oliver Lodge) and Modern Materialism in Relation to Immortality*. D. Appleton and Company, 1918.

Martineau, Harriet. *Letters on Mesmerism*. London: Edward Moxon, 1845.

McKerlie, Helen Graham. "Western Buddhism." *Asiatic Quarterly Review*, vol. 9, no. 17, Jan. 1890, pp. 192–227.

Mill, John Stuart. "The Negro Question." *Fraser's Magazine*, vol. 41, Jan. 1850, pp. 25–31.

"Modern Society and the Sacred Heart." *Dublin Review*, vol. 25, no. 49, July 1875, pp. 1–21.

Monier-Williams, Monier. *Buddhism, in Its Connexion with Brāhmanism and Hindūism, and in Its Contrast with Christianity*. John Murray, 1889.

"Mrs. Leonowens's Lecture: Buddhistic Art and Art Ideas—The Significance of the Chinese Emblems and Colors." *Boston Daily Advertiser*, vol. 83, 5 Apr. 1884, p. 4.

Müller, F. Max. *Chips from a German Workshop*. Vol. 1, *Essays on the Science of Religion*. Longman, Green, and Co., 1867.

———, editor. *The Dhammapada, A Collection of Verses, Being One of the Canonical Books of the Buddhists*. In *Sacred Books of the East, Translated by Various Scholars*. Vol. 10, part 1, Clarendon Press, 1881.

———. *Lectures on the Science of Religion; with a Paper on Buddhist Nihilism, and a Translation of the Dhammapada or 'Path of Virtue.'* Charles Scribner and Co., 1872.

———. *Natural Religion: The Gifford Lectures*. 2nd ed., Longmans, Green, and Co., 1892.

Nilan, Rev. J. "The Religion of Ancient Egypt." *Catholic World*, vol. 39, no. 232, Apr. 1884, pp. 557–64.

Olcott, Henry Steel. "The Genesis of Theosophy." *The National Review*, vol. 14, Oct. 1889, pp. 208–17.

Oldenberg, Hermann. *Buddha: His Life, His Doctrine, His Order*. 1881. Translated by William Hoey, Williams and Norgate, 1882.

Paley, William. *Natural Theology or evidence of the existence and attributes of the deity, collected from the appearances of nature*. 1802. Oxford UP, 2006.

Patterson, Charles Brodie. "The Spirit of Modern Christianity. *The Arena*, vol. 26, no. 4, Oct. 1901, p. 384.

Percival, Robert. *An Account of the Island of Ceylon, Containing Its History, Geography, Natural History, and the Manners and Customs of Its Various Inhabitants; to which is added the Journal of an Embassy to the Court of Candy*. C. and R. Baldwin, 1803.

Podmore, Frank. *Modern Spiritualism: A History and Criticism*. 2 vols. Methuen and Co., 1902.

Rattigan, William H. "Three Great Asiatic Reformers: A Study and a Contrast." *London Quarterly Review*, vol. 92, 1899, pp. 291–312.

Rhys Davids, Caroline. *Buddhism: A Study of the Buddhist Norm*. 1912. Asian Educational Services, 2000.

Rhys Davids, T. W. *Buddhism: Being a Sketch of the Life and Teachings of Gautama, the Buddha*. 1877. 21st ed., Society for Promoting Christian Knowledge, 1907.

———. *Buddhism, Its History and Literature*. 3rd ed., G. P. Putnam's Sons, 1896.
———, translator. *Buddhist Birth Stories; or, Jātaka Tales. The Oldest Collection of Folk-Lore Extant: Being the Jātakatthavaṇṇanā, for the First Time Edited in the Original Pāli*. Edited by V. Fausböll. Vol. 1, Houghton, Mifflin, & Co., 1880.
———. *The History and Literature of Buddhism*. 1896. Susil Gupta, 1962.
———. *Lectures on the Origin and Growth of Buddhism*. 1881. Hibbert Lectures. Rachna Prakashan, 1972.
Robertson, James. *The Rise and Progress of Modern Spiritualism in England*. Two Worlds Publishing Company, 1893.
Sabatier, Auguste. "Religion and Modern Culture." *The New World*, vol. 8, Mar. 1899, pp. 91–110.
Sargent, Epes. *The Scientific Basis of Spiritualism*. Colby and Rich, 1881.
Schopenhauer, Arthur. *The World as Will and Representation*. 1818 and 1844. Translated by E. F. J. Payne, 2 vols., Dover, 1966.
"Siam and the Siamese: An Interesting Conversational Lecture by Mrs. Leonowens." *Inter Ocean*, no. 210, 25 Nov. 1875, p. 2.
"Siam, Its Court and Religion." *The Open Court*, vol. 16, Jan. 1902, pp. 53–55.
Sinnett, A. P. *The Early Days of Theosophy in Europe*. Theosophical Publishing House Ltd., 1922.
———. *Esoteric Buddhism*. 7th ed., Houghton, Mifflin and Co., 1887.
Sirr, Henry C. *Ceylon and the Cingalese: Their History, Government, and Religion, the Antiquities, Institutions, Produce, Revenue, and Capabilities of the Island*. 2 vols., William Shoberl, 1850.
Snell, Merwin-Marie. "Modern Theosophy in Its Relation to Hinduism and Buddhism." *The Biblical World*, Mar.–Apr. 1895, pp. 200–205, 259–65.
Stephen, Leslie. *Essays on Freethinking and Plainspeaking*. London: Longmans, Green & Co., 1882.
Stewart, Balfour, and Peter Guthrie Tait. *The Unseen Universe: or Physical Speculations on a Future State*. 10th ed., London: MacMillan, 1881.
Stocker, R. Dimsdale. *Spirit, Matter and Morals*. London: A. Owen and Co., 1908.
Stoker, Bram. *Dracula*. 1897. Oxford UP, 1998.
Tennent, James Emerson. *Ceylon: An Account of the Island Physical, Historical, and Topographical with Notices of Its Natural History, Antiquities and Productions*. Vol. 1. 1859. *Project Gutenberg*. www.gutenberg.org/files/13552/13552-h/13552-h.htm. Accessed 28 Sept. 2004.
———. *Christianity in Ceylon: It's Introduction and Progress Under the Portuguese, the Dutch, the British, and American Missions: With an Historical Sketch of the Brahmanical and Buddhist Superstitions*. John Murray, 1850.
Townshend, Chauncey Hare. *Facts in Mesmerism: With reasons for a dispassionate inquiry into it*. Longman, Orme, Brown, Green, & Longmans, 1840.
Traill, H. D. "Neo-Christianity and Mr. Matthew Arnold." *The Contemporary Review*, vol. 45, Jan.–June 1884, pp. 564–76.
Trollope, Anthony. *An Autobiography*. 1883. Edited by Michael Sadleir and Frederick Page. Oxford UP, 1950.
———. *Barchester Towers*. 1857. Oxford UP, 1980.

———. *The Clergymen of the Church of England.* 1866. Trollope Society, 1998.
———. "The Fourth Commandment." *The Fortnightly Review*, vol. 17, Jan.–June 1866, pp. 529–38.
———. *The Vicar of Bullhampton.* 1870. Penguin, 1993.
Turnour, George. *The Maháwanso in Roman characters, with . . . an introductory essay on Páli buddhistical literature.* Vol. 1., Ceylon, 1837.
Tuttle, Hudson. *Arcana of Spiritualism: A Manual of Spiritual Science and Philosophy.* James Burns, 1876.
Walker, E. D. *Reincarnation: A Study of Forgotten Truth.* 1888. University Books, 1965.
Wilkinson, John Gardner. *The Manners and Customs of the Ancient Egyptians, including Their Private Life, Government, Laws, Arts, Manufacture, Religion and Early History.* John Murray, 1837.
Williams, Josephine. "The Religious Ideas of the Ancient Egyptians." *Westminster Review*, vol. 150, 1898, pp. 655–69.
Wilson, Harry Bristow. "Séances historiques de Genève—the National Church." *Essays and Reviews: The 1860 Text and Its Readings*, edited by Victor Shea and William Whitla, UP Virginia, 2000, pp. 275–344.
Woolf, Leonard. *The Village in the Jungle.* 1913. Edited by Yasmine Gooneratne, Edwin Mellen Press, 2004.

**Secondary Sources**

Adams, James Eli. *Dandies and Desert Saints: Styles of Victorian Masculinity.* Cornell UP, 1995.
Allen, Charles. *The Search for the Buddha: The Men who Discovered India's Lost Religion.* Carroll & Graf, 2002.
Almond, Philip C. *The British Discovery of Buddhism.* Cambridge UP, 1988.
Anderson, Amanda. "Trollope's Modernity." *ELH*, vol. 74, no. 3, 2007, pp. 509–34.
Andriopoulos, Stefan. "The Invisible Hand: Supernatural Agency in Political Economy and the Gothic Novel." *ELH*, vol. 66, 1999, pp. 739–58.
Aphornsuvan, Thanet. "The West and Siam's Quest for Modernity: Siamese Responses to Nineteenth Century American Missionaries." *South East Asia Research*, vol. 17, no. 3, Nov. 2009, pp. 401–31.
apRoberts, Ruth. *Arnold and God.* UP California, 1983.
———. Introduction. *The Clergymen of the Church of England*, by Anthony Trollope. Leicester UP, 1974, pp. 9–49.
Assmann, Jan. *Moses the Egyptian: The Memory of Egypt in Western Monotheism.* Harvard UP, 1997.
Bakhtin, Mikhail. *The Dialogic Imagination: Four Essays.* Edited by Michael Holquist; translated by Carly Emerson and Michale Holquist, UP Texas, 1981.
Banerjee, Sukanya. "Political Economy, Gothic, and the Question of Imperial Citizenship." *Victorian Studies*, Winter 2005, pp. 260–71.
Bankert, M.S. "Newman in the Shadow of *Barchester Towers*." *Renascence*, vol. 20, no. 3, 1968, pp. 153–61.
Batchelor, Stephen. *The Awakening of the West: The Encounter of Buddhism and Western Culture.* Parallax Press, 1994.

Beaumont, Matthew. "Socialism and Occultism at the *Fin de Siècle*: Elective Infinities." *The Ashgate Research Companion to Nineteenth-Century Spiritualism and the Occult*, edited by Tatiana Kontou and Sarah Willburn, Ashgate, 2012, pp. 165–80.

Beckerlegge, G. "Followers of 'Mohammed, Kalee and Dad Nanuk': The Presence of Islam and South Asian Religions in Victorian Britain." *Religion in Victorian Britain*, vol. 5, *Culture and Empire*, edited by John Wolffe, Manchester UP, 1997, pp. 221–70.

Beer, Gillian. *Darwin's Plots: Evolutionary Narrative in Darwin, George Eliot, and Nineteenth-Century Fiction*. Routledge & Kegan Paul, 1983.

Bevir, Mark. "Annie Besant's Quest for Truth: Christianity, Secularism and New Age Thought." *Journal of Ecclesiastical History*, vol. 50, no. 1, Jan.1999, pp. 62–93.

———. "A Theosophist in India." *Imperial Objects: Essays on Victorian Women's Emigration and the Unauthorized Imperial Experience*, edited by Rita S. Kranidis, Twayne, 1998, pp. 211–27.

———. "Welfarism, Socialism and Religion: On T. H. Green and Others." *The Review of Politics*, vol. 5, no. 4, Autumn 1993, pp. 639–61.

———. "The West Turns Eastward: Madame Blavatsky and the Transformation of the Occult Tradition." *Journal of the American Academy of Religion*, vol. 63, no. 3, Fall 1994, pp. 747–67.

Bhabha, Homi K. *The Location of Culture*. Routledge, 1994.

Bigelow, Gordon. "*Dracula* and Economic History." *Clio*, vol. 38, no. 1, 2008, pp. 39–60.

Bishop, Peter. *The Myth of Shangri-La: Tibet, Travel Writing and the Western Creation of Scared Landscape*. UP California, 1989.

Blake, Ruth. "Anna of Siam Lived in Canada." *The Maritime Advocate and Busy East Press*, Jan. 1951, pp. 9–12.

Blakeley, Phyllis R. "Anna of Siam in Canada." *The Atlantic Advocate*, Jan. 1967, pp. 41–45.

Botting, Fred. *Gothic Romanced: Consumption, Gender and Technology in Contemporary Fictions*. Routledge, 2008.

Bramble, John. *Modernism and the Occult*. Palgrave Macmillan, 2015.

Brandon, Ruth. *The Spiritualists: The Passion for the Occult in the Nineteenth and Twentieth Centuries*. Alfred A. Knopf, 1983.

Brantlinger, Patrick. "Imperial Gothic: Atavism and the Occult in the British Adventure Novel, 1880–1914." *Reading Fin de Siecle Fictions*, edited by Lyn Pykett, Longman, 1996, pp. 184–209.

———. *Rule of Darkness: British Literature and Imperialism, 1830–1914*. Cornell UP, 1988.

Braude, Ann. "The Perils of Passivity: Women's Leadership in Spiritualism and Christian Science." *Women's Leadership in Marginal Religions: Explorations Outside the Mainstream*, edited by Catherine Wessinger, UP Illinois, 1993, pp. 55–67.

Bridges, Meilee D. "Tales from the Crypt: Bram Stoker and the Curse of the Egyptian Mummy." *Victorians Institute Journal*, vol. 36, 2008, pp. 137–65.

Bristowe, W. S. *Louis and the King of Siam*. Chatto and Windus, 1976.

Brooke, John, and Geoffrey Cantor. *Reconstructing Nature: The Engagement of Science and Religion*. Glasgow Gifford Lectures, Oxford UP, 1998.

Brown, Callum G. *The Death of Christian Britain: Understanding Secularization 1800–2000*. 2nd ed., Routledge, 2009.

Brown, Michael. "The New Age and Related Forms of Contemporary Spirituality." *Religion and Culture, An Anthropological Focus*, 2nd ed., edited by Raymond Scupin, Pearson-Prentice Hall, 2008, pp. 455–66.

Brown, Susan. "Alternatives to the Missionary Position: Anna Leonowens as Victorian Travel Writer." *Feminist Studies*, vol. 21, no. 3, Fall 1995, pp. 587–614.

Budge, Gavin. "Mesmerism and Medicine in Bulwer-Lytton's Novels of the Occult." *Victorian Literary Mesmerism*, edited by Martin Willis and Catherine Wynne, Rodopi, 2006, pp. 39–59.

———. "'The Vampyre': Romantic Metaphysics and the Aristocratic Other." *The Gothic Other: Racial and Social Constructions in the Literary Imagination*, edited by Ruth Bienstock Anolik and Douglas L. Howard, McFarland & Company, 2000, pp. 212–35.

Bulfin, Ailise. "The Fiction of Gothic Egypt and British Imperial Paranoia: The Curse of the Suez Canal." *English Literature in Transition, 1880–1920*, vol. 54, no. 4, 2011, pp. 411–43.

Burfield, Diana. "Theosophy and Feminism: Some Explorations in Nineteenth-Century Biography." *Women's Religious Experience*, edited by Pat Holden, Barnes & Noble Books, 1983, pp. 28–51.

Burton, Antoinette M. "The White Woman's Burden: British Feminists and the Indian Woman, 1865–1915." *Women's Studies International Forum*, vol. 13, no. 4, 1990, pp. 295–308.

Byrne, Peter. *Natural Religion and the Nature of Religion*. Routledge, 1989.

Cadbury, William. "The Uses of the Village: Form and Theme in Trollope's *The Vicar of Bullhampton*." *Nineteenth-Century Fiction*, vol. 18, no. 2, Sept. 1963, pp. 151–63.

Campbell, Bruce F. *Ancient Wisdom Revisited: A History of the Theosophical Movement*. UP California, 1980.

Caracciolo, Peter. "Buddhist Teaching Stories and Their Influence on Conrad, Wells, and Kipling: The Reception of the Jataka and Allied Genres in Victorian Culture." *Conradian*, vol. 11, no. 1, 1986, pp. 24–34.

Cerullo, John J. *The Secularization of the Soul: Psychical Research in Modern Britain*. Institute for the Study of Human Issues, 1982.

Chadwick, Owen. *The Secularization of the European Mind in the Nineteenth Century*. Cambridge UP, 1997.

———. *The Victorian Church. Part 1: 1829–1859*, Oxford UP, 1966.

Cheng, Chu-Chueh. "Frances Trollope's America and Anna Leonowens's Siam: Questionable Traven and Problematic Writing." *Gender, Genre, & Identity in Women's Travel Writing*, edited by Kristi Siegel, Peter Lang, 2004, pp. 123–65.

Christensen, Allan Conrad. *Edward Bulwer-Lytton: The Fiction of New Regions*. UP Georgia, 1976.

Clausen, Christopher. "Victorian Buddhism and the Origins of Comparative Religion." *Religion*, vol. 5, 1975, pp. 1–15.

Coates, John. "*Zanoni* by Bulwer-Lytton: A Discussion of Its Philosophy and Its Possible Influences." *Durham University Journal*, vol. 76, no. 2, June 1948, pp. 223–33.

Coates, John D. "The 'Spiritual Quest' in Rider Haggard's *She* and *Ayesha*." *Cahiers victoriens et édouardiens*, vol. 57, 2003, pp. 33–54.

Cockshut, A. O. J. *Anglican Attitudes: A Study of Victorian Religious Controversies*. Collins, 1959.

Coe, Richard M. "It Takes Capital to Defeat Dracula: A New Rhetorical Essay." *College English*, vol. 48, no. 3, Mar. 1986, pp. 231–42.

*The Connected Discourses of the Buddha*. Translated by Bhikkhu Bodhi, Wisdom Publications, 1995.

Cottom, Daniel. *Abyss of Reason: Cultural Movements, Revelations, and Betrayals*. Oxford UP, 1991.

———. *Social Figures: George Eliot, Social History, and Literary Representation*. UP Minnesota, 1983.

Crabtree, Adam. *From Mesmer to Freud*. Yale UP, 1993.

Crook, Tom. "Putting Matter in Its Right Place: Dirt, Time and Regeneration in Mid-Victorian Britain." *Journal of Victorian Culture*, vol. 13, no. 2, Autumn 2008, pp. 200–22.

Dann, Caron Eastgate. *Imagining Siam: A Travellers' Literary Guide to Thailand*. Monash UP, 2008.

Darnton, Robert. *Mesmerism and the End of the Enlightenment in France*. Harvard UP, 1968.

David, Rosalie. *Religion and Magic in Ancient Egypt*. Penguin, 2002.

Davies, A. "The Aryan Myth: Its Religious Significance." *Studies in Religion*, vol. 10, no. 3, 1981, pp. 290–95.

Davies, Gwendolyn. "Anna Leonowens." *Dictionary of Literary Biography*, vol. 99, *Canadian Writers Before 1890*, edited by W. H. New, Gale, 1990, pp. 202–205.

Davis, W. and J. Helmstadterf, editors. *Religion and Irreligion in Victorian Society: Essays in Honor of R. K. Webb*. Routledge, 1992.

Dawson, Gowan, and Bernard Lightman, editors. *Victorian Scientific Naturalism: Community, Identity, Continuity*. UP Chicago, 2014.

Deane, Bradley. "Mummy Fiction and the Occupation of Egypt: Imperial Striptease." English Literature in Transition, 1880–1920, vol. 51, no. 4, 2008, pp. 381–410.

De Silva, K. M. "Religion and Nationalism in Nineteenth Century Sri Lanka: Christian Missionaries and Their Critics, A Review Article." *Ethnic Studies Report*, vol. 16, no. 1, Jan. 1998, pp. 103–38.

DeWitt, Anne. *Moral Authority, Men of Science, and the Victorian Novel*. Cambridge UP, 2013.

Dickerson, Vanessa D. *Victorian Ghosts in the Noontide: Women Writers and the Supernatural*. UP Missouri, 1996.

Dinnage, Rosemary. *Annie Besant*. Penguin, 1986.

Dixon, Joy. *Divine Feminine: Theosophy and Feminism in England*. Johns Hopkins UP, 2001.

———. "Modernity, Heterodoxy and the Transformation of Religious Cultures." *Women, Gender and Religious Cultures in Britain, 1800–1940*, edited by Sue Morgan and Jacqueline deVries, Routledge, 2010, pp. 211–30.

———. "'Out of your clinging kisses . . . I created a new world': Sexuality and Spirituality in the Work of Edward Carpenter." *The Ashgate Research Companion to Nineteenth-Century Spiritualism and the Occult*, edited by Tatiana Kontou and Sarah Willburn, Ashgate, 2012, pp. 143–63.

Dodson, Michael S. *Orientalism, Empire, and National Culture, India, 1770–1880*. Palgrave Macmillan, 2007.

Dowling, Andrew. *Manliness and the Male Novelist in Victorian Literature*. Ashgate, 2001.

Droit, Roger-Pol. *The Cult of Nothingness: The Philosophers and the Buddha*. Translated by David Streight and Pamela Vohnson, UP North Carolina, 2003.

Droogers, André. "Syncretism: The Problem of Definition, the Definition of the Problem." *Dialogue and Syncretism: An Interdisciplinary Approach*, edited by Jerald Gort, Hendrik Vroom, Rein Fernhout, and Anton Wessels, William B. Eerdmans, 1989, pp. 7–25.

Durey, Jill Felicity. *Trollope and the Church of England*. Macmillan, 2002.

"Early History." The Theosophical Society International Headquarters. www.ts-adyar.org/content/early-history. Accessed 24 Dec. 2016.

Ellmann, Maud. Introduction. *Dracula*, by Bram Stoker. Oxford UP, 1998, pp. vii–xxviii.

Ellwood, Robert, and Catherine Wessinger. "The Feminism of 'Universal Brotherhood': Women in the Theosophical Movement." *Women's Leadership in Marginal Religions: Explorations Outside the Mainstream*, edited by Catherine Wessinger, UP Illinois, 1993, pp. 68–87.

Endersby, Jim. "Odd Man Out: Was Joseph Hooker an Evolutionary Naturalist?" *Victorian Scientific Naturalism: Community, Identity, Continuity*, edited by Gowan Dawson and Bernard Lightman, UP Chicago, 2014, pp. 157–85.

England, Richard. "Natural Selection, Teleology, and the Logos: From Darwin to the Oxford Neo-Darwinists, 1859–1909." *Science in Theistic Contexts: Cognitive Dimensions*, special issue of *Osiris*, 2nd series, vol. 16, 2001, pp. 270–87.

Enns, Anthony. "Mesmerism and the Electric Age: From Poe to Edison." *Victorian Literary Mesmerism*, edited by Martin Willis and Catherine Wynne, Rodopi, 2006, pp. 61–82.

Evers, Hans-Dieter. "Buddhism and British Colonial Policy in Ceylon, 1815–1875." *Journal of Asian Studies*, vol. 2, no. 3, 1964, pp. 323–33.

Fichman, Martin. "Science in Theistic Contexts: A Case Study of Alfred Russel Wallace on Human Evolution." *Science in Theistic Contexts: Cognitive Dimensions*, special issue of *Osiris*, 2nd series, vol. 16, 2001, pp. 227–50.

Findlay, Ian. "Edward Bulwer-Lytton and the Rosicrucians." *Literature and the Occult: Essays in Comparative Literature*, edited by Luanne Frank, UP Texas at Arlington, 1977, pp. 137–46.

Foote, George A. "Mechanism, Materialism, and Science in England, 1800–1850." *Annals of Science*, vol. 8, no. 2, 1952, pp. 152–61.

Foster, Shirley. *Across New Worlds: Nineteenth-Century Women Travellers and Their Writings*. Harvester Wheatsheaf, 1990.

Fradin, Joseph I. "'The Absorbing Tyranny of Every-day Life': Bulwer-Lytton's *A Strange Story*," *Nineteenth-Century Fiction*, vol. 16, no. 1, June 1961, pp. 1–16.

Franklin, J. Jeffrey. "Anthony Trollope's Religion." *Routledge Research Companion to Anthony Trollope*, edited by Deborah Denenholz Morse, Margaret Markwick, and Mark W. Turner, Routledge, 2016, pp. 347–59.

———. "The Counter-Invasion of Britain by Buddhism in Marie Corelli's *A Romance of Two Worlds* and H. Rider Haggard's *Ayesha: The Return of She*." *Victorian Literature and Culture*, vol. 31, no. 1, 2003, pp. 19–42.

———. "The Economics of Immortality: The Demi-Immortal Oriental, Enlightenment Vitalism, and Political Economy in *Dracula*." *Cahiers victoriens et édouardiens*, vol. 76, 2012, pp. 127–48.

———. "The Evolution of Occult Spirituality in Victorian England and the Representative Case of Edward Bulwer-Lytton." *The Ashgate Research Companion to Nineteenth-Century Spiritualism and the Occult*, edited by Tatiana Kontou and Sarah Willburn, Ashgate, 2012, pp. 123–42.

———. "The Influences of Buddhism and Comparative Religion on Matthew Arnold." *Literature and Philosophy in Nineteenth-Century Britain*, special issue of *Literature Compass*, vol. 9, no. 11, Nov. 2012, pp. 813–25.

———. *The Lotus and the Lion: Buddhism and the British Empire*. Cornell UP, 2008.

———. "Memory as the Nexus of Identity, Empire, and Evolution in George Eliot's *Middlemarch* and H. Rider Haggard's *She*." *Cahiers victoriens et édouardiens*, vol. 53, 2001, pp. 141–70.

———. "The Merging of Spiritualities: Jane Eyre as Missionary of Love." *Nineteenth-Century Literature*, vol. 49, March 1995, pp. 456-82.

———. *Serious Play: The Cultural Form of the Nineteenth-Century Realist Novel*. UP Pennsylvania, 1999.

Frawley, Maira H. *A Wider Range: Travel Writing by Women in Victorian England*. Associated University, 1994.

Frost, Mark. "'The Circles of Vitality': Ruskin, Science, and Dynamic Materiality." *Victorian Literature and Culture*, vol. 39, no. 2, 2011, pp. 367–83.

Fulford, Tim. "Conducting the Vital Fluid: The Politics and Poetics of Mesmerism in the 1790s." *Studies in Romanticism*, vol. 43, Spring 2004, pp. 57–78.

Fuller, Sarah Canfield. *From Natural Theology to Scientific Materialism: Science Fiction and Victorian Philosophies of Science*. Dissertation, Indiana UP, June 2013.

Gabriel, Richard A. *Gods of Our Fathers: The Memory of Egypt in Judaism and Christianity*. Greenwood Press, 2002.

Gange, David. *Dialogues with the Dead: Egyptology in British Culture and Religion, 1822–1922*. Oxford UP, 2013.

———. "Religion and Science in Late-Nineteenth Century British Egyptology." *The Historical Journal*, vol. 49, no. 4, 2006, pp. 1083–1103.

Garreau, Joel. "Environmentalism as Religion." *The New Atlantis*, no. 28, Summer 2010, pp. 61–74. www.thenewatlantis.com/publications/environmentalism-as-religion. Accessed 3 Nov. 2017.

Gilmour, Robin. *The Idea of the Gentleman in the Victorian Novel*. George Allen & Unwin, 1981.

Glover, David. "The Lure of the Mummy: Science, Séances and Egyptian Tales in the Fin-de-Siècle England." *Australasian Victorian Studies Annual*, vol. 1, 1995, pp. 1–10.

———. "'Our Enemy Is Not Merely Spiritual': Degeneration and Modernity in Bram Stoker's *Dracula*." *Victorian Literature and Culture*, vol. 22, 1994, pp. 249–65.
Godwin, Joscelyn. *The Theosophical Enlightenment*. UP New York, 1994.
Goldfarb, Russell M., and Clare R. Goldfarb. *Spiritualism and Nineteenth-Century Letters*. Associated Universities, 1978.
Gomes, Michael. *The Dawning of the Theosophical Movement*. Quest Books, 1987.
———. *Theosophy in the Nineteenth Century: An Annotated Bibliography*. Garland, 1994.
Goodrick-Clarke, Nicholas. *The Western Esoteric Traditions: A Historical Introduction*. Oxford UP, 2008.
Gooneratne, Yasmine. *English Literature in Ceylon 1815–1878*. The Ceylon Historical Journal 14, Dehiwala, 1968.
———. "In Search of a Tradition: The Creative Writer in Ceylon." *English*, vol. 16, 1967, pp. 133–38.
Gopinath, Preseeda. "An Orphaned Manliness: The Pukka Sahib and the End of Empire in *A Passage to India* and *Burmese Days*." *Studies in the Novel*, vol. 41, Summer 2009, pp. 201–23.
Griswold, A. B. *King Mongkut of Siam*. The Asian Society, 1961.
Gyss, Claudia. "The Roots of Egyptomania and Orientalism: From the Renaissance to the Nineteenth Century." *French Orientalism: Culture, Politics, and the Imagined Other*, edited by Desmond Hosford and Chong J. Wojtkowski, Cambridge Scholars, 2010, pp. 106–23.
Hahn, H. Hazel. "Indian Princes, Dancing Girls and Tigers: The Prince of Wales's in India and Ceylon, 1875–1876." *Postcolonial Studies*, vol. 12, no. 2, June 2009, pp. 173–92.
Halberstam, Judith. *Skin Shows: Gothic Horror and the Technology of Monsters*. Duke UP, 1995.
Hall, Donald E., editor. *Muscular Christianity: Embodying the Victorian Age*. Cambridge UP, 1994.
Hall, N. John. *Trollope: A Biography*. Clarendon Press, 1991.
Hanegraaff, Wouter J. *New Age Religions and Western Culture: Esotericism in the Mirror of Secular Thought*. E. J. Brill, 1996.
Hanh, Thich Nhat. *Interbeing: Fourteen Guidelines for Engaged Buddhism*. 3rd ed., edited by Fred Eppsteiner, Parallax Press, 1998.
Harris, Elizabeth J. *Theravāda Buddhism and the British Encounter: Religious, Missionary, and Colonial Experience in Nineteenth-Century Sri Lanka*. Routledge, 2006.
Heelas, Paul. *The New Age Movement: The Celebration of the Self and the Sacralization of Modernity*. Blackwell Publishers, 1996.
Heimann, P. M. "*The Unseen Universe*: Physics and the Philosophy of Nature in Victorian Britain." *The British Journal for the History of Science*, vol. 6, no. 21, 1972, pp. 73–79.
Helmstadter, Richard J., and Bernard Lightman, editors. *Victorian Faith in Crisis: Essays on Continuity and Change in Nineteenth-Century Religious Belief*. Stanford UP, 1990.
Higgins, Lesley. "A 'Thousand Solaces' for the Modern Spirit: Walter Pater's Religious Discourse." *Victorian Religious Discourse: New Directions in Criticism*, edited by Jude V. Nixon, Palgrave Macmillian, 2004, pp. 189–204.

Honan, Park. *Matthew Arnold: A Life*. McGraw-Hill, 1981.
Hornung, Erik. *The Secret Lore of Ancient Egypt: Its Impact on the West*. Translated by David Lorton, Cornell UP, 2001.
Hume, Robert. "Gothic Versus Romantic: A Revaluation of the Gothic Novel." *PMLA*, vol. 84, 1969, pp. 282–290.
Humphreys, Christmas. *Studies in the Middle Way: Being Thoughts on Buddhism Applied*. 3rd ed., George Allen and Unwin, 1959.
Hurley, Kelly. "British Gothic Fiction, 1885–1930." *The Cambridge Companion to Gothic Fiction*, edited by Jerrold E. Hogle, Cambridge UP, 2002, pp. 189–208.
Jarrett-Kerr, Martin. "Arnold versus the Orient: Some Footnotes to a Disenchantment." *Comparative Literature Studies*, vol. 12, 1975, pp. 129–46.
——. "Indian Religion in English Literature, 1675–1967." *Essays and Studies*, vol. 37, 1984, pp. 87–103.
Jay, Elisabeth. *Faith and Doubt in Victorian Britain*. Macmillan, 1986.
Kaplan, Fred. " 'The Mesmeric Mania': The Early Victorians and Animal Magnetism." *Journal for the History of Ideas*, vol. 35, 1974, pp. 691–702.
Kemp, Daren. *New Age, A Guide: Alternative Spiritualities from Aquarian Conspiracy to Next Age*. Edinburgh UP, 2004.
Kepner, Susan. "Anna (and Margaret) and the King of Siam." *Crossroads*, vol. 10, 1997, pp. 1–32.
Kimball, Roger. "A Novelist Who Hunted the Fox: Anthony Trollope Today." *New Criterion*, Mar. 1992, n.p. www.newcriterion.com. Accessed 23 Oct. 2013.
Kincaid, James R. *The Novels of Anthony Trollope*. Oxford UP, 1977.
King, Richard. *Orientalism and Religion: Postcolonial Theory, India and the Mystic East*. Routledge, 1999.
Knight, Frances. *The Nineteenth-Century Church and English Society*. Cambridge UP, 1995.
——. *Victorian Christianity at the Fin de Siècle: The Culture of English Religion in a Decadent Age*. 2nd ed., I. B. Tauris & Co., 2016.
Kraft, Siv Ellen. " 'To Mix or Not to Mix': Syncretism/Anti-Syncretism in the History of Theosophy." *Numen*, vol. 49, no. 2, 2002, pp. 142–77.
Lane, Christopher. *The Age of Doubt: Tracing the Roots of Our Religious Uncertainty*. Yale UP, 2011.
Laqueur, Thomas. "Why the Margins Matter: Occultism and the Making of Modernity." *Modern Intellectual History*, vol. 3, no. 1, 2006, pp. 111–35.
Letwin, Shirley Robin. *The Gentleman in Trollope: Individuality and Moral Conduct*. Akadine Press, 1997.
Levine, George. "Paradox: The Art of Scientific Naturalism." *Victorian Scientific Naturalism: Community, Identity, Continuity*, edited by Gowan Dawson and Bernard Lightman, UP Chicago, 2014, pp. 79–97.
——. *Realism, Ethics and Secularism: Essays on Victorian Literature and Science*. Cambridge UP, 2008.
——. "Ruskin, Darwin, and the Matter of Matter." *Nineteenth-Century Prose*, vol. 35, no. 1, Spring 2008, pp. 223–49.
Lightman, Bernard. *Evolutionary Naturalism in Victorian Britain: The 'Darwinians' and Their Critics*. Variorum Collected Studies Series, Ashgate, 2009.

---. "On Tyndall's Belfast Address, 1874." *BRANCH: Britain, Representation and Nineteenth-Century History*, edited by Dino Franco Felluga, extension of *Romanticism and Victorianism on the Net*. www.branchcollective.org. Accessed 14 Dec. 2014.

---. *The Origins of Agnosticism: Victorian Unbelief and the Limits of Knowledge*. Johns Hopkins UP, 1987.

---. "Scientists as Materialists in the Periodical Press: Tyndall's Belfast Address." *Science Serialized: Representations of the Sciences in Nineteenth-Century Periodicals*, edited by Geoffery Cantor and Sally Shuttleworth, MIT, 2004, pp. 101–30.

---. "Unbelief." *Science and Religion Around the World*, vol. 1, edited by John Hedley Brooke and Ronald L. Numbers, Oxford UP, 2011, pp. 252–77.

---. "Victorian Sciences and Religions: Discordant Harmonies." *Science in Theistic Contexts: Cognitive Dimensions*, special issue of *Osiris*, 2nd series, vol. 16, 2001, pp. 343–66.

Lightman, Bernard, and Michael S. Reidy, editors. *The Age of Scientific Naturalism: Tyndall and His Contemporaries*, edited by Bernard Lightman and Michael S. Reidy, Pickering & Chatto, 2014, pp. 187–206.

Livingston, James C. *Matthew Arnold and Christianity: His Religious Prose Writings*. UP South Carolina, 1986.

---. "Matthew Arnold's Place in the Religious Thought of the Past Century." *Matthew Arnold in His Time and Ours: Centenary Essays*, edited by Clinton Machann and Forrest D. Burt, UP Virginia, 1988, pp. 30–39.

Lopez, Donald S., Jr. *Curators of the Buddha: The Study of Buddhism under Colonialism*. UP Chicago, 1995.

---. "Introduction to the Translation." In Eugène Burnouf, *Introduction to the History of Indian Buddhism*, 1844, translated by Katia Buffetrille and Donald S. Lopez Jr., UP Chicago, 2010, pp. 1–28.

Luckhurst, Roger. *The Mummy's Curse: The True History of a Dark Fantasy*. Oxford UP, 2012.

Machann, Clinton. *The Essential Matthew Arnold: An Annotated Bibliography of Major Modern Studies*. G. K. Hall & Co., 1993.

Magus, Simon. "Rider Haggard and the Imperial Occult." Unpublished essay, 2014.

Malalgoda, Kitsiri. *Buddhism in Sinhalese Society 1750–1900: A Study of Religious Revival and Change*. UP California, 1976.

Malfray, Hubert. "'There Is a Happy Land, Far, Far Away': Anna Leonowens or the (Re)Tracing of Harem Life." *In-Between Two Worlds: Narratives of Female Explorers and Travellers 1850–1945*, edited by Béatrice Bijon and Gérard Gâcon, Peter Lang, 2009, pp. 97–108.

Markwick, Margaret. *New Men in Trollope's Novels: Rewriting the Victorian Male*. Ashgate, 2007.

Mayne, Michael. Introduction. *The Clergymen of the Church of England*, by Anthony Trollope. Trollope Society, 1998, pp. vii–xix.

Mazlish, Bruce. "A Triptych: Freud's *The Interpretation of Dreams*, Rider Haggard's *She*, and Bulwer-Lytton's *The Coming Race*." *Comparative Studies in Society and History*, vol. 35, no.4, Oct. 1993, pp. 726–74.

McDonald, Beth E. *The Vampire as Numinous Experience: Spirituals Journeys with the Undead in British and American Literature*. McFarland & Company, 2004.
McGhee, Michael (Dharmachari Vipassi). "Regarding Matthew Arnold. . . ." *The Western Buddhist Review*, vol. 3, 2001, pp. 215–42.
McLeod, Hugh. *Religion and Society in England, 1850–1914*. St. Martin's Press, 1996.
McMahan, David L. *The Making of Buddhist Modernism*. Oxford UP, 2008.
Mead, Marion. *Madame Blavatsky: The Woman Behind the Myth*. G. P. Putnam's Sons, 1980.
Melnyk, Julie. *Victorian Religion: Faith and Life in Britain*. Praeger, 2008.
Melton, J. Gordon. "A History of the New Age Movement." *Not Necessarily the New Age: Critical Essays*, edited by Robert Basil, Prometheus Books, 1988, pp. 35–53.
Melton, J. Gordon, Jerome Clark, and Aidan A. Kelly, editors. "Introductory Essay: An Overview of the New Age Movement." *New Age Encyclopedia*, Gale Research, 1990, pp. xiii–xxxiii.
Mercer, Lorraine. "Anna Leonowens." *British Travel Writers, 1837–1875*, edited by Barbara Brothers and Julia Gergits, Thomson Gale, 1996, pp. 219–26.
Mills, Lennox A. *Ceylon under British Rule 1795–1932, With an Account of the East India Company's Embassies to Kandy 1762–1795*. 1933. Barnes & Noble, 1964.
Mills, Sara. *Discourses of Difference: An Analysis of Women's Travel Writing and Colonialism*. Routledge, 1993.
Mitchell, Leslie. *Bulwer Lytton: The Rise and Fall of a Victorian Man of Letters*. Hambledon and London, 2003.
Monroe, John Warne. *Laboratories of Faith: Mesmerism, Spiritism, and Occultism in Modern France*. Cornell UP, 2008.
Moore, James R. "Theodicy and Society: The Crisis of Intelligentsia." *Victorian Faith in Crisis: Essays on Continuity and Change in Nineteenth-Century Religious Belief*, edited by Richard J. Helmstadter and Bernard Lightman, Stanford UP, 1990, pp. 153–86.
Moretti, Franco. *Signs Take for Wonders: Essays in the Sociology of Literary Forms*. Translated by Susan Fischer, David Forgacs, and David Miller, Verso, 1988.
Morgan, Benjamin Joseph. *The Matter of Beauty: Materialism and the Self in Victorian Aesthetic Theory*. Dissertation, University of California, Berkeley, 2010.
Morgan, Susan. *Bombay Anna: The Real Story and Remarkable Adventures of the King and I Governess*. UP California, 2008.
Morse, Deborah Denenholz. *Reforming Trollope: Race, Gender, and Englishness in the Novels of Anthony Trollope*. Ashgate, 2013.
———. *Women in Trollope's Palliser Novels*. UMI Research Press, 1987.
Mullen, Richard, and James Munson. *The Penguin Companion to Trollope*. Penguin, 1996.
Neufeldt, Ronald. "In Search of Utopia: Karma and Rebirth in the Theosophical Movement." *Karma and Rebirth: Post Classical Developments*, edited by Ronald W. Neufeldt, State UP New York, 1986, pp. 233–55.
Neville-Sington, Pamela. *Fanny Trollope: The Life and Adventures of a Clever Woman*. Viking, 1997.

Noakes, Richard. "Spiritualism, Science and the Supernatural in Mid-Victorian Britain." *The Victorian Supernatural*, edited by Nicola Bown, Carolyn Burdett, and Pamela Thurschwell, Cambridge UP, 2004, pp. 23–43.

Norris, Richard A. "Theurgy." *Encyclopedia of Religion*, edited by Lindsay Jones, 2nd ed., vol. 13, 2005, pp. 9156–58.

Obelkevich, James. *Religion and Rural Society: South Lindsey, 1825–1876*. Clarendon Press, 1976.

Obeyesekere, Gananath. "Religious Symbolism and Political Change in Ceylon." *Modern Ceylon Studies*, vol. 1, no. 1, 1970, pp. 41–63.

Oppenheim, Janet. *The Other World: Spiritualism and Psychical Research in England, 1850–1914*. Cambridge UP, 1985.

Owen, Alex. *The Darkened Room: Women, Power and Spiritualism in Late Victorian England*. UP Pennsylvania, 1990.

———. *The Place of Enchantment: British Occultism and the Culture of the Modern*. UP Chicago, 2004.

Packham, Catherine. "The Physiology of Political Economy: Vitalism and Adam Smith's *Wealth of Nations*." *Journal of the History of Ideas*, vol. 63, July 2002, pp. 465–81.

Parramore, Lynn. *Reading the Sphinx: Ancient Egypt in Nineteenth-Century Literary Culture*. Palgrave Macmillan, 2008.

Parsons, Gerald, editor. *Religion in Victorian Britain*. Vol. 1, Manchester UP, 1988.

Pearl, Sharrona. "Dazed and Abused: Gender and Mesmerism in Wilkie Collins." *Victorian Literary Mesmerism*, edited by Martin Willis and Catherine Wynne, Rodopi, 2006, pp. 163–81.

Pearson, Richard. "Archaeology and Gothic Desire: Vitality beyond the Grave in H. Rider Haggard's Ancient Egypt." *Victorian Gothic: Literary and Cultural Manifestations in the Nineteenth Century*, edited by Ruth Robbins and Julian Wolfreys, Palgrave, 2000, pp. 218–44.

Pels, Peter. "The Modern Fear of Matter: Reflections on the Protestantism of Victorian Science." *Material Religion*, vol. 4, no. 3, Nov. 2008, pp. 264–83.

———. "Spirits of Modernity: Alfred Wallace, Edward Tylor, and the Visual Politics of Fact." *Magic and Modernity: Interfaces of Revelation and Concealment*, edited by Brigit Meyer and Peter Pels, Stanford UP, 2003, pp. 241–71.

Perkin, J. Russell. *Theology and the Victorian Novel*. McGill-Queen's UP, 2009.

Peters, John Durham. *Speaking into the Air: A History of the Idea of Communication*. UP Chicago, 1999.

Prasch, Thomas. "'All the Strange Facts': Alfred Russel Wallace's Spiritualism and Evolutionary Thought." *"Perplext in Faith": Essays on Victorian Beliefs and Doubts*, edited by Alisa Clapp-Intyre and Julie Melnyk, Cambridge Scholars Publishing, 2015, pp. 6–38.

Prothero, Stephen. "From Spiritualism to Theosophy: 'Uplifting' a Democratic Tradition." *Religions and American Culture*, vol. 3, no. 2, Summer 1993, pp. 197–216.

———. *The White Buddhist: The Asian Odyssey of Henry Steel Olcott*. Indiana UP, 1996.

Rahula, Walpola. *What the Buddha Taught*. Grove Press, 1974.

Ransom, Josephine. *A Short History of the Theosophical Society*. Theosophical Publishing House, 1938.

Reed, Edward S. *From Soul to Mind: The Emergence of Psychology from Erasmus Darwin to William James*. Yale UP, 1997.
Reill, Peter Hanns. "Vitalizing Nature and Naturalizing the Humanities in the Late Eighteenth Century." *Studies in Eighteenth-Century Culture*, vol. 28, 1999, pp. 361–81.
Richards, Thomas. *The Imperial Archive: Knowledge and the Fantasy of Empire*. Verso, 1993.
Said, Edward W. *Orientalism*. Pantheon, 1978.
Schlossbert, Herbert. *Conflict and Crisis in the Religious Life of Late Victorian England*. Transactions Publishers, 2009.
Schwab, Raymond. *The Oriental Renaissance: Europe's Rediscovery of India and the East, 1680–1880*. Translated by Gene Patterson-Black and Victor Reinking, Columbia UP, 1984.
Scott, David. "Conversion and Demonism: Colonial Christian Discourse and Religion in Sri Lanka." *Comparative Studies in Society and History*, vol. 34, no. 2, Apr. 1992, pp. 331–65.
Shaw, Rosalind, and Charles Stewart. "Introduction: Problematizing Syncretism." *Syncretism/Anti-syncretism: The Politics of Religious Synthesis*, edited by Charles Stewart and Rosalind Shaw, Routledge, 1994, pp. 1–26.
Shea, Victor, and William Whitla. *Essays and Reviews, The 1860 Text and Its Readings*. UP Virginia, 2000.
Siebers, Alisha. "Marie Corelli's Magnetic Revitalizing Power." *Victorian Literary Mesmerism*, edited by Martin Willis and Catherine Wynne, Rodopi, 2006, pp. 183–198.
Siegel, Kristi. "Intersections: Women's Travel and Theory." *Gender, Genre, & Identity in Women's Travel Writing*, edited by Kristi Siegel, Peter Lang, 2004, pp. 1–11.
Sivasundaram, Sujit. "Buddhist Kingship, British Archaeology and Historical Narratives in Sri Lanka c. 1750–1850." *Past and Present*, vol. 197, Nov. 2007, pp. 111–42.
Smith, Karen Manners. "Anna and the King." Review of *Anna and the King*, directed by Andy Tennant. *The American Historical Review*, vol. 105, no. 3, June 2000, pp. 1060–61.
Stanley, Matthew. *Huxley's Church and Maxwell's Demon: From Theistic Science to Naturalistic Science*. UP Chicago, 2014.
——. "Where Naturalism and Theism Met: The Uniformity of Nature." *Victorian Scientific Naturalism: Community, Identity, Continuity*, edited by Gowan Dawson and Bernard Lightman, UP Chicago, 2014, pp. 242–62.
Suleri, Sara. *The Rhetoric of English India*. UP Chicago, 1992.
Sussman, Herbert L. *Victorian Masculinities: Manhood and Masculine Poetics in Early Victorian Literature and Art*. Cambridge UP, 1995.
Sutcliffe, Steven J. *Children of the New Age: A History of Spiritual Practices*. Routledge, 2003.
Swingle, L. J. *Romanticism and Anthony Trollope: A Study in the Continuities of Nineteenth-Century Literary Thought*. UP Michigan, 1990.
Tartar, Maria M. *Spellbound: Studies on Mesmerism and Literature*. Princeton UP, 1978.
Terry, R. C., editor. *Trollope: Interviews and Recollections*. St. Martin's Press, 1987.

Tomaszewska, Monika. "Vampirism and the Degeneration of the Imperial Race: Stoker's *Dracula* as the Invasive Degenerate Other." *Journal of Dracula Studies*, no. 6, 2004, pp. 1–8.

Tromp, Marlene. *Altered States: Sex, Nation, Drugs, and Self-Transformation in Victorian Spiritualism*. SUNY Series, Studies in the Long Nineteenth Century, State UP New York, 2006.

———. "Spirited Sexuality: Sex, Marriage, and Victorian Spiritualism." *Victorian Literature and Culture*, vol. 31, no. 1, 2003, pp. 67–81.

Turner, Frank Miller. *Between Science and Religion: The Reaction to Scientific Naturalism in Late Victorian England*. Yale UP, 1974.

———. *Contesting Cultural Authority: Essays in Victorian Intellectual Life*. Cambridge UP, 1993.

———. "The Victorian Crisis of Faith and the Faith that was Lost." *Victorian Faith in Crisis: Essays on Continuity and Change in Nineteenth-Century Religious Belief*, edited by Richard J. Helmstadter and Bernard Lightman, Stanford UP, 1990, pp. 9–38.

Vance, Norman. *The Sinews of the Spirit: The Ideal of Christian Manliness in Victorian Literature and Religious Thought*. Cambridge UP, 1985.

van der Veer, Peter. *Imperial Encounters: Religion and Modernity in India and Britain*. Princeton UP, 2001.

van Huyssteen, and J. Wentzel Vrede, *Encyclopedia of Science and Religion*. Macmillan, 2003.

Viswanathan, Gauri. *Outside the Fold: Conversion, Modernity, and Belief*. Princeton UP, 1998.

Vitzthum, Richard C. *Materialism: An Affirmative History and Definition*. Prometheus Books, 1995.

Warren, James H. "Contesting Colonial Masculinity/Constituting Imperial Authority: Ceylon in Mid-Nineteenth-Century British Public Debate." *New Zealand Journal of Asian Studies*, vol. 6, no. 2, Dec. 2004, pp. 39–62.

Warren, William. "Who Was Anna Leonowens?" *Travelers' Tales: Thailand, True Stories*, edited by James O'Reilly and Larry Habegger, Travelers' Tales, Inc., 1993, pp. 85–93.

Washington, Peter. *Madame Blavatsky's Baboon: A History of the Mystics, Mediums, and Misfits Who Brought Spiritualism to America*. Schocken Books, 1993.

Waters, Karen Volland. *The Perfect Gentleman: Masculine Control in Victorian Men's Fiction, 1870–1901*. Peter Lang, 1997.

Welbon, Guy Richard. *The Buddhist Nirvāna and Its Western Interpreters*. UP Chicago, 1968.

Wessinger, Catherine, Dell deChant, and William Michael Ashcraft. "Theosophy, New Thought, and New Age Movements." *Encyclopedia of Women and Religion in North America*, edited by Rosemary Skinner Keller, Rosemary Radford Ruether, and Marie Cantlon, Indiana UP, 2006, pp. 753–68.

Whitlark, James. "Matthew Arnold and Buddhism." *The Arnoldian*, vol. 9, no. 1, Winter 1981, pp. 5–16.

Wicke, Jennifer. "Vampiric Typewriting: *Dracula* and Its Media." *ELH*, vol. 59, 1992, pp. 467–94.

Wilburn, Sarah A. *Possessed Victorians: Extra Spheres in Nineteenth-Century Mystical Writings*. Ashgate, 2006.
Williams, Anne. "Natural Supernaturalism in *Wuthering Heights*." *Studies in Philology*, vol. 82, no. 1, Winter 1985, 104–27.
Willis, Martin. *Mesmerists, Monsters, & Machines: Science Fiction and the Cultures of Science in the Nineteenth Century*. Kent State UP, 2006.
Winter, Alison. *Mesmerized: Powers of Mind in Victorian Britain*. UP Chicago, 1998.
Wise, M. Norton, and Crosbie Smith. "Work and Waste: Political Economy and Natural Philosophy in Nineteenth Century Britain (I)." *History of Science*, vol. 27, 1989, pp. 263–301.
Wolff, Robert Lee. *Strange Stories, and Other Explorations in Victorian Fiction*. Gambit, 1971.
Wordclay. "Differences Between Memoir and Autobiography." www.wordclay.com/genre/memoirautobiography.aspx. Accessed 2 Oct. 2012.
Wyatt, David K. *Thailand: A Short History*. 2nd ed., Yale UP, 2003.
Wyse, Bruce. "Mesmeric Machinery, Textual Production and Simulacra in Bulwer-Lytton's 'The Haunted and the Haunters; or, the House and the Brain.'" *Victorian Review*, vol. 30, 2004, 32–57.
Young, R. F., and G. P. V. Somaratna. *Vain Debates: The Buddhist-Christian Controversies of Nineteenth-Century Ceylon*. Institut für Indologie der Universität Wien, 1996.
Young, Robert J. C. *White Mythologies: Writing History and the West*. Routledge, 1990.
Zirkoff, Boris De. "Preface." *H. P. Blavatsky: Collected Writings 1874–1878*, vol. 1, Theosophical Publishing House, 1966, pp. vii–xxii.
Zlotnick, Susan. "Jane Eyre, Anna Leonowens, and the White Woman's Burden: Governesses, Missionaries, and Maternal Imperialists in Mid-Victorian Britain." *Victorians Institute Journal*, vol. 24, 1996, pp. 27–56.

# Index

*Aberglaube* (extra-belief), 76–77, 80–81
Abhidharma Piṭaka, 71
Aestheticism movement, 13, 43, 214n9, 227n21
aesthetics, 35, 43
agnosticism, 8, 17–18, 47, 63
Akhenaten, 150–52, 156, 160, 202, 224n7, 224n10, 224n12
Alabaster, Henry, 68; *The Wheel of the Law*, 119–20, 220n15, 227n15
alchemy, 30, 33, 38, 41, 192
*All the Year Round* (periodical), 28
Almond, Philip C., 219n4; *British Discovery of Buddhism*, 91
alternative religions. *See* hybrid religions
Amarna, 150–51
Amenemhat, 158
Amenhotep IV, 151
Amiel, Henri Frédéric, 74

Amun or Amun-Ra (Amon, Amen), 151, 153, 159
*anatman* (Buddhist dogma), 79, 82
Anderson, Amanda, 64
Andreae, Johannes, 28
Angkor Wat, 131
Anglican clergymen, 46, 51–66, 217n4. *See also* Church of England
Anglicism, 88–91, 103, 198
animal magnetism, 13, 30–31, 39, 168, 172
Anthroposophy, 30, 185–86, 211, 226n3
Anti-Idolatry Connexion League, 90
Anti-State-Church Association, 217n5
apRoberts, Ruth, 216n1
Arcane School, 204
archaeology, 143–44, 147–50, 154, 157, 162
"argument from design," 5, 12–15, 20–21, 39, 78, 106, 109, 216n18

Aristotle, 167
Arnold, Edwin, 214n16; *The Light of Asia*, 69, 227n15
Arnold, Matthew, 67–82; Buddhism and, 6, 72–75, 86; Christian theology, 22, 62, 75–81; comparative religion and, 72–75, 86, 105; orthodox/heterodox boundary and, 45–46, 82, 194; religious position, 49, 69; spiritualism versus materialism, 82; Theosophy and, 194–97
—works: "Amiel," 74; "Consolation," 74; *Culture and Anarchy*, 78; "Empedocles on Etna," 73, 79; *Literature and Dogma*, 67–68, 75–81; *Merope*, 73; "Resignation," 73, 79; "Sohrab and Rustum," 73; "The Scholar Gypsy," 73
Arnold, Thomas, 49
art: Buddhist, 132; Bulwer-Lytton and, 35–36; spiritualism and, 43; supernatural and, 216n23; syncretism and, 206–7
Aryan metaphysics, 80
Aryans, 70, 88, 227n13
Asian religions: environmentalism and, 208; New Age beliefs and, 205, 208. *See also* Buddhism; Hinduism
Asians: stereotypes about, 99–101, 107, 122. *See also* Ceylon (Sri Lanka); India; Siam (Thailand)
Assmann, Jan, 143, 153, 224n10
Aten, 151–52, 155
Atenism, 152–56, 202, 224n12
atheism, xi–xii, 7–9, 15, 17, 19, 37, 217n5
atonement, 57, 111, 161, 196, 198
Augustine, 20

Baildon, Henry, 11
Bailey, Alice, 204
Baker, Samuel White, 98; *Eight Years of Wanderings in Ceylon*, 89
Bankert, M. S., 217n7
Baptists, 3

Barthélemy-Saint-Hilaire, Jules, *Buddha and His Religion*, 73, 129
Batchelor, Stephen, 70
Beal, Samuel, 222n26
Besant, Annie, xiii, 189, 191, 199–201, 208–10; *The Evolution of Life and Form*, xiii, 207
Bevir, Mark, 197
Bhabha, Homi, 207
Bible: historicist criticism of, 143, 194–95; King Mongkut's critiques of, 128; literalism, 75; New Criticism, 93; nonliteral readings of, 22, 61, 69, 75–77; textual origins and, 70
Bigandet, P., *The Life or Legend of Gaudama*, 68
Bigelow, Gordon, 174, 179
Blackwood, William, 27
blasphemy, 69, 82
Blavatsky, Helena Petrovna, 29, 33, 41, 189–206, 209–10, 225n3; ancient Egyptian religion and, 146, 153, 192, 194; Buddhism and, 94, 137, 198–99; use of "Spirit," 162. *See also* Theosophy
—works: *Isis Unveiled*, xiii, 143, 191–98, 202, 226n12, 227n20; *The Key to Theosophy*, 191; *The Secret Doctrine*, 191
body/soul dualism, 10–11, 164, 167, 180
Bonnet, Charles, 168
Boothby, Guy, 164
Bowring, John, 222n4; *Kingdom and People of Siam*, 121
Bradlaugh, Charles, 7
Braid, James, 38
Breasted, James Henry, 151
Bridgewater Treatises, 12
British Empire: colonial masculinity, 89–91, 93–103, 113; counterinvasion by Buddhism, xiii, xv, 69, 82, 86, 105, 114, 198 (*see also* Buddhism); Egypt, occupation of, 144, 147, 162; global prominence of, xiii, 142; Orientalist-versus-Anglicist debate,

88–91, 103; progress and, 107–8; superiority, discourses of, 118, 124, 198; uprisings and reprisals, 89, 92–93, 97–98, 107–8, 111, 207. *See also* Ceylon (Sri Lanka); Great Britain; imperialism; India
Broad Church Anglicanism, xiv, 23, 47, 49–50, 52, 57, 59, 67, 69, 114, 172, 194, 196–97
Broad Church compromise, 61–62, 218n19
Brontë, Charlotte, 3
Brown, Callum, 214n14
Brown, Susan, 116
Brownrigg, Robert, 91
Buddha, 70–72, 82, 95–96, 114, 227n13
Buddhism: animal fables, 94–103; as atheistic, 72; Christianity, dialogue with and influence on, xiii–xvi, 3, 21–22, 67–69, 72–82, 86–88, 103–12, 114, 127–35, 195, 198; descriptions of, 129–31; environmentalism and, 208; ethics, 72–73, 93, 109, 129; European "discovery" of, 67–72, 85; influence on hybrid religions, 186; morality, 72; "prehistoric Buddhism," 198–99; Protestant Buddhism, 85–86, 94, 113–14, 198, 220n3; reincarnation, 33; science and, 105, 120, 187; self-renunciation, 79–80; in Siam, 119–20, 126–35; textual past of, 219n4; Victorian discourse of "good" and "bad" Buddhism, 75, 80, 135
"Buddhist Catechism," 199
Buddhist modernism, 220n3
Buddhists: conversion to Christianity, 111–12; monks, 119–21, 127, 134; stereotypes about, 99–100
"Buddhist Temporalities Question," 92
Budge, E. A. Wallis, 150, 157, 224n6, 224n12; *Easy Lessons in Egyptian Hieroglyphics*, 149; *Egyptian Religion*, 149

bully masculinity, 89–90, 95–98, 101–3, 113, 221n19
Bulwer-Lytton, Edward, xii, xiv–xv, 27–44, 192, 215n2; esoteric and occult traditions, 28–30, 41–44; metaphysical novels, 34–41; rescue of Christian spirituality by occultism, 41–42, 142, 165, 178; spiritualism versus materialism, 44, 142
—WORKS: *The Caxtons*, 27; *The Coming Race*, 43; *The Last Days of Pompeii*, 27; *Paul Clifford*, 215n1; *A Strange Story*, 28–29, 37–40, 43, 164–70; *Zanoni*, 28–29, 34–37, 39–40, 43, 165, 215n3, 215n5, 216n16
Burnouf, Eugène, 90, 134, 223n8; *L'introduction à l'histoire du Buddhisme Indien*, 68, 71–73, 79–82, 128–30, 219n10, 220n13
Burton, Antoinette, 124
Butler, Samuel, 15

Cadbury, William, 51–52
capitalism: Christianity and, 179; consumerism, x, 170, 174, 179–81; free-market, 176–77, 179, 181; individualism and, 174, 187; monopolistic corporate, 177, 179–80; opposition to, 201
Carlyle, Thomas, 13, 37, 89, 101, 216n16; *Past and Present*, 32
Carnegie, Dale, 210
Catholicism, 17, 23–24, 48, 75, 172. *See also* Tractarians
*Caxtons, The* (Bulwer-Lytton), 27
Celtic lore, 192
Census of Religious Worship (1851), 40, 217n5
Ceylon (Sri Lanka): British colonial rule, 85–112; national politics, 86, 94, 112; Sinhalese Buddhist revival, 85–86, 92–94; uprisings, 86, 92–93, 98, 111
Chaldeans, 42, 194, 197
Champollian, Jean-François, 148
Charcot, Jean-Martin, 169–70

Cheng, Chu-Chueh, 222n5
Christ figure. *See* Jesus Christ
Christianity, orthodox. *See also* Church of England; faith; theology: ancient Egyptian religion and, 146–48; capitalism and, 179; conversion to, 111–12; crisis of faith in, ix, xvii, 1–2, 6, 40, 141–42, 165, 177–78; ethics, 51–52, 65, 82, 196; intolerance of paganism, 153, 196; liberal forms of, 211; links to preceding religions, 153, 195–96, 227n14; physicotheologies and, 11–18; rational, 22, 77; revitalized spirituality, occultism and, 40–42, 142, 165, 177–79; Spirit and, 2–6, 142; supernaturalism, 38–39; traditional spirituality, 61–66, 82; Trollope and, 45–52, 61–66; truth-telling authority, 6, 9, 17, 141–42
Christian Science, 188, 200
Chulalongkorn, King, 125, 130
Church of Christ, Scientist, 185
Church of England: ecclesiastical "abuses," 47, 217n4; high-and-dry Church, 48–49, 56; schism within, 6, 17, 30, 47–51; Tudor settlement, 218n19. *See also* Broad Church Anglicanism; evangelicals; High Church; Low Church; missionaries
Church of Jesus Christ of Latter-day Saints, 42
Church of Scientology, 42, 186
*Chymical Wedding of Christian Rosenkreutz* (Andraea), 28
civilization, 110
Clausen, Christopher, 70
*Cleopatra* (Haggard), xiii, 141–43, 145, 156–63, 181, 202
Clifford, W. K., 7, 20
Cockshut, A. O. J., 50, 218n13
Colenso, John William, 58, 60–61; *Pentateuch*, 48, 50
Coleridge, Samuel Taylor, 49, 74

colonial masculinity, 89–91, 93–103, 113
colonial violence, 89, 97–98, 107–8, 207
colonies, British. *See* British Empire; imperialism
comparative religious studies, xiii, xv–xvi, 21–22; Buddhist use of, 93; emergence of, 68–72, 88; hybrid religions and, 186; influence on Christianity, 75–82; in Leonowens, 127–35; missionaries and, 85; Orientalism in, 90; primacy of textual origins, 69–70, 81, 91, 130, 147; syncretism and, 206; Theosophy and, 198
compassion, 114
Confucianism, 192
Congregationalism, 3
consumer capitalism, x, 170, 174, 179–81
conversion to Christianity, 111–12
Corelli, Marie, x–xi, xiv, 29, 42–43, 164, 194, 225n6; *The Life Everlasting*, xi, 166; *A Romance of Two Worlds*, 166, 169
cosmotheism, 156, 181, 187, 197, 202
Cottom, Daniel, 216n23
critical thinking, 22
Cubism, 206

Dalai Lama, 69
damnation, eternal, 20, 109, 196
Dann, Caron, 122
Daoism, 192
Darwin, Charles, 7, 12, 16, 20, 156; *The Descent of Man*, 107, 221n24; *On the Origin of Species*, xiii, 2, 6, 48, 70, 105. *See also* evolutionary science
Darwin, Erasmus, "The Temple of Nature," 156
David, Rosalie, 151
Davis, Mary F., 215n10
De Alwis, James, 221n22
Decadent movement, 43, 225n6, 227n21
Defoe, Daniel, *Robinson Crusoe*, 220n7

degeneration theory, 225n6
Deism, x, 11, 31, 39, 146, 156, 162, 186
demi-immortal Oriental, 165–70; Blavatsky and, 190, 202; in Bulwer-Lytton, 34–35, 38, 40, 43; description of, 43; in martial-arts Buddhism films, 216n24; vampires, 164–69, 172–74, 180
Democritus, 7
De Quincy, Thomas, "Ceylon," 89
Descartes, René, 20, 168
design. *See* "argument from design"
Dhammapada, 95–96, 98
Dhammayutika Nikaya, 130
dharma (dhamma), 73, 107, 197, 214n16
dharmachakra, 75
Dickens, Charles, 13, 27–28
Diderot, Denis, 7
Disraeli, Benjamin, 27
divine feminine principle, 159, 163, 196, 199–200, 202. *See also* Goddess; Isis
Dixon, Joy, 200
Dodson, Michael S., 88
dogma, 76, 81, 220n13
doubt, 2, 20
Dowling, Andrew, 220n9
*Dracula* (Stoker), xiii, 164–65, 169–81, 202; Christianity and, 172–73; economics and, 170–81
Driesch, Hans, *History and Theory of Vitalism*, 167
dualisms, 208. *See also* body/soul dualism; spirit/matter dualism
Durey, Jill Felicity, 51–52, 64
Dutch School, 35

Ecclesiastical Commission, 217n4
economics, x, 170–81
Eddy, Mary Baker, 200
Edwards, Amelia, *A Thousand Miles up the Nile*, 148
Egyptian Exploration Fund, 148, 151
Egyptian religion, ancient, xiv, 141–63; cosmotheism, 146, 152, 162; heterodox responses to, 154, 162; monotheism, 145–53, 160, 202; orthodox responses to, 154–56, 162; polytheism, 145, 147, 149–52, 163, 192, 202; spiritualism versus materialism, 147, 154–56, 162–63; trinitarian resurrection, 152–53, 155–56, 160–61, 202
Egyptology, 143, 148–49
Egyptomania, 143
Eitel, Ernest J., 68, 221n23
electricity, 170, 194
electromagnetism, 187
elephants, in Buddhist fables, 94–96, 98
Eliot, George, 53, 69
Eliot, T. S., 73; *The Waste Land*, 206
Elliotson, John, 31, 39
Emerson, Ralph Waldo, 131
Engaged Buddhism, 211
*English Governess at the Siamese Court, The* (Leonowens), xiii, xv, 115–37; as comparative religious study, 127–35; as Gothic romance, 123–27, 135; "harem-slave episodes," 119–20, 126, 132, 135; as memoir, 118–23, 135
English language, 70
Enlightenment period, 11; skepticism, 37; vitalism, 30, 167–70 (*see also* vitalism). *See also* Deism
Enns, Anthony, 225n11
entelechy, 167
environmentalism, 208–9
Epicurus, 7, 9
esoteric beliefs and practices, 2, 29–30. *See also* heterodox religious and spiritual discourses; new occultism; occultism
esoteric Christianity, 31, 40, 192
esoteric philosophy, 192
esoteric science, 193
*Essays and Reviews* (1860), 48, 50, 61, 69
ethics: Buddhist, 72–73, 93, 109, 129; Christian, 51–52, 65, 82, 196

evangelicals, 5–6, 48, 58, 64, 217n6; biblical literalism, 75; Low Church, 4, 6, 47–48, 53; revival, 3–4, 90; revival movement, 3–4. *See also* missionaries
Evans, Marian. *See* Eliot, George
evil, 108–10
evolutionary science, xiii, 2, 186; Buddhism and, 22–23, 94, 106–7; Christianity and, 6, 12, 14, 21, 70, 194–95; New Age religion and, 205; vitalism and, 168 (*see also* vitalism)
*Evolution of Life and Form, The* (Besant), xiii, 207
Exodus, 143
Eyre, John, 97

faith: aboriginal source of, 193; crisis in, ix, xvii, 1–2, 6, 40, 141–42, 165, 177–78; as private, 50, 65, 218n12; public expression of, 65, 218n12; salvation by, 80; spiritualism and, 32; traditional Christian spirituality, 19–20, 61–66, 82; Trollope on, 50–52, 61–66
fallen women, 53, 57–58
fatalism, 75
Fausbøll, Viggo, 221n16
feminine divine. *See* divine feminine principle; Goddess; Isis
feminization of religion, 200. *See also* women
*Forest Life in Ceylon* (Knighton), xiii, xv, 86–88, 93–114
forgiveness, 161
Forster, E. M., *A Passage to India*, 101
Foster, Shirley, 126
Frawley, Maria, 223n5(chap.6)
free will, 109
Freud, Sigmund, 169, 188; *Moses and Monotheism*, 224n7
Fyshe, Anna, 127

Gabriel, Richard A., 152
Gaia hypothesis, 209
Galton, Francis, 7, 17

Gange, David, 144, 150
Gaskell, Elizabeth, 53
gender: Victorian assumptions on, 214n14. *See also* women
genre, xiv–xv, 86. *See also* Gothic-romance subgenre; memoir; theology; travel writing genre
German Romanticism, 13, 146, 156
globalization, 207
Gnosticism, 192, 194
Goddess, 161, 196, 202
God's design. *See* "argument from design"
Goethe, Johann Wolfgang von, 74
Gogerly, Daniel J., 90, 221n16; *Kristiyāni Prajñapti* (Christian Institutes), 92
Golden Dawn. *See* Hermetic Order of the Golden Dawn
Gooneratne, Yasmine, 87, 99
Gopinath, Preseeda, 98
Gothic-romance subgenre, xiv–xv, 35, 141, 224n1; Bulwer-Lytton as father of, 43; Egyptian elements in, 144; Leonowens' use of, 123–27, 135; realism and, 216n13; spiritual de-evolution, 225n6; "thrifty metaphoricity" of, 165
Great Britain: colonial governance (*see* British Empire); national politics, 85–86, 112
*Great Expectations* (Dickens), 28
Great Wheel, 74–75
Greeks, 35, 70, 194, 223n1
green movement, 208–9
Guṇānanda, Mohoṭṭivattē, 94

Haggard, H. Rider, xiii, xv, 29, 40, 194, 224n7; demi-immortal characters, 164, 167
—WORKS: *Cleopatra*, xiii, 141–43, 145, 156–63, 181, 202; *The Days of My Life*, 156; *Morning Star*, 157; *Smith and the Pharaohs*, 157; *The Way of the Spirit*, 157
Halberstam, Judith, 165, 174

Hall, N. John, 64
Hanegraaff, Wouter, 204, 210, 226n4
Hanh, Thich Nhat, 209
*Hard Times* (Dickens), 13
Hardy, R. Spence, 90; *A Manual of Buddhism*, 68, 95, 129, 221n11
Hardy, Thomas, 53
harem, 118, 121–22, 124–26, 199
Harmachis, 157–59
Harris, Elizabeth J., 86, 220n3
Harrison, Frederic, 7
Hawthorne, Nathaniel, 131
Heelas, Paul, *The New Age Movement*, 210
hell, 109–11
heresy, 50, 69, 82, 103, 114, 194
Hermetic Order of the Golden Dawn, 30, 42, 143–44, 146, 154, 158, 162, 185, 223n1
Herodotus, *An Account of Egypt*, 146
heroes, religious, 52–61
heterodox religious and spiritual discourses: cultural and historical context, 1–19; new occultism, links to, 185–203; overview, x–xvii. *See also* Bulwer-Lytton, Edward; Mesmerism; occultism; orthodox/heterodox boundary; Spiritualism
High Church, 4, 6, 47–48, 64, 73, 75, 217n7
higher self, 79–80, 188, 209–11
Hilton, James, 43
Hinduism, 127, 137, 206, 226n3; influence on Christianity, xv, 3, 73, 195; influence on hybrid religions, 186; Theosophy and, 199
historicism, 69, 72, 76, 81–82, 143, 155, 194–95
Hobbes, Thomas, 8
Hodgson, Brian Houghton, 68, 219n2
Hodgson, Richard, 226n7
holism, 187, 204–5, 207–9
Holy Trinity (Christian), 153, 161, 202
Home, Daniel, 28
Home, Madame, 28

Horus, 153, 160, 202
Hughes, Thomas, 49; *Tom Brown's Schooldays*, 52
Humphreys, Christmas, 226n8
Huxley, Thomas Henry, 7–9, 16–17, 19, 70
hybrid religions and spiritualities: formation of, 30, 33; New Age spiritualities, links to, 203–11; new occultism and, 185–203; overview, x–xiv, 1–2; syncretism, 206–7; women-centeredness, 199–200. *See also* Theosophy
hypnotism, 38, 169–70
hypocrisy, 58–59

ideal, 35–36
idolatry, 90, 143, 149, 153, 161
immanence, 147, 154, 156, 161–63, 181
immanentism, 186–87, 189, 196, 198, 201–2; New Age beliefs, 204–5, 207–9
immortality, 43. *See also* demi-immortal Oriental
imperialism: First and Second Empire, 221n19; originating texts and, 70, 91; progressivism and, 107–8; religious syncretism and, 206
Incarnation, 57, 196, 198
India, 94, 127, 199, 227n13; colonial rule in, 85, 88
individualism: capitalism and, 174, 187; liberal, 187, 201, 209; Protestant, 41, 216n20; utilitarian, 210
Indo-European, 70, 80, 88, 146, 220n13, 227n13
influence, 150, 154
interdependence, 208–9
Isis, 143–46, 150, 152–53, 156, 159–62, 196, 202
*Isis Unveiled* (Blavatsky), xiii
Islam, 127

*Jakatas* (Buddha birth stories), 95–96
Jamaica, Morant Bay rebellion, 89, 97

James, William, 2, 5, 187–88
*Jane Eyre* (Brontë), 3, 39
Jesus Christ: as historical figure, 69, 72, 76, 82; as ideal gentleman, 114; Osiris and, 155; righteousness, 78–79; Theosophy and, 196
Jones, William, 88
Joshua, Book of, 223n2
Jowett, Benjamin, 69
Judaism, 143, 145, 152, 155, 160
Judge, W. Q., 225n1, 225n3
Jung, Carl, 187, 207
Jupp, William, 207

Kabala, 192, 194
Kandy, 91–92
karma (kamma), 69, 109, 197, 214n16; ethics of, 93; as materialistic, 72; science and, 106–7; in Theosophy, 199
Kelvin, Lord, 10
Kepner, Susan, 117, 125
Kimball, Roger, 218n11
Kincaid, James R., 218n15
*King and I, The* (Rogers and Hammerstein), 115
Kingsley, Charles, 49; *Westward Ho!*, 52
Kipling, Rudyard, 157; *Jungle Book*, 96; *Just So Stories*, 96
Knighton, William, xiii, xv, 22, 85–114, 198, 201; colonial masculinity and Buddhist animal fables, 93–103, 113; dialogue between Christianity and Buddhism, 103–13; *Forest Life in Ceylon*, xiii, xv, 86–88, 93–114; spiritualism versus materialism, 86, 106, 113
Knox, Robert, *An Historical Relation of the Island of Ceylon*, 220n7

*Lancet, The*, 31
Landon, Margaret, *Anna and the King of Siam*, 115
Langdon, Samuel, *Punchi Nona*, 220n7
*Last Days of Pompeii, The* (Bulwer-Lytton), 27

latitudinarianism, xiv, 48, 50, 54, 65, 69, 194–95. *See also* Broad Church Anglicanism
law: of the dharma, 22, 227n15; God's law, 22–23; of nature, 22; of progress, 107–8; rule of law, 97, 221n18; scientific, 22, 107; Theosophy and, 197
Leadbeater, C. W., 225n3
"Legend of the Maha Naghkon," 136
Leibnitz, Gottfried Wilhelm, 168
Leonowens, Anna, xiii, xv, 22, 115–37, 198–99, 201; accuracy of, 116–17; biography, 115–16, 125–26, 131–32, 136–37; *The English Governess at the Siamese Court*, xiii, xv, 115–37; *The Romance of Siamese Harem Life*, 118
Leo XIII, 20
Letwin, Shirley Robin, 217n8
Lewes, G. H., 7
Lhasa, 74
liberal individualism, 187, 201, 209
liberal-intellectual masculinity, 90, 97–98, 101–2, 105, 221n18
Liberation Society, 217n5
life after death, 152, 166
life force, 31, 168–69, 171
Lightman, Bernard, 9, 16
*Light of Asia, The* (Arnold), 69, 214n16, 227n15
Lilly, William Samuel, 81; *Ancient Religion and Modern Thought*, 19–24, 40
literary criticism, Biblical interpretation and, 76–77
*Literature and Dogma* (Arnold), xiii, 67–68, 75–81
London Mesmeric Infirmary, 31
Lopez, Donald S., Jr., 81
Lotus Sūtra, 73, 219n10
Lovelock, James, 209
Low Church, 4, 6, 47–48, 53, 73, 75
Lucas, Judith C., 219n10
Lucretius, 7, 9

Macaulay, T. B., *Minute on Indian Education*, 89
MacDonald, Frederika, 227n16
magic, 33, 41, 194
Magus, Simon, 224n12
Mahatmas, 190–91, 198, 202, 226nn7–8
Mahayana Buddhism, 129, 211
*maitrî* (loving-kindness or charity), 134
mammonism, 32
"Manual of Spiritual Science and Philosophy" (Tuttle), ix
Markwick, Margaret, 49, 217n9
Marsh, Richard, 43, 164
"martial-arts Buddhism" films, 69, 216n24
Martineau, Harriett, 215n5; *Letters on Mesmerism*, 28
Marx, Karl, 170
masculinity, 175–76, 220n9; bully, 89–90, 95–98, 101–3, 113, 221n19; colonial, 89–91, 93–103, 113; liberal-intellectual, 90, 97–98, 101–2, 105, 221n18
materialism, x, 19, 165, 168, 213n2; critiques of, 13, 34, 39, 193; metaphysical, x, 12, 165; scientific naturalism and, 7–11; supernaturalism and, 39. *See also* scientific materialism; spiritualism versus materialism; spiritual materialism
materialist spiritualism, 37
Maurice, F. D., 49, 69
Maxwell, James Clerk, 10
Mayne, Michael, 217n10
McDonald, Beth E., 178
mediums, 28
Melton, Gordon, 204
memoir, 118–23, 135
Menka-Ra, 158
Mercer, Lorraine, 222n3
Mesmer, Franz Anton, 30
Mesmerism, xiii, 3, 192, 225n11; communication and, 177; history of, 4, 29–34; influence on hybrid religions, 186, 193; materialists and spiritualists, 31, 39; vitalism, 13, 41, 168–72, 187
metaphysics, 8, 15–16, 71, 78, 80–81, 220n13
Methodism, 3, 53, 218n19
Mill, James, *History of British India*, 89
Mill, John Stuart, 20, 89, 97, 101–2, 174, 221n18
Mills, Sara, 116
mind, scientific understandings of, 14–15
miracles, 71, 75–78, 81, 220n13
missionaries, 198; in Ceylon, 85, 90–94, 103, 118; in Siam, 120, 128
Mivart, St. George, 21
modernism: globalism of, 201; spiritual malaise of, 35–36; subjectivity and, 210; syncretism and, 206
Mongkut, King, 117, 119–22, 126–28, 132–37, 223n8
Monier-Williams, Monier, 68, 72
monism, 9–10, 187
monkeys, in Buddhist fables, 94, 96, 98, 107
monotheism, 202
morality: Buddhist, 72, 110; Christian, 52, 82
morality/emotion, 49, 62, 65–66, 77–78, 196
Morant Bay rebellion (Jamaica), 89, 97
Moretti, Franco, 170, 177, 224n2
Morgan, Susan, 117
Mosaic Distinction, 143, 145–55, 160–61, 163, 202, 206
Moses, 94, 146, 148, 151–52, 154, 158, 224n7
Mullen, Richard, 217n3, 217n7
Müller, Friedrich Max, 21–22, 68–70, 129, 187, 195, 219n2, 221n16
mummies, 143; "curse of the mummy," 144, 158–59, 162; racial features of, 147, 223n6(chap.7)
Munson, James, 217n3, 217n7
muscular Christianity, 52

Napoleon, expedition to Egypt, 146, 148
naturalism: defined, 213n4. *See also* scientific naturalism
natural supernaturalism, 13, 37, 39, 41, 202
Natural Theology, x, 3, 31; Anglican Church and, 105; Buddhism and, 86; development of, 11–12; scientific naturalism and, 16, 23, 168, 187. *See also* "argument from design"
*Natural Theology* (Paley), 12
nature, 10–16, 19, 31, 35, 41, 106, 152, 224n10; alienation from, 204; divine and, 186, 189, 191, 196, 208; laws of, 22, 195; as mechanical system, 168; scripture versus, 147, 154, 156
*New Age, The* (journal), 227n21
*New Age Encyclopedia*, 204
New Age spiritualities: features of, 204–11; formation of, xii, xiii, 2–3, 203–4; Higher Self and, 188; hybrid religions, links from, 203–11; social/political reformism, 201; women in, 200
Newman, Francis, 18
Newman, John Henry, 20, 74; *Apologia*, 48
new occultism: dissolution of spirit/matter dualism, 186–87, 201–2; formation of, 185–86; heterodox religious and spiritual discourses, links from, 185–203; social/political reformism and, 200–201; subjectivity and, 187–89. *See also* hybrid religions
New Testament, 78
New Thought movement, 188, 204
New Woman, 224n15
nihilism, 75, 79–81, 114
Nilan, J., 146–48
nirvana (nibbana), 69, 75, 79–82, 214n16
Noble Eightfold Path, 72
Nonconformists, 3, 6, 17, 30, 47–48, 53–54, 75, 111

non-Western religions, 3, 192. *See also* Buddhism; Egyptian religion, ancient; Hinduism
Norse mythology, 192
North England physicists, 10, 13, 23

Obeyesekere, Gananath, 220n3
occultism, xi, xv, 2; ancient, 42; spiritual phenomena and, 39–40; variety of Victorian esoteric and occult beliefs and practices, 29–30. *See also* Egyptian religion, ancient; esoteric beliefs and practices; heterodox religious and spiritual discourses; new occultism; vampirism
occult romance novels. *See* Gothic-romance subgenre
Oken, Lorenz, 168
Olcott, H. S., 86, 94, 113, 190, 199, 204, 225n3
Oldenberg, Hermann, 68, 75
*On the Origin of Species* (Darwin), xiii, 2, 6, 48, 70, 105
Oppenheim, Janet, 33, 215n13
Orage, A. R., 227n21
Orientalism, 198–99; ambivalence of, 100; versus Anglicism, 88–91, 103
Orientalist imaginary, 122
originality, 150
orthodox/heterodox boundary, 19, 24, 82, 114, 194. *See also* heterodox religious and spiritual discourses
Osiris, 149–50, 152–54, 159–60, 202
Owen, Alex, 33
Oxford movement, 218n12

Packham, Catherine, 176, 225n9
pagan beliefs and practices, 4–5, 53, 56, 63; ancient Egyptian, 143, 149, 155, 163 (*see also* Egyptian religion, ancient); Christian intolerance of, 153, 196
Paley, William, 12, 216n18
pantheism, 16
paranormal phenomena, 32, 38, 193

patriarchy, abusive, 126, 135, 199
Pearson, Richard, 224n14
Pels, Peter, 11, 18
penance, 161
Petrie, W. M. Flinders, 157, 224n6; *Tell el Amarna*, 150–51
Pettigrew, Thomas "Mummy," 223n6(chap.7)
philology, 70, 76–77, 81, 88, 92
philosophy, 36–37
physicotheologies, x, xv, 11–18, 181, 186, 209
physics, modern, 187, 193
physics, Epicurean, 9–10
Picasso, Pablo, 206
Plato, 20
Plutarch, *On Isis and Osiris*, 146
Podmore, Frank, 215n13; *Modern Spiritualism*, 33
political economy, 170–81
political reformism, 200–201
polytheism, 145, 147, 149–52, 163, 192, 202
postmodernism, 207
progress, 12, 107–10, 166–67, 174–76, 199; New Age religions and, 205, 211
prosperity, 171, 173–75, 179, 201, 210
Protestant Buddhism, 85–86, 94, 113–14, 198, 220n3. *See also* Buddhism
Protestant Christianity: alternatives to, x–xvii; antimaterialism, 10–11; individualism, 41, 216n20; Reformation, 1, 17. *See also* Christianity, orthodox; Church of England
psychical research, 193–94
psychology, 15, 38, 187–88, 193, 206–7, 210
Ptah, 153
Pusey, Edward, 217n7

Quakerism, 211

racial difference, 99–101
Radcliffe, Ann, 224n1

Rattigan, William H., 81
Re, 153
realism, xv, 35–36
redemption, 78, 80, 196
Reill, Peter Hanns, 168
reincarnation, 69, 109, 161; hybrid religions and, 186; as materialistic, 72; in New Age beliefs, 205; progressivism and, 108; science and, 105–7; in Theosophy, 197, 199
religion: Victorian conceptions of, 1–19, 50, 52. *See also* comparative religious studies; heterodox religious and spiritual discourses; hybrid religions and spiritualities; New Age spiritualities; occultism; spiritualism versus materialism; *individual religions*
religious heroes, 52–61
Resurrection, Christian, 153, 173
revelation, 147, 153–56, 161, 191, 206
revolutionary politics, 36–37
Rhys Davids, Caroline, 22, 74
Rhys Davids, T. W., 22, 68, 75, 219n7
righteousness, 77–78, 81, 161, 196–97, 219n10
Robertson, James, 32
romance. *See* Gothic-romance subgenre
Roman Empire, 145–46, 157
Romanticism, 13, 146, 156
Rosicrucianism, 28, 33–34, 41, 192, 215n3
Ruskin, John, 13

Sabbath-breaking, 58–59
Said, Edward, *Orientalism*, 88
Śākyamuni Buddha, 71, 198
Samaj, Arya, 199
Sanskrit, 70, 128, 214n16
Schopenhauer, Arthur, 20, 75
science, modern, x, 2, 193. *See also* evolutionary science; ambivalence about, 44; gendered as male, 214n14; as metaphysics, 8; as method, 8; physicotheologies and religion, 11–18;

science, modern *(continued)*
  professionalism of, 16; spirituality and, 209; truth-telling authority of, 6, 9, 17, 22, 37, 141–42, 197
scientific empiricism, xv
scientific law, 22
scientific materialism, 7–8, 32, 44, 197, 204
scientific naturalism, x–xi, xiii–xiv, 3; Buddhism and, 86, 94; emergence of, 105; materialism and, 7–11; physicotheologies and, 12, 14–18; social relationship with Church of England, 16–17; Spirit and, 193
Scientology, 42, 186
scripture versus nature, 147, 154, 156
séances, 28, 31–33, 192
secularization thesis, 15–16
self-expression, 125–26
self-help movement, 188
selfhood, 187–89
self-renunciation, 79–80
sexuality, as sin, 57–58
Shea, Victor, 61
Siam (Thailand), 115–37; Buddhism in, 119–20, 126–35; independence from colonial rule, 120; missionaries in, 120, 128. *See also* Mongkut, King
Siddhartha Gautama, 70, 227n13
sin, 57–58, 78, 80, 110–11, 159, 161, 196
Sinnett, A. P., 195, 225n2; *Esoteric Buddhism*, 198; *Occult World*, 225n3
Sirr, Henry C., 222n30
skepticism, 37–38
slavery, 118, 121–22, 124, 126
Smiles, Samuel, *Self Help*, 188
Smith, Adam, 170, 225n9; *The Wealth of Nations*, 176
social Darwinism, 201
socialism, 201, 207, 211
social reformism, 200–201
Society for Psychical Research, 32, 38, 187, 190, 226n7

Sokaris, 153
soul, 167, 209; scientific investigation on, 32, 210; vampires and, 173. *See also* body/soul dualism
Spencer, Herbert, 7, 20
Spinoza, Baruch, 7
Spirit: mesmeric phenomena as evidence of, 31; self and, 210–11; summarized, ix–x; Theosophy and, 188; in Victorian period, 2–6, 142
*Spirit, Matter, and Morals* (Stocker), 9–10
spirit channeling, 43
spirit/matter dualism, xiv, 106, 108, 181, 201–2
*Spirit of Nature, The* (Baildon), 11
spiritual evolution, 32–33, 186, 195, 205; de-evolution, 167, 225n6
spiritualism: ambivalence about, 44; use of term, 213n2. *See also* spiritualism versus materialism
Spiritualism (movement), xiii, 3, 187, 190; in Bulwer-Lytton, 41; champions and opponents, 39; evolution and, 14; history of, 4, 29–34; influence on hybrid religions, 186, 193; opposition to materialism, 32; souls and, 173; use of term, 213n2; as women-centered, 33
spiritualism versus materialism: ancient Egyptian religion and, 147, 154–56, 162–63; capitalism and, 179 (*see also* capitalism); dissolution of dichotomy, xiv, 142, 161–62, 168, 186–87, 201–2; materialism and scientific naturalism, 7–11; orthodox/heterodox boundary and, 19–24; overview, ix–xvii; physicotheologies and religion of science, 11–18; Spirit and orthodox Christianity, 2–6; vampirism and, 164–65, 181; vitalism and, 168 (*see also* vitalism)
spirituality, Christian: revitalized by occultism, 40–42, 142, 165, 177–79; traditional, 61–66, 82
spiritual materialism, 37, 181, 202

spiritual progress, 167, 186, 189, 197, 201
spiritual science, xi, 186, 192
Sri Lanka. *See* Ceylon
Stahl, Georg Ernest, 168
Stanley, Matthew, 213n4
Steiner, Rudolf, 226n3
Stephen, Leslie, 8, 20
Stewart, Balfour, 13
Stocker, Dimsdale, 9
Stoker, Bram, xiii, xv, 43; *Dracula*, xiii, 164–65, 169–81, 202; spiritualism versus materialism, 141–42
Stowe, Harriet Beecher, 131; *Uncle Tom's Cabin*, 121
*Strange Story, A* (Bulwer-Lytton), xii, 28–29, 37–40, 43, 164–70
Strauss, David Friedrich, *Das Leben Jesu*, 69
subjectivity, modern, 187–89, 209–11
suffering, 108–10
supernatural events, 5, 38, 71
supernaturalism, 194. *See also* natural supernaturalism
Sussman, Herbert J., 220n9
Sutcliffe, Steven, 204, 226n4
Sūtra Piṭaka, 71
Swedenborgianism, xiii, 186, 192
syncretism, 70, 192, 205–7

Tait, Peter Guthrie, 13
Tartar, Maria, 31
technology, 177–78
Tennent, James Emerson, 93, 98
textual origins, primacy of, 69–70, 81, 91, 130, 147
Thailand, 120. *See also* Mongkut, King; Siam
thaumaturgy, 77
theistic scientists, 10, 13–14, 17, 23
theological metaphysics, 16
theology, xiv, 22, 62, 67–82. *See also* comparative religious studies; Natural Theology

Theophilus, 145
Theosophical Society International, 29, 143, 215n6, 225n1; founding of, 30, 33, 41, 190. *See also* Theosophy
Theosophical Society International (Wheaton, Ill.), 225n1
Theosophical Society Pasadena, 215n6, 225n1
Theosophy, xi, xiii–xiv, 3, 185–206; ancient Egyptian religion and, 144, 155, 162, 202; Buddhism and, 94, 198–99; Ceylon and, 85; comparative religion and, 195; egalitarianism, 200; impact of, 185; moral system, 197; New Age spiritualities and, 203–6; scandals, 190, 226n12; social/political reformism, 200–201; spirit/matter dualism and, 186; on spiritual de-evolution, 225n6; subjectivity in, 188–89, 209–11, 225n2; trinity in, 227n20; women-centeredness, 199–200
Theravada Buddhism, 91, 95–96, 129
theurgy, 77, 216n22
Thipakon, Chao Phya, 220n15
Thomas Aquinas, 20
Thomson, William, 10
Tingley, Katherine, 200
tolerance, 114
Tories, 48, 217n7
Torrington, Lord, 93, 98, 101, 111
Townshend, Chauncey Hare, 28, 39
Tractarians, Anglo-Catholic, 3, 20, 30, 47–49, 217n9
Transcendentalism, 13, 156
transcendental materialism, 16
travel writing genre, xiv–xvi, 117–18. *See also* women's travel writing
trinitarian resurrection, Egyptian, 152–53, 155–56, 160–61, 202
trinity: in Christianity, 153, 161, 202; in Theosophy, 227n20
Tripiṭaka, 71

Trollope, Anthony, xii–xiii, 6, 45–66; orthodox/heterodox boundary, 45–46, 63–66, 194; religious position, 46–51, 64–65; spiritualism versus materialism, 60, 65; Theosophy and, 194–97
—WORKS: *An Autobiography*, 53; *Barchester Towers*, 48, 51; *The Bertrams*, 48; *The Clergymen of the Church of England*, xiii, 48, 50, 55–56, 58–59; *The Eustace Diamonds*, 51; *The Last Chronicle of Barset*, 48; *The Vicar of Bullhampton*, xii–xiii, 48, 51–66; *The Warden*, 48; *The Way We Live Now*, 51
truth-telling authority: of orthodox Christianity, 6, 9, 17, 141–42; of science, 6, 9, 17, 22, 37, 141–42, 197
Turner, Frank Miller, 8, 12, 18, 214nn7–8
Turnour, George, 90; "*Mahawanso*", 95
Tutankhaten/Tutankhamun, 151
Tuttle, Hudson, ix; on spiritual evolution, 32; on Spiritualism, 40
Tylor, Edward, 8
Tyndall, John, 7–9, 16, 23

unbelief, 62, 66. *See also* atheism
United States, 2, 156, 188, 204
unity, 10, 106, 156, 201, 207–8, 210–11
*Unseen Universe, The* (Stewart and Tait), 13
utilitarian individualism, 210

Vajrayana Buddhism, 129
values, 51–52
vampirism, 43, 164–65, 169–70; Christianity and, 172–73; economics and, 170–81; novel series, 225n10; spiritualism versus materialism, 164–65, 181
Vance, Norman, 217n9
van der Veer, Peter, 86, 94
*Varieties of Religious Experience, The* (James), 2
vengeance, 161

*Vicar of Bullhampton, The* (Trollope), xii–xiii, 48, 51–66; fallen woman subplot, 52–53, 55, 62; religion subplot, 53, 62; religious heroes, 52–61, 63, 65–66; romance subplot, 53–55, 62
Vinaya Piṭaka, 71, 131
violence: colonial, 89, 97–98, 107–8, 207; interdependence and, 208
vitalism, 31, 164–76, 179–82, 202; mesmeric, 13, 41, 168–72, 187

Wace, Henry, 67, 81
Wallace, Alfred Russel, 14, 23
Ward, James, 10, 15
Warren, James H., 89, 221n18
Weber, Max, 174
Whitla, William, 61
Whitlark, James, 79
Wicke, Jennifer, 170
Wilburn, Sarah A., 216n20
Wilde, Oscar, 43, 164, 166–67
witchcraft, 33
Wodehouse, Philip, 93
Wolff, Caspar Friedrich, 168
women: fallen, 53, 57–58; in harem (Siam), 118, 121–22, 124–26, 199; protection of British womanhood, 175; sexuality, 57–58; Spiritualism and, 33; Victorian New Woman, 224n15
women's rights, 118, 121, 124, 132, 199–200
women's travel writing, 116–18, 124, 126, 135, 223n5(chap.6)
Woolf, L., *Village in the Jungle*, 220n7
World Wide Web, 207

Young, Robert, 16

*Zanoni* (Bulwer-Lytton), xii, 28–29, 34–37, 39–40, 43, 165, 215n3, 215n5, 216n16
Zlotnick, Susan, 124
*Zoist, The*, 31